Life is what you make it

Iain Esslemont

Published by

MELROSE BOOKS

An Imprint of Melrose Press Limited
St Thomas Place, Ely
Cambridgeshire
CB7 4GG, UK
www.melrosebooks.com

FIRST EDITION

Cover designed by Matt Stephens

ISBN 978-1-906561-42-0

Printed and bound in Great Britain by:
The MPG Books Group, Bodmin and King's Lynn

"THE EARTH IS BUT ONE COUNTRY
AND MANKIND ITS CITIZENS,"

BAHA'U'LLAH.

Contents

Contents (cont.)

PART TWO: REFLECTIONS AND PERCEPTIONS

Preface

"When the foundation stone is laid, the architect appears with his plans, and struts for an hour before the public eye. So with the writer in his preface ... It is best, in such circumstances, to present a delicate shade of manner between humility and superiority: as if the book had been written by someone else, and you had merely run over it and inserted what is good."

Robert Louis Stevenson, *An Inland Voyage;*
(London, 1878; repr. London, 1929), p. xxi.

What is this book about, or, to be grammatically correct, about what is this book? Who is the author; what kind of a life has he had; why does he feel that his life-story is of interest to others?

The world population is around 6.6 billion, and I am one of them. I am not a celebrity, just an ordinary man, a general medical practitioner, dealing with ordinary people, who are; after all, more interesting than celebrities, who are, after all, also mortal human beings.

It is a good idea not to become dependent on others although interpersonal association is necessary and I soon learned to be largely self-sufficient. Hence the title.

After early ideas of becoming a conventional general practitioner in a Scottish country town, events changed my ideas and I embarked on an overseas career which I found much more interesting and, I might add, often entertaining.

People are interesting, other cultures are fascinating, and I gathered such a variety of experiences that, prompted by a remark from a colleague of different race and nationality, it seemed a good idea to share my "adventures" with others.

During all these years, from reading, experiences and evaluation, I developed my own ideas and perceptions, and these have been added for readers to consider. Exchange of ideas in the university of life is beneficial provided that everyone accepts that each person is an individual and is worthy of respect. A number of individuals – Dr M. J. Rajakumar, Neville Stone, my wife's cousin, Peter Glendinning Gibb – have suggested that I write my autobiography, and our local newspaper's Senior Journalist, Janine Beacham, wants to read my "memoirs". To them I dedicate this book.

To my wife, Mary, who, after the initial shock at finding I was serious about publishing my autobiography, has been especially supportive, I wish to give a special dedication.

Thanks are necessary to Mr Alan Wilkinson, a stranger to me, who severely criticized some of the style, resulting in me doing self-evaluation and revision, less, I think, than he might have liked.

Acknowledgements to the publisher, Mr Austin Kehoe and his staff, who have been very supportive, are gratefully given.

As I did my own typing no acknowledgement to any stenographer is necessary!

I have enjoyed reliving my experiences and I hope that you may have equal enjoyment reading them.

> Dr MK Rajakumar, one of those to whom this book is dedicated, passed away, unfortunately, on the night of 21st November, 2008, before the book was published. Dr Rajakumar was a very gentle man but passionate about general medical practice. The dedication continues to his memory.

PART ONE:

The Chronicle

Chapter 1

The Broad Canvas

"The first night I spent in Malaya, I slept on a *charpoi* in a gardener's shed under an *attap* roof."

Three of us were sitting by the poolside at the New Club in Kuala Lumpur, M. J. Rajakumar, my wife and me.

It was 1997, the sun was dazzlingly bright, the grass tropical green, the air hot and steamy, the backs of our shirts were soaked with sweat.

Rajakumar had just asked me how I came to be in Malaysia and that was my answer.

I thought of those days in 1957 when things were so different from the pristine ostentation of this, one of Malaysia's newest clubs.

I had first met this doctor some twenty-three years previously when the College of General Practitioners, Malaysia, was being formulated and he had asked me, as a newly qualified Member of the Royal College of General Practitioners, London, to be involved. Now, here I was, about to be awarded the Fellowship of the Academy of Family Physicians, Malaysia, which had evolved from the Malaysian College.

He said, "You know, you should write your autobiography. That could be the first line."

My mind went back over my life, walking over the rocks and heather of the Cairngorm hills at the top of Scotland, walking in very different scenery through the wet jungle on the dividing range in Malaya, walking over the very different burnt umber earth of outback Australia, of travelling the eighty-six mile journey to Singapore with a very sick nephew of Malaysia's prime minister, of being taken by launch through Penang Straits, to illness on board a ship and many other experiences.

Since then, a patient, a barrister and another friend have suggested that I should write the story of my life.

However it could be confusing to start in the middle.

> *The White Rabbit put on his spectacles. "Where shall I begin, please your Majesty?" he asked.*
>
> *"Begin at the beginning," the King said gravely, "and go on till you come to the end: then stop."*
> **Lewis Carroll, *Alice's Adventures in Wonderland***

This seems a good idea, but where is the beginning?

Life is a continuum. The germs of our existence start somewhere in a melting pot a long time ago and are passed on through our ancestors, our grandparents, our parents, to us.

I order to establish where I stand on the map, I would like to outline my origins.

The house on the right is 3 Newlands Crescent, Aberdeen, decorated for the Coronation of King George VI on 12th May, 1937. It is the house in which I was born

In Scotland, ancestry is hard to find, as after the '45 Rebellion, the Redcoats under the "Butcher", the Duke of Cumberland, burned the Parish Records.

The furthest back I can trace my family tree is to Peter Esslemont, also known as Patrick, who married Isobel Manson on the 8th December 1743 at Tarves, Aberdeenshire.

He was my great-great-great-great grandfather and was a farmer.

Two of his great-grandsons ventured into Aberdeen City to found mercantile businesses. Peter, who was the sixth child in a family of nine, began what was to become a very successful clothing business, which became Esslemont and Mackintosh. He later became a Lord Provost of the city and a Member of Parliament.

The seventh child, John Ebenezer, also left the farm to seek his fortune in Aberdeen, founded a retail and wholesale grocery business, including the blending of tea and the manufacturing of confectionery.

John Ebenezer lived from 1839 until 1927. He married Margaret Davidson, the daughter of a tailor, in 1866, and their family history paints a picture of conditions in the nineteenth century. Then, one hundred out of ten thousand mothers died in childbirth and, of children born, over one hundred in every thousand were dead by the age of one year. In this day and age, the respective figures are one in ten thousand and less than ten in a thousand. Of this couple's seven offspring, three died in childhood.

John and Margaret's second child, Peter, was the eldest of the four surviving children. This was my grandfather. He took over the family business. William, the next, became a lawyer. Then came John, who graduated as a doctor, became interested in the Baha'i religion, was secretary to Shoghi Effendi, grandson of Baha' u'llah, the founder of the religion, and wrote the book *Baha' u'llah and the New Era*. The Baha'i faith proclaims the necessity and the inevitability of the unification of mankind, and has spread to practically every country of the world. John died in 1926 at the age of fifty-one years and is buried on Mount Carmel. His book has survived and is described in *Encyclopaedia Britannica* (15th Edition, 1974) as the "classic introduction to the Baha'i faith, giving a general view of its history and teachings". I am still approached by people of various nationalities who ask if I am related.

My grandparents' first baby, Margaret, was born in November 1896. Her father did not believe in immunization and Margaret developed diphtheria and died in January 1901.

Charlotte Gordon was born a year after that, went into the family business, never married and died many years later, in 1987.

The third child was a boy, Alexander Gordon. He joined the Heinz Company, and eventually became Secretary and Director to the Company. He married and had two children, Peter and John, my cousins.

My father, John Connon, was born next, in 1905. He graduated as a Bachelor of Commerce at Aberdeen University and also went into the family business, becoming Managing Director.

The last child of this family was named Mary Gerrie (Molly), born in 1908. In September 1931 she married Dr Robert (Bob) Scott, who died as a relatively young man in 1935. Ironically, his death was at about the time when the antibacterial properties of the sulphonamide drugs became known and, as the cause of his death was bacterial endocarditis, he might have been helped by these drugs. Aunt Molly herself studied medicine and became a doctor. She later remarried another doctor but there were no children from either marriage.

Thus is painted my paternal background.

My brother has been compiling the family tree, in which is found an Archbishop of Canterbury, Davidson of Lambeth, Randall Thomas Davidson, 1st Baron. The Archbishop's uncle, Lord Henry Cockburn, was Solicitor General for Scotland in the nineteenth century.

In his book *The Seven Daughter s of Eve*,[1] Professor Bryan Sykes discusses the importance of our maternal ancestry but, unfortunately, much less is known about my mother's side of the family.

My maternal grandfather, John Milne, born in 1874, was from Dundee. He had five sisters and two brothers. From the 1881 British Census, he was the son of John and Margaret Milne, who lived at 15 Strawberry Bank, Dundee. His father was a flour and provision merchant. My grandfather spent the first few years of his life in a house overlooking the River Tay. He described how, when he was a small child, he was playing on the floor one night when there was a terrible storm. One of the older members of his family was watching the storm and the lights of the train crossing the bridge through the window. He stated that the train lights vanished. It was the night of the Tay Bridge disaster in 1879. He also remembered how William McGonagall, the well-known

---

1   Sykes, B. *The Seven Daughters of Eve*, Corgi Books, Great Britain, 2001.

writer of dreadful poetry, came round the doors, selling his broadsheets.

He married Emily Jackson. I can find little about her but the family appears to come from the region of Lockerbie, in the Borders.

My grandfather's brother in America lost all his money in the Wall Street crash. When this occurred, he was in Niagara, and went out, all dressed up for dinner, for a splendid meal. Having dined, he jumped over the falls.

There were two children of the marriage, John, known as Jack, and my mother Grace Muriel. John Connon Esslemont married Grace Muriel Mine on 1st August 1931, completing the sketch of the background of my existence.

Chapter 2

Antebellum

In the sketch of the family tree was mentioned my great-grandfather's older brother, Peter, who became a Lord Provost.

His granddaughter, Mary, was born in 1891. She was engaged to be married but, unfortunately, before the wedding, her fiancé died. As was a custom in those days, she took a year off and travelled round the world. On returning to Aberdeen, because of her misfortune, she studied medicine, and became a general practitioner.

She had quite a determined personality, and was the first woman president of the men's Student Union of Aberdeen University. The author, Eric Linklater, describes this in his biography, *Fanfare for a Tin Hat*.

She ran a general practice in Aberdeen, with a branch surgery in Torry, one of the poorest areas of the city. She had patients who were so poor that they would delay calling the doctor until they were practically at death's door, too late to be saved. Often, instead of leaving a bill, she would leave a currency note on the kitchen table. She was the only Scot, and the only woman, to be on the Committee setting up the National Health Service.

Dr Mary received many honours, including the Freedom of the City of Aberdeen.

She was the doctor who delivered me, at home, on 2nd September 1932.

Evidently I was overdue, and the Professor of Midwifery attended my birth. At first I had difficulty in breathing and the Professor suggested trying some whisky. It worked!

As I wrote at the beginning, life is a continuum. Logically, in the womb, the first nerve cells, the neurons, develop. When electrical discharges between them begin, our thought processes begin, either consciously or subconsciously. At the other end of life, when these discharges cease, all thought processes come to an end. What we call "life" is, in fact, conscious existence, what we see as our "being".

Memories of the first few years of life are a little like patches of light in the mist.

I gather that my mother was very ill for the first year of my life and that I was cared for during this period by my paternal grandparents in Aberdeen.

There are very early memories, of sitting on a wicker chair, my legs being hurt by the ends of the canes; of being picked up to be kissed by my grandfathers, who had moustaches, the bristles rough on my face.

There is the recollection of a visit to the West Coast of Scotland, of dark rock and the sea washing in, with froth, "like daddy's shaving soap".

In 1936 we visited the Empire Exhibition in Glasgow, which had, as part of it, a fun-fair. I remember being on the bumper cars with my father, catching his spirit of enjoyment as we careered round the floor, and, in the street outside, excited at seeing the famous Graf Zeppelin, one of a series of rigid airships built by Graf Ferdinand von Zeppelin of Germany.

My playmate was our dog, Kuno, a black cocker spaniel, very kind and quiet, who put up with me using him as a horse without any complaint.

Back in Aberdeen, I started at the local primary school, Broomhill, at the age of four. The teacher smiled a lot. She was very kind and understanding and very likeable. We started learning the alphabet from almost the first day.

In the patchwork of memories, a series of "snapshots" include recollections of the "woodie" opposite the school, of running home from school one day for some reason, of learning to tie shoelaces, of the school gymnasium and being taught to "breathe in through the nose, out through either the nose or the mouth".

About then came my first awareness of death. My mother said that a boy I had entered school with had died. I remember that he was a small, rather scruffy boy in a woollen jersey. I rather think that he died of meningitis, probably of the tuberculous kind. I had difficulty going to sleep that night. I had not been close to the boy but I felt sorry for him, and was aware that I would not see him again.

There is a memory of the gates of Glamis Castle and of the King driving through – it was the old king, George V, so it must have been prior to 1935.

The coronation of King George VI I can remember well as there was a splendid procession and we had a first-class view from the windows of the family business in King Street in Aberdeen.

On 8th February 1937, my brother Alan was born. During the time of his birth I was looked after at my Aberdeen grandparents' house. I have a memory of wanting to see my baby brother but it was several days before I returned home. It was a bit disappointing to have to wait to see him.

Memories are few and far between, but I recall that Walt Disney's film, *Snow White and the Seven Dwarfs* came out for the first time about then.

In 1939 it seems that I learned some words at school not considered suitable for a polite child's vocabulary. Apparently I tried one on my aunt and my stay at Broomhill School came to a speedy end.

At the end of June, just prior to the finish of term, we were all given gas masks and were shown how to use them.

Sometimes I went to my father's office and well remember my aunt's little cubicle with all its Chinese and Indian ivory souvenirs, overlooking the tea blending floor with its dry, astringent, crisp smell of the fresh tea leaves imported from the Far East. From there I would go through to the confectionery factory with its completely different heavy, sweet smell, mixed with cinnamon and peppermint.

In July, the annual holiday was on a farm in Glen Fincastle, near Loch Tummel. I had great fun, riding farm horses, helping to round up the cattle, playing with the dog. We visited friends on a close-by farm, on the shores of Loch Tummel. That farm is now under the waters of the loch, which was later vastly expanded when the hydroelectric scheme came into being after the war.

It was then that we visited Blair Castle, and I was fascinated by a pair of large china nodding mandarins.

Chapter 3

Things Begin to Happen

The 2nd of September 1939 was the seventh anniversary of my birth. It was a Saturday. Next day was warm and sunny, and in the morning I was playing in the garden. My father came out and said that we were at war. He explained that Germany had invaded first Czechoslovakia, and then Poland, and that now Britain had declared war on Germany.

For an unknown reason, I experienced a feeling of *déjà vu*. I did not know what *déjà vu* was but felt that I had been here before and that it had all happened before.

The following day I started at my new school, the Aberdeen Grammar School, one of the oldest institutes in the country, having been founded prior to 1256. In early times it was closely associated with the town's kirk of St. Nicholas. It originally stood near the aforementioned church, in the Schoolhill, a little to the west of where now stands Gray's School of Art. The archery prizes still hang in the office of the Rector.

In the Roll of Pupils is an entry: "Gordon, George Byron. Entd. II. 1795-1798. (In 1798 name appears as Geo. Dom. de Byron.)". In 1785 Catherine Gordon of Gight married the Hon. John Byron and their son, Lord Byron, lived in a house in Broad Street, Aberdeen, for some years after his birth.

At the new school I felt a stranger. Again, in my first day, the teacher, Miss Gracie, was patient and kind. I can recall that four of the pupils stayed at the boarding house as their parents were overseas.

I soon learned that I was ahead of the rest of the class in what I had been taught, in spite of the fact that I was one of the youngest.

I had my first set of football clothes and football boots and, two days after starting at the new school, I ran up to the sports field, which was not far from home.

I entered the back gate and was running across the playing fields when someone shouted at me. It was the sports master. I had been looking forward a great deal to playing football but was completely put off and have disliked all forms of sports ever since.

The war very soon had an effect on the school. The building of one of the other educational establishments, the Central School, was taken over for war business so both schools functioned from the Grammar. So that each establishment could retain an identity, during one month classes would begin in the morning and the following month, in the afternoon. This meant starting at 8.30 am or finishing at 5.30 pm on alternate months. In the winter, it would be dark when we started or when we finished. The school lunches, which were held in what was formerly the chapel, were discontinued and the building was used for the wood and metalwork classes.

Birthday parties of pupils, because of the onset of food rationing, came to an end. I only attended one or two of them.

At home, much of the garden was dug up to plant vegetables. Just prior to the onset of hostilities a new large, glass play room had been built, and this was subdivided to form a greenhouse to grow tomatoes, and the large part which remained was used for whist drives and concerts to raise money for the war effort.

In the street, there was a fire practice so that we could learn how to use the new stirrup pumps. The most exiting complication was the fact that the tarmacadam road surface went on fire and had to be extinguished!

I can remember the last banana and, for one to two years, the only meat was mutton. The public was no longer able to use the beach and use of cars was drastically curtailed. In May to June 1940, Dunkirk fell, and we wondered when the invasion of Britain would take place. Otherwise, apart from the restrictions, little exciting happened during that first year.

The July holiday in 1940 was spent on a farm in Glen Clova. The restrictions of the war were beginning to show. The only available confectionery was a sherbet – there were, by this time, no lemonades. However we once again enjoyed farm life. Watching the sheep-dipping was a new experience.

While we were out walking one day, there was a massive explosion over the hills. It sounded like a bomb but we never discovered what it was. The other bit of excitement, which we missed as we were on holiday, was the crash of a German aeroplane into the new ice-rink which was being built near our house.

In January 1941 my great-grandmother Gordon, Grandfather Peter's mother-in-law, died aged 99 years. I remember her as a spare, somewhat forbidding old lady. After church on Sunday mornings Alan and I walked up to Louisville Avenue where she lived with my grandparents; to be paraded before her; and she would ask what we learned in church that day. She had suffered a stroke some months previously and was bed-bound and cared for at home until her demise, I think of pneumonia.

In 1941 we laughed at Charlie Chaplin's film, *The Great Dictator*. It was a welcome, hilarious relief in those early dark days.

I had a long illness at that time and was two months off school. In the course of the illness, with so much bed rest, I developed a dropped arch in my left foot, which has given me some trouble since then.

Summer holidays in 1941 were a full two months spent on a farm in Finzean. I had learned how to ride a bicycle by then and we had an energetic holiday cycling up to the Forest of Birse, walking through the woods to the sounds of the wood pigeons, fishing with a bent pin and catching nothing. I also started to learn angling. Each day the children of the farm and I took the milk up to a cottage on the hill, over the hay field after the haymaking. We gathered wild raspberries and made jam. One evening there was a film show at the village hall followed by a dance. At Finzean, for the first time, I saw tinkers – "tinkies" as they were called. My mother made me stay inside until they had gone. She said they were always fighting.

The Battle of Britain took place between 16th July and 15th September, 1940. However, after that, the Luftwaffe maintained a bombing offensive, attacking Britain's larger cities. One of the main targets was the Glasgow docks, and the Clydebank blitz is well remembered. On the return journey the German planes would jettison their remaining bombs on Aberdeen, the railway junction, Kittybrewster, being a favourite target.

Our "air-raid shelter" was the cupboard under the stairs. The sirens would waken us and we would go downstairs to the shelter, in which there was a bed. The raids were so frequent that for days on end we would be sleepy for the next day and night.

One particularly bad raid was memorable, as there was a fantastic display of the Northern Lights (Aurora Borealis) that night. We stood outside, mesmerized by the sight, made more spectacular by the glow of the burning beach fairground, which had been hit. It was somewhat imprudent to be standing outside but it was a sight not to be forgotten.

The foolhardiness of venturing outside was soon brought home to me. At one of the birthday parties in the first few months of the war, I had met, and played with, a particularly fun-loving pupil. At school, we were shocked to learn that he had been killed by the German planes that were machine-gunning the streets.

It was towards the end of that year of raids when we had a particularly bad bombing attack. My cousin from Dundee and her mother were visiting at the time, and when the sirens went off we all gathered in the cupboard under the stairs which was used as our air-raid shelter.

Most of the bombing was in the more industrialized area of the city, but at one point there was a bang, closer at hand. The next bomb explosion sounded nearer, and then the next was nearer still. We sat, wondering what was going to happen. Suddenly the repeated bangs stopped. My aunt and cousin left the next day, cutting short their visit. I gather that there were few or no raids on Dundee!

Next day, we curious children went to where the bombing had occurred, to stare at the empty space where a house in a row of tenements had been, with a bed still perched precariously on an upstairs floor and a telephone receiver dangling over the edge.

News of the war was not good. One by one, the countries fell – Holland, Belgium, Denmark and half of France. It was a very frightening time. Then came the fall of Norway and Hitler began his fated march to Russia. My father had built a valve radio prior to the war and on it we followed the advance of the German Army to Moscow and to Stalingrad.

During these years I caught all the childhood illnesses. I cannot remember whooping cough, but measles was nasty, mumps unpleasant, chicken pox very uncomfortable. The best of all was german measles as I did not feel particularly ill but had a fortnight off school. They were some of the best days of spring, the sun shining and all the daffodils blooming.

The garden had a pond and a burn running through it, which was great fun. On one occasion, one of my friends fell into the pond. We trailed up to the house and it was pointed out that his feet were dry. We explained that he had fallen in head first.

The pond and burn were also of great interest to me as I enjoyed learning about all the water creatures, and yearly watched the progressive development of frog spawn, from tadpole to young, then grown-up frogs. Thus began my life-long interest in biology.

For our summer holiday in 1942, we stayed on a farm near Torphins. I took part in the harvesting at the end of August and since then have never lost the joy of harvest-time.

In October 1942, one evening when I was in bed – I am unsure if I had been unwell – my father came up to see me and said that, that evening, a big battle was taking place in the desert in North Africa at a place called Alamein.

School memories were of learning poems such as "Young Lochinvar". The first songs we sang were "The Flight of the Earls", "Hearts of Oak" and "The Bluebells of Scotland". We learned multiplication and division tables, some history and geography.

There was no television in those days and listening to the radio filled the evenings.

The fortunes of war, by this time, had begun to turn. After the bombing of Pearl Harbor by the Japanese, the Americans had come into the fight. The Allied Forces were now fighting their way back across North Africa, back to Tunis; landings had taken place in Sicily; and then into the toe of Italy.

About that time my aunt, Molly, took up her resident's job as a doctor at the Aberdeen City Hospital, the local fever hospital. I was invited for Sunday lunch each week and, after lunch it was my delight to visit the laboratory, where there were all the specimens, cultures of germs in Petri dishes and, of course, rats, mice, guinea pigs and a monkey. My interest in medicine was kindled and continued from there. One of the other residents married Aunt Molly in April 1944 and so I then had three doctors in my life not including a more distant cousin, also a doctor.

In 1943, Italy discontinued her participation in the war. My parents, Alan and I were then on our summer vacation in Huntly. That holiday was when I continued to learn to fish, not very successful angling, my only catch being an undersized trout.

It was about then that I joined the Wolf Cubs, for the second time. I had joined the 17th Pack in 1939 but that Pack had folded up by my second or third visit, not as a result of my joining, I hope! This time I became a member of the 9th Pack and my life in the Scouts, which was to become invaluable to me later, had begun.

At school, informal discussion on current events was much more exciting than the school curriculum. The bombing of the Ruhr dams was particularly interesting despite the modern condemnation of this action and the retrospective judgment that the result had little significant impact on the war effort. In those days, after what Britain had experienced over the last few years, any action which damaged Germany was considered good.

On 6th June 1944 began the Normandy landings that were the forerunner to the end of the war, and the day-to-day progress was eagerly watched.

I can remember summer holidays more acutely than the daily grind of the schoolwork, and that year we stayed in Bellabeg, Strathdon. We spent a lot of time cycling, and climbing the local hill to pick blaeberries (blueberries) but ending up picking cranberries which were much more plentiful. I had made a model aeroplane with a small jet engine and I enjoyed flying it in a small glen locally. The jet propulsion soon came to an end, which was disappointing.

It was there that we attended the Lonach Highland Games for the first time. This Gathering is made all the more spectacular as it is preceded by a march of all the local highlanders, in full highland dress and carrying pikes and banners, for seven miles up the glen, visiting the big houses on the way, where they would be refreshed by a drop of malt whisky, manufactured in a nearby glen.

1944 to 1945 was the last year of the war and my last year of primary school. In the newsreels viewed in the local News Cinema, films of the taking of Belsen and other German concentration camps disclosed the awful sights of piles of starved bodies, the results of the treatment by the concentration camp staff. The war rapidly came to an end, and on 29th April 1945, the instrument of unconditional surrender was signed by two German plenipotentiaries and the war in Europe was over. In Aberdeen, however, wartime restrictions of blackout at night etcetera continued for another month or so because Aberdeen was a port and there remained the danger of Nazi U-boats and other shipping which could continue hostile acts.

We spent our annual holiday in 1945 at Dinnet in Deeside. My paternal grandparents were there and my aunt and uncle and cousin Peter from London, whom I had not seen since before the war. I thoroughly enjoyed that holiday and spent it exploring the two nearby lochs and the remains of prehistoric houses in the area.

In early August, over the radio came the news that an atomic bomb, a bomb of unprecedented power, had destroyed Hiroshima. Political correctness condemns such an action taking place, but in those days of stress, the event was wonderful news.

Two days later, a second bomb was dropped on Nagasaki. There seems little doubt that these two bombs shortened the war and saved countless lives, despite the lives lost in the explosions. In the light of the atrocities committed by the Japanese until then, often not revealed until later, the war was over not too soon. On 2nd September, 1945, my birthday, Japan signed the peace treaty.

What do I recall of the war?

Two main things acutely stay in my memory. One was the songs, "The White Cliffs of Dover", "We'll Meet Again", "Run Rabbit Run", "You Are My Sunshine", "Wish Me Luck", and many others. There was no television, and the radio was almost the only evening entertainment, closeted inside with the blackout outside. The other memory was the *camaraderie*. Neighbours spoke to neighbours, whist drives were organised in the district to raise money for the war effort. It was a different world then.

Chapter 4

Postbellum

The next transition in my life was the summer holiday of 1945; for it was then that I entered secondary school and metamorphosed from a Cub to a Scout.

In Primary school the class had one teacher who could be stimulating or punitive for the course of a year. In secondary school different teachers taught different subjects. All gave out homework, so that at the end of the day, there were six to eight sets of reading and writing to do. Latin could involve one to two hours work in the evening. The math's teacher made a point of allocating only fifteen minutes to his after-hours work.

Boy Scout activity was a different learning curve. I mastered the skills of survival and how to look after myself when camping, besides being fun and making new friends, friendships that have lasted better than school friends.

Entering the third year of secondary school, we had to choose what subjects would be best for passing the leaving certificate. Higher English was mandatory. Science was an obvious choice, as was Maths. A language was obligatory for university entrance, so French was chosen as Latin seemed too difficult to my way of thinking. History or Geography was also necessary. I chose History. Higher Art was also chosen as a higher subject due to a certain skill I had in drawing and painting.

1948 was the year we "flitted". My "Dundee" grandparents were aging and it was decided to move house to a larger one where the grandparents could be accommodated in some of the rooms, and we became a larger family. Gone was the burn and the pond but the new place was very suitable in many other aspects, centrally heated, pleasant rooms, nice neighbours, nearer school. A couple of streets away lived Mary Garden, the opera singer.

Strangely enough, I have much less recollection of where we spent holidays. Perhaps Scout camps were more memorable. I recall that they were held at Braemar, Haddo House, Loch Morlich near Aviemore, Glen Esk, Dinnet and Braemar again. In 1948 I spent two weeks in London. It was an exciting and educational fortnight. The weather was beautiful and every day was spent seeing something new, visiting the Tower of London, Hampton Court, the Science Museum at Kensington and the countryside around the city. I visited Bray but did not meet the Vicar!

In September 1948 occurred an unforgettable experience. I do not know how many pupils were involved but we had a block booking as spectators at a cricket match between Australia and a Scottish team. It was the last match that Don Bradman played in Britain, after his last test match, in which he scored a duck. The match lasted two days and Bradman certainly scored no duck on this occasion. Once he gained his century, he really hit out at the ball, sending it over the grandstand a number of times. It was unforgettable playing. Only once since then have I watched cricket, a test match at Headingly at Leeds between the West Indian team and England. Very little happened and it was deadly boring, despite the presence of the West Indian steel band.

At the end of the fifth year of secondary school, I gained Higher English, Higher Science, Higher Art, Lower Mathematics and Lower History. It was considered advisable that I gain at least one, and if possible two, further Higher subjects in an extra year at school so I aimed at converting the Lower Maths and Lower French into Highers. My Lower French had been gained by coaching. The coaching had been so good and the mark had been so high that I was advised to go on to the Higher examination. It did not work! The conversion of Lower to Higher Maths also almost came unstuck. Correct enunciation of a theorem gained twenty marks, thus answering three theorems correctly achieved a pass mark. Deductions involved thinking rather than memory, and so were chancier, scoring fewer marks. In the examination, I completely forgot how to work out the Corollary to the Theorem of Pythagoras. Fortunately I solved two deductions so I passed the examination.

I considered that it was not worthwhile sitting the Bursary Competition as I did not have any realistic chance of passing and so my sixth year at school entailed very little work.

However, this year of comparative leisure was full of interest. A visit was organised to the Edinburgh Festival. The year was 1949 and it was the third Festival. I can remember seeing a play by Peter Ustinov, who was relatively unknown at that time; "Un Ballo in Masquera" by Verdi; attending a recital for viola and piano played by Fritz Busch and Rudolph Serkin respectively; and sitting in the orchestra stalls to watch and listen to a concert conducted by Sir Thomas Beecham. The latter was quite extraordinary. Beecham shouted at the orchestra. Presumably his vocal efforts were unheard in the main body of the Usher Hall, which was the concert venue. The newspaper reviews added to the entertainment on the railway journey home next day. For the Busch and Serkin recital it was noted that in playing from memory, in the last semiquaver before the recapitulation, Fritz Busch played F-sharp instead of E-flat! In the review of the Beecham concert, it started by saying that Beecham began with a variation of his own on an original theme, "God Save the King".

For the rest of the school year, besides the two subjects studied for the Highers, I, with two other pupils, was involved in painting murals for one of the classrooms, the subject being Chaucer and the Canterbury Tales. Some sixteen years later, the murals were there but they were damaged by a fire in the school many years after that, and destroyed.

Another extracurricular subject was biology, as I, and a few others, were going to study Medicine.

The last year at school was therefore full of fun and interest.

During my school years, the Art Master introduced me to a film society held on Sunday evenings at another school. Famous films of the history of the cinema were shown, *The Birth of a Nation*, *Intolerance*, *The Battleship Potemkin*, *Ivan the Terrible*, *Rembrandt* and many others. There was probably no significant film in the history of the cinema that I did not see. I have continued to be interested in film art but during my working life it became more difficult to pursue this hobby until the advent of classical videos and DVDs. Now again I have been able to see how film-making has progressed.

About this time, the play, *Castle in the Air*, by Alan Melville, visited Aberdeen. My mother had mentioned that Jack Buchanan was some sort of relation. His entrance, almost dancing down the steps of the stage, was evocative of his sparkling personality.

It was during the final years at school that we had a talk by Eric Linklater, a former pupil of the school, and now a well-known author. His talk, about his experiences in the Second World War, was spell-binding. A born raconteur, he described how he worked as a journalist in Italy, once, by misadventure, meeting General Eisenhower as the result of tripping over that senior officer's tent guy rope. Years later, he recounted his adventures in his biography, *Fanfare for a Tin Hat*.

Thus the most interesting year at school brought to an end my school career.

Chapter 5

Alma Mater

University was very different from school. In those days matriculation fees were paid and I learned afterwards that the family had clubbed together to pay for my medical education. My father made it plain to me that, should I fail the exams, I would have to leave university and look for a job.

The University of Aberdeen was originally two Universities. What is now King's College, Old Aberdeen, was founded by William Elphinston, Bishop of Aberdeen from 1483 to 1514. In 1495 Bishop Elphinston obtained a Bull from Pope Alexander VI (Alexander Borgia) granting authority to establish a University. One of the original faculties was Medicine, which made Aberdeen the oldest medical school in the English speaking world.

Marischal College was founded in 1593 by a Protestant, George Keith, 5th Earl Marischal, in opposition to King's College, which was under the control of the Catholic Earl of Huntly. Aberdeen now had as many universities as the whole of England. The two Colleges were united as the University of Aberdeen in 1860.

The very first day at University I remember well. We were gathered in a group in Marischal College quadrangle outside our first lecture room. A few of the students I knew. One third were from Scotland, one third from elsewhere in the British Isles and the other third from the rest of the world.

Lectures were given but it was our responsibility to read the textbooks and to learn. The subjects were chemistry including organic chemistry, physics and biology, which consisted of zoology and botany.

The lecturer in chemistry was Dr Strathdee, who introduced us into the university system. It was said of him:

Virtuous and wise he was – but not severe
He still remembered that he once was young.

Armstrong.

The quotation is very apt. He was very human, and acted as a counsellor to the fledgling students.

Dr Griffiths was the physics lecturer. He was more aloof, but with a sense of humour. His first lecture began: "Imagine a beetle crawling along a metre rule. That is velocity." Later, when explaining electrical frequency, he demonstrated very high frequency by holding an electric light bulb in his hands and touching the contacts with his fingers, making it light up.

The zoology lecturer, Dr Neill, would walk into the lecture room, exactly at the start of his lecture, lock the door behind him and proceed with the lecture. At the end, he would finish his sentence exactly on time, unlock the door and leave. The next lecture would start with the next sentence, where he had left off.

During the first year we were all medically examined by the university doctor, Dr John Macklin, who, many years before, had been on Shackleton's expedition to the Antarctic.

For me, the first university year was very quiet, learning to adjust. At the end of the year we sat the first professional examination.

The summer holidays were long, three months, so in mid-August, I, with some friends started a job, grouse-beating up in Strathdon.

I enjoyed walking, so, if I was going to be paid for it, it would be most enjoyable. Two of us lived in a tent, at the Cock Brig, Corgarff.

The estates we worked on were Candacraig Estate, the laird of which was Major "Dandy" Wallace, and Delnadamph Estate, the owner of which was Mr Thessinger, at that time the Lord Mayor of London.

We walked over the heather-clad hills about twenty miles a day, all in a line, waving white flags at the ends of sticks, driving grouse. The keeper who looked after us was Fettes Tindal. We were paid one pound, a piece of cake, and a bottle of beer per day.

We worked there for two months and, by the beginning of October, would wake up in the morning with frost on our sleeping bags. Dressing and cooking in our sleeping bags became an art form.

The next stage of our medical career took one and two-thirds years, encompassing anatomy, physiology and biochemistry, with psychology and statistics thrown in.

As can be imagined, anatomy was the most dramatic and daunting of the subjects. The professor was Professor R. D. Lockhart, and his lecture on the skin was our introduction to the second year of the medical course. Prior to the lecture, he took the roll, reading our names at fast conversation speed. Our job was to know where our names were in the list, and to answer without a break, so that the roll-call took not more than two minutes. He described the skin as a magician's mantle, a waterproof, an overcoat, a sunshade, a suit of armour, a refrigerator, sensitive to the touch of a feather, to temperature and to pain, withstanding the wear and tear of three score years and ten, and executing its own running repairs.

After the lecture, we were introduced to the dissecting room and to the body we were to dissect over the next year. We were all somewhat subdued at the prospect, but spent hours over the one and two-thirds years at the job of dissecting and memorising.

Besides the professor, there were three lecturers, the most senior of whom was Dr G. F. Hamilton, an expert in neurology. He was an intimidating examiner, who would ask a question and, on receipt of an answer, say "Ye-es?" in a rising tone, then wait, whereupon you would try to add more, he would again say "Ye-es?" and go on, until you had thoroughly incriminated yourself.

The next most senior lecturer was Dr F. G. Fyfe, a rather taciturn man, until, at one lecture, he was explaining how one side of the body was more dominant than the other, demonstrated by the fact that he could wink better with his left eye than his right. When he realised that all the girls were seated on his left, he was seen to faintly smile.

The third lecturer was Dr J. McKenzie, a good looking young man and the blandest of the three, without the others' eccentricities.

There were also demonstrators who would help out in showing parts of the anatomy when we were in doubt. One of these demonstrators insisted on spelling out the anatomical names – "This is the Temporal Bone; T-E-M-P-O-R-A-L, Temporal, B-O-N-E, Bone."

Physiology, how the body works, was more difficult. The practical experiments were interesting and I discovered that I could hold my breath for four minutes, which was useful to know as I was keen on swimming at that time.

Besides swimming, I took lessons in fencing (épée), Scottish Country Dancing and American Square Dancing.

Biochemistry was the worst of all and the reason for most of the failures in the second professional examination.

I developed a system for swotting. I had discovered that, if I worked all night, I was useless next day, so I worked until midnight then went to bed. At one of the university "hops" (Saturday night dances) I had met a very nice girl. She was a trainee nurse and worked five nights then had one night off. Thus I would swot for five nights then take the evening off. We went out for a bit over a year then stopped meeting. I was not in the position yet to settle down and felt it was unfair to monopolise this girl when she could be meeting others more promising.

The year was 1953 and the secrets of RNA and DNA were just being revealed. The very last biochemical lecture before the examination was on the molecular structure of RNA. Many of the students were doing last-minute "swotting" and skipped the lecture. It had not yet reached the textbooks but was an examination question! Fortunately I had even memorised the formula.

The second professional examination was such a *pons asinorum* that, when a few of us discovered that we had passed, we went to the local bar and had a few beers before going home to lunch, the first time in my life I had done such a thing.

The course for the second professional examination covered one and two thirds years so it was broken by the three-month long summer vacation, where again I went grouse beating.

This time, after the first two weeks, the laird let us use an old disused inn on the Strathdon end of the Glengairn road, which made things a bit more comfortable. On the days when there was no shooting and therefore no beating, we worked on the farm. Most of the time, we harvested.

Occasionally, Major Wallace would visit to see how we were doing. In 1946 or 1947, during the outbreak of Poliomyelitis, he had contracted the disease. He was determined not to be beaten by disablement, and would be carried up to the shooting butts where he would be seated on a piano stool and shoot the birds, using the stool to swivel himself round for the shots. He was quite a remarkable marksman. I saw him shoot two birds, one with each barrel, in front of the butts, grab another gun, shoot two birds as they flew over the butts, and then, with yet another gun shoot two behind the butts as they flew away – six birds in one covey.

On the harvest field, he would throw down his sticks, pick up two sheaves of corn and throw them up to the man building the corn rick. Despite his infirmity, he was working faster than any of us.

On the days when there was no harvesting because of rain, we worked with the quantity of pigs that were being reared. One of the students had loaded a truck with vegetables and came in, standing on the fodder, pleased at having a little rest. The driver started to tip the truck, unnoticed by the student who even steadied himself with his hand on the tipping load, until all the vegetables, student and all, slid off the back, down among the pigs. It was a smelly job and the odour of pig clung to these particular clothes for years afterwards.

Back to university and, the second of the major exams completed, studies in pathology, bacteriology, *materia medica*, medicine and surgery began at the medical school at Forresterhill instead of Marischal College.

It was about this time that I went with my parents on a holiday in the southwest of Scotland. We visited a cousin of my mother, John Maxwell, at Dalbeattie. He was an artist and painted pictures for his living. On this visit, he said that he was due four pictures in all to the various Scottish art galleries, for which he would be paid a thousand pounds each. He was also interested in the new hi-fi gramophones, not long introduced, and showed us his Leak amplifier and an old horn gramophone, the horn of which was six feet in diameter. We were introduced to "Pictures at an Exhibition" by Mussorgsky and "The Four Seasons" by Vivaldi. His other interest was his garden and he took us out to show it to us, laid out in a Roman style with a rectangular pool with paving round the pool and a row of pencil pines on each side. He said that he had laid this out three years previously, that he was getting a bit tired of it as it was, and that he was going to dig the whole lot up and replant it in a completely different, informal style. He said that he did that every three years!

Only one term of the third year was left, after which, this year, I tried a change in holiday work, as a hospital orderly at Aberdeen City Hospital, the hospital for infectious diseases, "the fever hospital".

Now it was face-to-face with patients, in the humble role of a very junior member of staff. I also had to learn the intricacies of avoiding transfer of infection, to myself and to other patients.

A patient with Weil's disease, deeply jaundiced, with small spots of bleeding into his skin, had to have his urine checked daily for blood cells. There was a girl, not yet in her teens, who died of tuberculous meningitis, whose post-mortem I attended. There was a boy who was admitted with poliomyelitis. It was quite dramatic how he could sit up from the recumbent position, his spine as rigid as a poker, all in one movement.

Another man came in and died of subarachnoid haemorrhage. The doctor did all he could physically to revive him and I am uncertain as to whether such violent methods are warranted in someone who is at the point of death. With him, I learned how to prepare a body for funeral.

There was a girl of about eight who looked very sunburnt as she had Addison's disease, which, in those days, was often due to tuberculosis of the adrenal glands.

A woman was admitted with a high fever. I was given the job of tepid sponging her and her temperature fell from 104° F to a normal 98.4° F immediately. It was not the sponging which was effective – she had Hodgkin's disease and was demonstrating Pel-Ebstein fever. The late Dr Richard Asher, in his book *Talking Sense*, stated that no such condition as Pel-Ebstein existed as he had never seen it. Having seen it, I could have assured him that it did.

The patient whom I remember most vividly was a boy of fourteen, who had fallen into a stream about eight days previously and grazed his head. He was developing stiffness of his muscles. He had attended his doctor but, for some reason, had not been given ATS (anti-tetanus serum). Active immunisation of tetanus had not yet begun. Culture of his scalp wound confirmed tetanus bacilli. Treatment for tetanus – apart from sedation – had not then started. I was given the job of "specialling" – sitting with him, observing and reporting any problems. I had to be absolutely quiet as any stimulus, including sound, would set off a tetanic spasm. It was rather eerie. He lay there motionless with a quiet smile – the *risus sardonicus* – occasionally going into a tetanic spasm, where his whole body would arch in acute muscle spasm. Muscles can snap, such is the strength of the contraction. The spasms became more frequent, until it was time for me to go off-duty. The boy died during the night.

Somewhat sobered by my holiday job, I started my fourth year of medicine; pathology, *materia medica*, bacteriology, public health, forensic medicine. The last was always well attended, partly because law students were also at the lectures and partly because of the nature of the subject. I also had to attend a certain number of post-mortem examinations. One of these was particularly interesting. *Muir's Textbook of Pathology*[1] gives the following account:

> *In newborn lambs, the condition known as "sway-back" is an acute demyelinating disorder which is usually fatal. It is met with in the offspring of ewes kept on pastures deficient in copper, and the administration of small amounts of copper to the ewes before lambing prevents the disorder. An unexplained coincidental finding is the development of symptoms suggestive of disseminating sclerosis in four out of seven research workers engaged in the study of sway-back (Innes).*

This post-mortem was on the fourth of these research workers. It is also of interest that disseminating sclerosis, or multiple sclerosis, is common in northeast and southwest Scotland, sheep-rearing areas, and is rare in Singapore, which does not rear sheep.

During the next summer holiday, I returned to the City Hospital as an orderly, this time in one of the TB (tuberculosis) wards. Patients were in there for two to five years, with the disease in various stages, from small cavities in the lung to half the lung eaten away by the disease. Treatment then was by drugs; streptomycin, para-amino salicylic acid (PAS) and isonicotinic acid hydrochloride (INAH): and by procedures; artificial pneumothorax and pneumoperitoneum. The work was harder and there was less variety than there had been on the previous holiday.

Back to medical school and the course now felt long. Still medicine and surgery, psychiatry, clinical chemistry, bacteriology, ophthalmology, tuberculosis, radiology, infectious diseases, anaesthetics, dermatology, ENT (ear, nose and throat), dental surgery, venereal diseases, radiotherapy, paediatrics, midwifery and gynaecology, the list seemed endless.

---

1   *Muir's Textbook of Pathology*, sixth edition, revised by D. F. Cappell, London; Edward Arnold, 1951.

In spite of the amount of work, on recollection I seemed to be more rather than less active in extra-curricular activities. I had continued in Scouts, as a Scouter. I joined the Lairig Club, in which, for a minimal joining fee, there was a bus laid on once a month, on a Sunday, to take us up into the hills. The bus would arrive at a convenient spot – Derry Lodge, Loch Muick, or wherever – at about eight o'clock in the morning and remain there until about seven in the evening, leaving us to our own devices, whether it be hill-walking, rock-climbing, fishing or just sitting in the bus, reading a book. The first Sunday, a group of us climbed Ben MacDhui, the second highest hill in Scotland.

Another time, from Loch Muick, we climbed Lochnagar. On that occasion, we crossed over into the corrie of Lochnagar to climb up the face of the cliff by the Black Spout. I can remember that the blaeberries were in fruit and we spent some time guzzling them. In the Black Spout, the fellow ahead of me began to slip. I got into a good stance, with my feet in good holds, and caught him in my arms. We were very lucky, as the foot of the cliff and the loch were some hundreds of feet below.

The "Black Spout", Lochnagar.
"Oh for the crags that are wild and majestic!
The steep frowning glories of dark Loch na Garr."
George Gordon (Lord) Byron.

Looking back, down the "Black Spout!

Snow cornice at the top of the "Black Spout".

We reached the top and enjoyed the view, to return to Loch Muick by another route. We were walking down through the glen, when one of the girls asked if any of us had any paper, as she needed to answer a call of nature. From my rucksack I produced a toilet roll. However, her problems were not quite over. The glen was typical of a Cairngorm glen, gouged out eons ago, with smooth heather-covered slopes and neither a tree nor a shrub in sight where the poor girl could conceal herself. I told her that we would walk on and that we would not look round. We were true to our word.

Some years previously, another friend had had a similar call but all he had was the cellophane wrapper of a packet of dates. When he returned from his "call", he ruefully stated that he had used the wrong side of the cellophane! Without thinking he had held the unsticky side. After that, I always went prepared, and a roll of toilet paper really does not take up much space.

We also had one glorious day when we climbed Cairn Toul and went on to Braerhiach, a journey of some twenty-two miles and a climb to over four thousand feet. The sky was spotlessly blue, the sun poured down and the rocks were too hot to touch.

At the end of each Sunday's climb, the bus would take us to the Inver Inn where we had a meal and then a sing-song round the piano on the bar.

I have very vivid and fond memories of these days, the exercise, the highland scenery, the fresh air, and, lastly, the relaxing mood of having satisfied our hunger, a beer, and the companionship of us all singing together.

During the winter holidays and at Easter, a group of the Scout troop and I would go up by bus to Braemar and stay for a week at the Youth Hostel there, going out each day, climbing. We had our bicycles with us, would cycle to the climb, and start walking from there.

The climbs on Lochnagar were the most interesting. We would approach from the west, across a corner of Balmoral, the Queen's estate, and go to the most western tip of the corrie where we would jump over into the deep snow slope then traverse round to the foot of the Black Spout, from where we could start the climb.

On one occasion, there were four of us and we had climbed to just below the top, where we found that the snow overhang was too pronounced to climb over. We stayed on the ledge below the overhang, working out what to do. To go back down would have been precarious as it was so sheer. I stuck my ice-axe into the ice at the edge of the overhang and the others used that as a foothold.

Then I had to climb up, using the chip in the ice as a meagre foothold and with the help of an ice-axe dug well in to the snow on the summit.

Another time, two of us had decided to tackle the Red Spout, another, slightly more difficult ascent. We had just reached the foot of it when we heard a crack, like a rifle shot, above us. We looked up and saw what had the appearance of a ball of snow at the top of the Red Spout. We realised that the cornice had broken away and was coming down on us. I thought that I should get a photo of this, then I thought the situation was much too serious to take photographs, and put the camera away. We traversed to our right as quickly as possible to try to get out of the way of the avalanche but it was coming down too fast. We dug in our ice-axes up to the hilts and got our heads down. The avalanche passed over us because of the steepness of the slope and the only problem was that we were enveloped by tiny dust particles of ice crystals which made it hard to breathe for a minute or two. Then I thought, damn, I should have taken a picture after all!

One Easter, two of us had spent every day climbing for a week and on the next day, had gone out as usual but had decided that we'd had enough climbing so went and bought the morning newspaper and went and read it in a hut on the snow-covered golf course. It was coming up to lunch time so we entered one of the cafés in Braemar for something to eat. It was then that we discovered that we had only sixpence between us. We therefore asked for one cup of tea and two straws and explained our predicament. The lady brought us two cups of tea and a couple of scones.

Having maintained an interest in the Scout troop, each year there was the summer camp, the various camping-grounds being Fraserburgh, Glen Clova, Glenesk, Braemar again, The Isle of Mull, Plockton.

At Fraserburgh, one of our experiences was going out to sea on a North Sea drifter. We had left the harbour when the captain said that it was a pity that we were on board a coal drifter and had boarded on a Monday because, if the catch was not sufficient, they would throw it overboard and go on fishing every day until they had a big enough catch – we might be out at sea until Friday! The sea was quite rough and we remained at sea until Wednesday, when we were landed at Peterhead. There was always a kettle on the coal-fired stove, and it was constantly replenished with more tealeaves and more water. The tea was very black and strong and tasted of coal.

As a student I had ten shillings a week as pocket money. All my transport was by pedal bicycle, which cost nothing but was fairly hard work, and wet in inclement weather. When I was about half-way through university, I approached my father to see if I could use his car sometimes. The answer was in the negative so I tried a bit of blackmail by saying that in that case I would have to buy a motor bicycle. By that time, I had saved enough money in grouse beating and hospital orderly work to possibly afford one. To my surprise, my father said that would be a good idea! The garage man who serviced the vans of my father's business had a second-hand Norton 500 cc which was in good condition and for which he was looking for a buyer, so I bought it for a very good price. Many years later I discovered that my father was thinking along the lines of a BSA 250 cc.

A motor bicycle broadened my horizons a great deal. I continued to use my pedal bicycle round Aberdeen but used the Norton to go for trips down to England and over to the west coast of Scotland, accompanied only by a tent. I arrived in Oban one evening after dark. The problem with travelling from town to town, which is the normal practice, is that, once there, it is somewhat impractical to try to pitch a tent on the tarmacadam. I went up one of the side roads looking for a place to camp. The darkness made it harder to see a place but I eventually found a nice level patch of grass. I pitched the tent, crawled inside and went to sleep. Wakened by the morning light, I put my head out of the tent and looked around. Over me was the railway viaduct and I was camped on the green of the golf course. The tent was packed and I was away within five minutes. It was fortunate that the tent pegs were metal, leaving little trace.

Motorcycling is the ideal form of travel for the West Highland roads, which are very often single track. It meant that I needed little room to pass cars travelling in the opposite direction, and sometimes even in the same direction, without having to reach a passing place. One time I was taken unawares was on the Isle of Mull. The tarmac suddenly came to an end and the road continued as two concrete strips, one for each wheel of a car! I had to continue driving my motor bicycle along one of the concrete strips – it felt like I was on a tightrope.

Motorcycling was less attractive in wet weather when the norm was to be soaked to the skin.

On the summer holiday between the fifth and sixth years at University, I decided that the exercise involved in grouse-beating would be the last chance I would get for a long time. Lord Cowdray, at Skene, which was only ten miles west of Aberdeen on the divide between Deeside and Donside, was looking for beaters. Most of the students working there were accommodated on the estate, and Lord Cowdray, being the man he was, charged for the accommodation. With the motor bicycle, I could live at home and travel each day the ten miles to work. This was agreed to, as I recall, with some reluctance, and I had to be sure that I turned up every day on time.

Lord Cowdray was one of the richest men in Britain at the time and a hard task-master. He certainly obtained his "pound of flesh", having us deal with the burning remnants of the forest fires, which had set light to the peat in the ground; collecting fallen trees from a severe gale some years previously, rain or shine; and farming.

The estates on which we beat were interesting and included estates on Clach-na-ben (hill of the rock), with the hundred-foot rock crowning the top; Dunnotar Castle; and back to Strathdon, where we beat on Edinglassie Estate and I met up with the gamekeepers I had come to know three years previously.

Back to my final year at University, I disciplined myself to read the text-book of surgery and the textbook of medicine and worked every night of the week, finishing at midnight. I would play Brahms' four symphonies as background music.

Saturday was the exception, when I stopped at ten at night, drove down to the Students' Union (after they stopped collecting the entrance fee), had a few dances and escorted home the partner from the last dance. With a motor bicycle it was easy and there was no more looking up the student guide to see where she lived!

This was also the year when it was my turn to stay at the quarters at the hospital, to do my stint at maternity for six weeks. I also did two locum jobs, one at the City Hospital on one of the medical wards and the children's ward, and the other in the maternity hospital.

While I was doing the latter job, the senior professorial lecturer, Dr McGillivray, was examining a patient. Suddenly he stopped and asked me to feel the abdomen, where the scar of a previous Classical Caesarian Section was dehiscing and the baby was starting to be extruded into the abdominal cavity. He then asked me to take the end of the bed and we ran with the bed through to the operating theatre. An anaesthetic was rapidly given, the abdomen was opened and the baby was delivered alive. The whole procedure, from examining the abdomen to the delivery of the baby took four minutes.

One of the junior registrars at that time was an Irishman, Dr Colin Hodge. He was determined that I should learn how to do a hind-water rupture of the placental membranes to induce labour. In the determination, we induced about ten labours. The labour ward maternity sister was furious.

The maternity professor at that time was Professor Dugald Baird, later to become Professor Sir Dugald Baird, both of whose sons had been at school with me. He was a good teacher and full of common sense. I can remember his discussion of the merits of blood transfusion and reminding us that four hundred patients had died as the results of blood transfusion in the previous year. It was a sobering thought and emphasized the need to take seriously whether or not to administer a transfusion.

He was conducting a ward round one day and had come to a patient whom I had clerked. This patient was very full of herself and had spent time impressing on me how her first baby had been delivered by Professor Baird. She did not explain why her current delivery was a public and not a private one. At the ward round, she stated that her first baby had been delivered by the professor. He replied that he did not remember her.

That year also I spent a lot of time in the psychiatric department, where we could watch the patient-doctor session through a viewing screen.

I also attended evening classes at the Arts School, doing portrait painting in oils.

This year passed all too quickly and we came to the final examinations, which took place over two weeks. In the middle of the exams, I developed a tooth root abscess and managed to obtain an emergency dental appointment. The dentist asked how I had come to the dental surgery and I replied that it was by motorbike. However, he gave me a short anaesthetic and removed the tooth. After half an hour I was allowed to return home. I attended the obstetric examination that afternoon, having missed no exams.

At that time, I had started to smoke cigarettes and on the last day of the finals, smoked a hundred of them. I can remember Professor Baird passing and telling us not to smoke ourselves to death.

My last examination finished at 5.30 on the Friday afternoon. The pass list was posted up at Marischal College at 6.00 pm. I had passed!

That evening was spent very quietly. I took my current girlfriend, a very pretty girl, later to become Arts Queen, to the bar at the Athenaeum, where we had three drinks, then walked home.

Graduation took place on 4th July, 1956.

Chapter 6

Post Graduation

"Life is what you make it."

What had I made of my life so far?

I had been very lucky. I had achieved my ambition and had become a doctor but could not have done so without having a very supportive family. My parents, although they administered discipline and sometimes corporal punishment, had not believed in showing emotion and did not consciously show love, but they must have given love by letting me pursue an approved course of career.

Thus, so far, I had been dependent.

Now, I was on my own.

This was expressed very incisively to me. Having graduated, I now had to obtain the means to achieve gainful employment, provisional registration, references, apply for a job. At one point, one of the administrators whom I approached said quite bluntly that I had to do it myself, that I could not expect other people to do the work for me. How much that remark was deserved, I am unable to say but it certainly had an effect.

At graduation, various posts at Aberdeen hospitals had been offered to those who had graduated. I had looked for a position at the City Hospital, where I had felt familiar, but was offered the job as a house surgeon in the thoracic surgery unit at Woodend hospital. I wanted to be a general practitioner and considered that training in thoracic surgery would not be of any value. The senior thoracic surgeon was known to be a pig of a man who did not delegate any work likely to be of any practical learning. I therefore declined that job and started to look for another position. All hospital jobs began on 1st August so I did not have long in which to work.

One of my friends in the class mentioned that Ayr County Hospital was looking for a house surgeon. Ayr is a lovely small town with generally good weather as it lies in the rain shadow of the Isle of Arran.

> "Auld Ayr, wham ne'er a town surpasses
> For honest men and bonnie lasses."
>
> ***Tam O' Shanter,*** **Robert Burns**

Furthermore, the very attractive girl that I was dating lived at Stephenson, not far from Ayr!

I applied for the job and was accepted.

I motorcycled to Dunlop, Ayrshire, where the church minister, Mr Andrew Easton, who was formerly our next door neighbour in Aberdeen, had his parish. There I stayed overnight and was pleasantly surprised when I was brought breakfast in bed by the minister himself!

It was the 31st July and the start of the big adventure.

It was a beautiful morning to be motorcycling among the green rolling hills of north Ayrshire. I reached the town of Ayr, drove up through the square and reached the hospital. I was shown my room and the doctors' common room, which served as a living and dining room. I met the two other doctors, Dr Dykes, who was also doing his first house job as orthopaedic resident, and Dr Aitkenhead, who worked as casualty officer during the day and at the weekends, allowing the two residents the weekends off.

Next morning, I met the surgical registrar, Dr Cameron, and my surgical chief, Mr Cormack.

My duties were that I was to clerk the patients when they were admitted, assist at the surgical operations, assist at the gynaecological operations with Dr Richard de Soldenhoff, who was the obstetrician and gynecologist for the county, and be the casualty officer on call on alternate evenings and nights.

The days were full and it was a steep learning curve. The evenings and nights on casualty were the most daunting, as what might appear in casualty was unknown until it was there. A number of years later it was realized that it was risky to have inexperienced doctors working as casualty officers, as a result of which, only medical officers with several years' experience were allowed to work in such a department unsupervised. On the other hand, the demanding nature of the job necessitated concentrated learning.

I had been at the hospital for about two or three weeks, and had just finished clerking the new admissions in the gynaecological ward for operation next day, when the telephone rang. The nurse answered it, looked at me and said that it was the church minister from Alloway, who wanted to speak to me. The Alloway kirk, with its association with Robert Burns, was one of the more prestigious in the district. I had never met this clergyman, who was a Mr Donaldson, but it turned out that he was a friend of Mr Easton, who had given him my name. I was being invited to lunch next Sunday, and it was the start of a pleasant friendship.

I visited the girlfriend in Stephenson once but it was a relationship that did not come to anything. At a University dance once, the partner with whom I was dancing at the time asked me why I was scared of girls. I was not aware of feelings of this nature, not having had very much to do with them in my childhood. The only women in my life had been my mother, female relatives, my cousin and a rather bossy girl up the road where we lived. At University, I was respectful of them and came to prefer female to male company. I could understand Burns' love of all women.

(Some time after writing this, I came upon Sir Walter Scott's description of Robert Burns, whom he had met in Edinburgh: "I was told, but did not observe it, that his address to females was extremely deferential, and always with a turn either to the pathetic or humorous, which engaged their attention particularly.")

But it was the days before the pill, so that sexual activity, nowadays so prevalent, had to be kept within reasonable bounds. In those days, pregnancy could be a distinct possibility, and the boy and the girl had to maintain a certain degree of self-discipline to prevent any accident.

Burns was well aware of consequences:

> "Whene'er to drink you are inclined,
> Or cutty-sarks rin in your mind,
> Think! Ye may buy the joys o'er dear;
> Remember Tam o' Shanter's mare."
>
> *Tam O' Shanter*, **Robert Burns.**

On the other hand, he was the most human of men:

> "Ae fond kiss, and then we sever!
> Ae fareweel, alas, for ever!"
>
> ***Ae fond kiss,* Robert Burns.**

It is of interest that the Bahá'á faith is the only religion where men and women are accepted as equals.

But I digress.

On my two-week holiday in Aberdeen later in the year, I met the girl from Stephenson again and she visited me at home, together with another girl from Plockton whom I had met the previous year. Both girls were studying at the Dunfermline School of Physical Education in Aberdeen at the time.

I explored the Burns countryside, and found the Ayrshire people to be very hospitable. A number of the nurses invited me along to their homes for meals, in particular for Christmas and New Year dinners.

The most unusual and memorable experience was an afternoon when a patient was brought in, quite intoxicated, laughing and carrying on. It transpired that he had been mowing the grass, was almost finished and had called to his wife to pour him a shandy. She had made up a shandy with beer and the contents of a lemonade bottle, which turned out to be, not lemonade, but trilene (trichloroethylene) which was used as an industrial solvent in the colourless form and, coloured blue, as an anaesthetic in hospitals. His intoxication was practically instantaneous and he was brought to the hospital. I passed a stomach tube into his stomach and emptied the gastric contents (he unfortunately had had tripe for lunch), whereupon he recovered immediately with absolutely no memory of the preceding two hours.

Another lesson I learned was that, if a patient was brought in unconscious because of too much alcohol, intravenous pyridoxine would bring them back to consciousness. The state of consciousness only lasted a few minutes but it would be enough to ask a few questions and obtain a very brief history.

Thus, the six months at Ayr passed reasonably enjoyably and I was sorry when it was drawing to a close.

However, I had to move on and I applied for jobs in Devon, Lincolnshire and Yorkshire. The Devon job was a complete non-starter. I discovered that it was a much sought-after post, the consultant being a distinguished physician and author.

There was a phone call to the hospital from Dewsbury in Yorkshire, asking me to come for an interview. I obtained leave and travelled down overnight. When I arrived in Leeds to change trains, the sky was yellow and the houses were black, and I wondered what I had come to.

The Dewsbury General Infirmary, as it was called, was reasonably up-to-date; I was interviewed and was employed as a house physician (paediatrics and general medicine). The previous house physician, who was also a Scot, showed me round the wards, we had some supper, and then he took me down to the pub to meet the landlord. After that I got on the night train to return to Ayr and the operating session the next day.

The new job, in addition to children and medicine, included casualty again, so that, when the time came for full registration, I had completed a full year of casualty.

Paediatrics is very uplifting but, at the time, can be heartbreaking. One day a child is ill, next day, he or she is bouncing about – or dead. Recovery or death can be so rapid.

My consultant was Dr Atherton, a youngish, very supporting chief. On the medical side was Dr Rae. He admitted very few patients and most of the work was in outpatients. He was a brilliant diagnostician. He would ask about four questions and then send the patient into the examination room, where I would do a full examination. Usually, before I told him the results of the examination, he would produce the diagnosis!

I can remember a patient who had been referred to the orthopaedic consultant with a suspected gangrene of one leg. The leg was almost black. I did the examination, and pulses were certainly present in all places and equal. When I returned to the room, Dr Rae asked if I had ever seen scurvy. The only laboratory test for scurvy we had in those days was to saturate the body with large doses of ascorbic acid and find how many days it took to return to a normal value.

Casualty kept me very busy. The consultant surgeon took a great deal of interest in my work and wanted me to take up orthopaedic surgery as a career. There were many fractures to set and I learned the various minor forms of plastic surgery, grafting, pedicle grafting, which we did ourselves.

We also administered anaesthetics, in those days using nitrous oxide, oxygen and trilene, or, alternatively, ethyl chloride. I can recall having a young patient with a Colles fracture and there being no other doctor available to give the anaesthetic. I gave the patient an ethyl chloride anaesthetic and while the patient was out, went round to reduce the fracture and plaster it while the patient slowly came round. The fracture healed well and there were no complications, but I imagine taking such action would not be allowed in the present day.

During my term at Dewsbury, we had a change of resident surgical registrar. There was an interim locum from Manchester, who stayed for one month. As I did most of the casualty work, we got to know each other quite well.

He had returned to Manchester one weekend and, on his way back in the car over the moors, had spotted a pheasant. As he had his rifle with him, he had left the car and shot the pheasant. Unfortunately he was seen by the police and was charged with nine offences – shooting a bird out of season, poaching, using a firearm within a certain distance of the public highway – the others I have forgotten!

At that hospital was my first opportunity to see television. We never had it at home in Aberdeen and it was not at the hospital at Ayr.

The next permanent registrar was due to arrive and the locum and I were watching a show on the screen – it was *Les Belles de Nuit*, directed by René Clair, in black and white, which was fortunate as it was only a black and white television. The film was due to end in ten minutes when the new registrar arrived. We were both engrossed and his predecessor just said, "Sit somewhere!"

Despite this very rude introduction, the new registrar and I became very good friends. His name was Yusuf Kodwavwalla, he was an Ismaili Muslim and we continued our friendship after we had both left the hospital.

Dewsbury is a small town in the heart of the industrial part of the West Riding of Yorkshire. It is in the centre of a ring of industrial towns – Leeds, Bradford, Huddersfield, Wakefield – and there were almost continuous black, smoke-grimed houses filling in that ring. However, despite the surroundings, Dewsbury was a good place to get out of. I had left my motor bicycle at Aberdeen and so was dependent on public transport. A bus or train ride would take you out into the various picturesque parts of Yorkshire: Ilkley Moor, Bolton Abbey, York, Harrogate, Knaresborough, Haworth and others.

I only visited Haworth once. I took buses to the nearest point and walked the two miles through the drizzling rain to the village. I climbed the steep village street to the top end of the town, considering walking further to the farm on which *Wuthering Heights* was thought to be based. At this point I decided not to go further, which was just as well as it would have been a long walk through the rain. However, the atmosphere was exactly as described in the Brontë novels.

On other weekends I would travel to Leeds to hear the Hallé Orchestra, conducted by Sir John Barbarolli.

When I was rostered on casualty on Saturday and Sunday, I wrote out the whole of *Tam O' Shanter* in script and memorized the poem. I can also recall the relief that the rugby season was ended, with all the associated fractures, only to be faced, in one day, with two broken jaws resulting from cricket balls!

About that time, our dog in Aberdeen died. He was the third we had, another black cocker spaniel, very docile and quiet, who posed for me long enough to let me complete a drawing in scraperboard. His death comes particularly to mind as I had one of those experiences of extrasensory perception that occasionally happened to me and I knew that he had died before the news came by letter from Aberdeen.

About two or three months before I would finish at Dewsbury, I was conscripted to undergo my two years of National Service in the army. I had been exempted in order to study medicine, which was then the policy. I had to go to Leeds for medical examination. The manners of the non-commissioned officers who conducted the marshalling of those to be examined were on the borderline of politeness. Stripped off to the underpants, each examinee went to a different doctor to have each system examined. From time to time, when the doctor found that I was registered, they would become very friendly, and some were curious to know if I was related to Dr Mary Esslemont.

When I reached the end of the examinations and was being assessed, the doctor doing the assessing came upon the fact that I had suffered from a duodenal ulcer about two years previously, when I was a student. With a history of peptic ulcer, two years was the cut-off point between being accepted and not accepted into the forces, and the doctor gave me the choice of whether to do my National Service or be excused. I felt well, felt that I had some moral duty, that to use the ulcer to skip National Service would be somehow cheating, so I elected to go ahead and do my two years.

Scraperboard portrait of our third dog, a black cocker spaniel named "Garry".
I have not mentioned the three cocker spaniels much. The first, Kuno, was in the first
about twelve years of my life; the second was a golden cocker spaniel who did not
survive very long; the third, Garry, was with us during the latter part of my school days
and lived for about twelve years until 1957.

About a month after that, I was called for an interview by a colonel in York. He explained that there would be three possible postings: in the UK, in Germany or in the Far East, known as FARELF. There would be two weeks of square-ground training, two weeks of training at the School of Tropical Medicine at Millbank in London and two weeks of field training. He asked about my hobbies and interests. I had a lot of questions, particularly about overseas, and spent about two hours at the interview.

Eventually, the six months at Dewsbury came to an end on 31st July 1957 and I returned to Aberdeen.

I sold the motor bicycle and recovered about £100 for it, which was what I had originally paid.

Almost immediately I received word to report for army service either within a week or a week after that. There seemed little point in putting off the date so I chose the first option.

Chapter 7

On Her Majesty's Service

I could not afford a third-class sleeping compartment on the night train to London, the *Flying Scotsman*. An old friend from scouting and beating days was also travelling, so we shared each other's company.

In London or at Aldershot, we were asked which posting we wanted, UK, Germany or FARELF (Far Eastern Land Forces). I chose FARELF.

There was an opinion that, in the army, you did not get what you wanted and, instead, got what you did not want. However, my posting was indeed to the Far East.

Our basic training was at Crookham Barracks at Aldershot. We were taught marching. The drill corporal shouted terse commands: "Attention", "Stand at ease", "Stand easy – legs apart – you won't drop anything!" Orders, orders, orders! We were taught all the various military manoeuvres, but did not learn very well. However that was expected. Years later, there was a sequel.

It was very boring but only lasted a fortnight.

Our next two weeks was spent at the London School of Tropical Medicine at Millbank on the Thames Embankment next to the Tate Gallery. That was much more interesting, learning about malaria and other tropical diseases. It was the first time we encountered the Director General of the Royal Army Medical Corps (RAMC) who told us that, if we did not like our lot, then we could spend the next two years in the ranks!

The London School of Tropical Medicine was founded by Sir Patrick Manson, born in Old Meldrum, Aberdeenshire in 1844, and educated at

Marischal College. He was the first to discover that the mosquito was the host to the worm *Filaria bancrofti*, and to the malarial parasite. This was verified three years later by Ronald Ross, whom he mentored. He also instituted the Medical School of Hong Kong, which developed later into the University of Hong Kong. One of the early students was Sun Yat-sen, the future president of the Republic of China.

Being in the heart of London, we did not miss the opportunity of visiting all the shows and I remember seeing *At the Drop of a Hat*, visiting the Windmill, and spending a lot of time in the Tate Gallery. I think that in those two weeks, I spent more money than I earned.

At that time, there was a problem finding employment in medical practices. The best practices were of course fully occupied and available practices were not always the best. Many doctors were emigrating to find decent jobs. While in London I went to BMA House in Tavistock Square to ask about opportunities in the future after I had finished National Service. I was told that I could get a job provided I settled where I was placed, which was the very situation I feared. The adviser and I discussed overseas and it seemed to me that Australia would be the best bet. The advisor also said that, if I could gain a diploma in obstetrics, it would help. A diploma in child health would also be useful, but, unfortunately, the hospital at Dewsbury was too small to qualify. Obstetric jobs were difficult to obtain, but I thought that I might write to Dr de Soldenhoff, who was the gynaecological consultant at Ayr, to see if I could get a job when I left the army.

The field training during the next two weeks was at Farnham, near Aldershot. It was quite interesting but the opportunity was taken to visit the pretty countryside of southeast England, Surrey, Sussex and Guildford. The new cathedral was being built at Guildford, a roofless building of brick at that time. We also visited the Farnborough Air Display.

All those going to the Far East were given two weeks' embarkation leave, during which time we had to obtain passports and other travel necessities.

During the two weeks' leave, I had the opportunity to attend a concert at Haddo House. These concerts were held from time to time and a local orchestra took part with visiting musicians. I can remember a production of *The Pirates of Penzance*, with, in the orchestra, Leon Goosens playing the oboe and Dennis Brain the French horn. At the concert I attended on the eve of my departure for the Far East, Benjamin Britten was conducting and Peter Piers was singing. The Queen Mother was a member of the audience.

Over the news we learned that the Russians had beaten the Americans in the space race and that the first Sputnik had been successfully launched.

In early October, we started the flight to Singapore. In those days it took four days.

The first stop was at about eleven that evening, at Brindisi, where we were given a meal, pasta. Then we stopped at Ankara, and then on to Bahrain. At Bahrain, when we went out through the door, the heat hit us. I at first thought that it was heat reflected from the side of the plane but it was not long before it was realized that this was the outside temperature. I did some sketches of the flat-roofed buildings and of two women, all swathed in black – it must have been stiflingly hot.

We flew on to Karachi, where we spent the night, the first under a fan in that hot, dry climate. We flew over India, landing at Rangoon. The airport there was air-conditioned, another first experience. From Rangoon we travelled to Bangkok, where we arrived at first light for a breakfast of a very light fluffy white bread. The last stage of the flight was down the east coast of Malaya, and we had our first aerial views of the jungle-covered hills and the sandy coastline.

And so we eventually landed at Singapore, where we were transported to the RAMC Mess.

The Mess was very pleasant, a large colonial-style building with large airy rooms, high on a hillside overlooking the Straits of Singapore. The Tiger Balm Gardens were below us among the trees at the foot of the hill. Beyond that, the sea was silver, dotted with islands.

One of the new things we learned to become used to were geckos, known as chit-chats, because of their distinctive call – *tch tch tch* – like someone tutting, on the walls.

We waited to find out where our eventual posting was. The favourite was Hong Kong, next came Singapore. The Emergency was being fought in Malaya, so it was considered a possible trouble spot.

We spent about four days in Singapore and I learned that I would be going to the British Military Hospital, Taiping, in Malaya.

In the next few days, a group of us, bound for Malaya, were taken to the Singapore railway station to board the train for Kuala Lumpur.

Sketch from the 'plane of Bahrain.

Sketch from the 'plane of two Arab women crossing the airfield runway at Bahrain.

The train travelled north past rubber plantations and secondary jungle. From time to time we would pass through a village and there were frequent barbed-wire fences with ominous signs picturing trespassers being shot. The scenery was fairly monotonous. The train usually had an armed coach as one of the carriages, and I gathered that this was the first train to not have this safeguard.

At lunchtime a menu was produced. Not knowing what to expect, for much of it appeared somewhat foreign, I chose *nasi goring* (fried rice), as it seemed innocuous. The doctor who was at the same table decided that he would try *nasi goring* "special", which was a dollar dearer. *Nasi goring* "special" was nasi goring with a fried egg on top!

After many hours of travel, we reached Kuala Lumpur railway station, a flat-topped building in eastern style with minarets and onion domes. When the station was originally built, apparently the plans were turned down by the office in London because such an extent of flat roof would collapse if there was a lot of snow!

From the railway station we were taken to an army camp near Batu Caves where we would spend the next two nights. There were not enough rooms and beds for us all. I was the unlucky last and the only place that could be found for me to sleep was a *charpoi* erected for me in a thatched shed, used for holding gardening implements. "The first night I spent in Malaya, I slept on a *charpoi* in a gardener's shed under an *attap* roof."

Chapter 8

Malaya

As I lay on the taut strings of the *charpoi* the thoughts tumbled through my mind – might there be snakes? Among the sacks containing vegetables piled in the corner of the wooden building there were plenty of places where a cobra might hide. While I was showering that evening, a tropical storm began. The shower block was outside, the lightning was spectacular, and I wondered if it was wise to be showering with lightning about.

However, I survived.

Next day, we were taken by truck to Seremban, about forty miles south of Kuala Lumpur. The truck had a canvas canopy, we were supplied with a rifle, and part of the road went through a jungle-covered hillside, bringing us face-to-face with the fact that we were in a war zone.

In Seremban, we were further briefed, and then returned to Kuala Lumpur.

After another night under the *attap* roof, we were taken to the station again, to continue our journey north. The scenery became more spectacular. The hills of the central mountain range began to appear and the dramatic limestone cliffs round Ipoh eventually came into view. Through the coconut palms and the rubber trees, these spectacular vertical hills rose steeply, just like the ones depicted in Chinese paintings.

Next stop was Taiping, where two of us, posted there, disembarked. At the station, we were met by an RAMC Captain, Bernard Knight, who was to take us to the hospital, BMH Kamunting. As we approached the hospital, there was an ambulance travelling in front of us. Bernard, who was the

LIFE IS WHAT YOU MAKE IT

hospital pathologist, told us that it was carrying the body of a British soldier who had been shot by the Communist terrorists.

We were shown our rooms and the officers' mess. All was reasonably comfortable. We were given tea and bananas, which were green. Although green, they were ripe.

What about the heat? And the mosquitoes?

I enjoyed the warmth. It was hot, and the humidity was high. There were mosquito nets over the beds and we were supplied with daily Paludrine to prevent malaria.

Besides me, the medical staff consisted of a physician; a surgeon who lived outside the hospital in Taiping; an anaesthetist who also looked after the skin diseases; the pathologist; a general duties medical officer who looked after the sick parade of the local garrison and dealt with admissions to the hospital; a dentist; and a non-medically qualified administrative officer, Major Haynes. There was also a quartermaster, who also lived in the nearby village outside the BMH.

My duties at the hospital were to look after two medical wards, one for general medical patients, and one for Malay soldiers suffering from tuberculosis.

The main medical diseases were leptospirosis and scrub typhus, both caught in the jungle. The leptospirosis was potentially serious (there was one death) but could be treated with penicillin, although this was contrary to medical advice at that time. The scrub typhus was treated with Aureomycin. Every patient's blood was checked for malaria every four hours for two days.

One patient had glandular fever, which caused enlarged lymph glands and enlargement of the spleen, just like scrub typhus. His white blood cell count dropped to a significant degree. Captain Knight and I wrote it up for the *British Medical Journal* but it was rejected. After the illness, his condition recovered.

Another set of patients who were puzzling at first were a group of Gurkhas who ran high fevers and a rash. Then I found tiny white spots inside one man's mouth. These are known as Koplik's spots, which only occur in measles.

The Director General, Lieutenant General Drummond, visited us one day. He was known to be tricky, and when he reached my ward, the question he asked me was if the ward sister had everything she needed. I immediately answered yes – she only had to ask – and I saw her behind General Drummond, vigorously nodding her head.

BMH Kamunting.

Limestone hills round Ipoh.

Chinese cemetery.

Malayan Kampong scene.

I also assisted at operations and well remember the soldier who was admitted with his tibia projecting out the front of his leg. At operation, three cubical shaped pellets, a sort of dum-dum, were removed from his calf. During his convalescence crêpitus could be felt in the muscles of his leg, a sign of gas gangrene.

One night, when I was on emergency duty as orderly medical officer, we were informed that a soldier who had been shot in the chest was to be flown in by helicopter. He did not materialise that night, and I went to bed, to be woken up at 2.00 am because another soldier, an Iban tracker, had arrived, shot through the chest. I spent the rest of the night aspirating the blood from his thorax. Next morning the originally expected patient arrived. The bullet had entered the left side of his neck, had gone down, missing vital structures and major blood vessels on the way, and finished up in the right side of his chest. He was lucky to be alive.

There was enough time for me to do some studying and I used it to read a textbook of psychiatry and a textbook of surgery.

If the medical side was interesting, the social life was enjoyable. We went one evening to the best restaurant in Taiping. It was a canvas-covered area beside the main sewer in Taiping and I tasted for the first time shark fin soup, sweet and sour pork, finishing with fried rice.

Major Haynes, who introduced us to this eating place, and taught me how to use chopsticks, was a soldier of long experience who remembered, before World War II, standing on the Great Wall of China and seeing Chinese prisoners being beheaded.

One day, outside the perimeter fence of the hospital compound, there was a cacophony of noise, and a brass band appeared. There was clashing of cymbals and banging of drums, then, behind the band, came the coffin. The Chinese coffin is huge, made of wood. A group of people, dressed in sackcloth, walked in procession behind the coffin. Major Haynes explained that this was a Chinese funeral and that the sackcloth-clad individuals were the professional mourners, hired for the occasion.

The family, dressed in black, followed the mourners. White is the colour of mourning, so the family wore black so that the ghosts of the dead would not plague them. However, they wore a small white patch on one shoulder as a sign of respect.

Lorries with paper representations of houses, cars and all manner of things, which would all be burned so they would accompany the dead person to heaven, came in the parade.

My room in the hospital overlooked the Chinese cemetery. The tombs were made as a large three-quarter circle, to signify the shape of a womb.

I learned that the right hand only is used if shaking hands with a Malay. The right hand is used for eating, the left for washing the perineal area after a bowel motion – the right hand is clean, the left hand dirty.

The Malay people are very courteous and there is a very definite code of etiquette.

Early on, I learned how to wear a sarong, and since then, I have always worn a sarong in the evening and in bed. It is very comfortable, more so than pyjamas, and easier to wear.

The hospital was a fairly closed community, so we held parties, to which the ward sisters were invited, and the ward sisters held parties to which we were invited.

In Taiping, besides restaurants, there were a couple of cinemas, to which we sometimes went.

We once visited Ipoh, which I found not very interesting, and once visited Penang, which I found wonderful, and where I bought some Daler board so that I could do a bit of painting.

The Lake Gardens at Taiping were beautiful: broad green lawns, the lakes themselves, some filled with lotus plants. Rain trees (*Enterolobium*) overhung the road; clumps of Travelers' Palms, Hibiscus and Bougainvillea were everywhere. Splashes of scarlet were added by the Flame of the Forest (*Delonix regia*, Flamboyant Tree or Royal Poincana). Beyond the gardens, Maxwell Hill, blue in the steamy air, rose as a backdrop.

Behind all this, on the lowest slopes, was the Swimming Club, a pool where a small river had been dammed at the foot of a waterfall. We spent Christmas Day there. Strictly speaking, the Swimming Club was in "Black" territory, areas that had not been definitely cleared of Communist terrorist activity. On the path up to the swimming pool, the track climbed through jungle, with trailing creepers hanging from the tree tops.

Halfway up, beside the river, was a Sikh temple and it was common to see the Sikhs washing and tending their long hair. In the seventeenth century, the execution of two Gurus and persecution by the Mughals provoked the Sikhs to take up arms. Five Sikhs were baptised into a new fraternity known as the Khalsa, "the pure" (from the Persian, also meaning "pure".) Khalsa is a concept of a "chosen" race of soldier-saints. The men have a common surname, Singh ("lion"); and the corresponding name given to all Sikh women is Kaur ("lioness"). The five emblems of Khalsa, all beginning with the letter *k*, have no scriptural basis but are written in the *Rahatnamas*. The most important is *kesa* ("hair"), which the Khalsa must retain unshorn. Then come the *kangha* ("comb"), *kaceh* ("drawers"), *kirpan* ("sabre") and *kara* ("bracelet") of steel, commonly worn on the right arm.

In the New Year, we went up the 4,000-foot-high Maxwell Hill, overlooking Taiping, to Maxwell's Rest House in the Land Rover provided, then walked up to Speedy's Rest House at the top of the hill. The jungle scenery, tree ferns predominating, was beautiful. The cry of the gibbons could be heard – *wak-wak-wak* – from which they get their local name, *wakwak*.

A painting in oils that I completed of the view of Maxwell Hill from my bedroom is a reminder of my days in Taiping.

In January, I was shocked to learn that I had now been posted to Hong Kong. I did not want to go. I was very happy in Taiping, and happy that I was settled (or so I thought) in one place for any length of time. However, there was no arguing, and so it was.

Oil painting by the author of the view from his room at BMH Kamunting. Maxwell Peak and the hills behind the Waterfall Gardens in Taiping, are in the distance.

*Road through
the jungle to the
Swimming Pool.
The top of the Sikh
temple can be seen.*

The Swimming Pool

The waterfall feeding the Swimming Pool

Chapter 9

Hong Kong

It was drizzling, cold, grey and miserable when I landed in Hong Kong in February.

I probably had a night at BMH Kowloon, and then was taken by Land Rover, over about twenty-three miles of a road named TWSK (Tsun Wan to Sek Kong) to the Field Ambulance at Sek Kong.

It continued to be drizzling, cold, grey and miserable.

Our quarters were nissen huts, a large leaking one for the mess, and smaller, dusty ones for our bedrooms. The landscape was flat, parched (despite the drizzle), grey, quite different from the lush, exuberant greenery of Malaya.

The other officers were a short-service commissioned officer, who acted as adjutant or registrar and was resolved to do as little as possible, and three other National Servicemen, who were doctors who were not too happy with their lot.

My job was to look after the sick parade at the Field Ambulance at Sek Kong and teach first aid. It was deadly boring and I began counting the number of days left in the army. As I hoped that I would some day return to Malaya, I began to learn Malay, and also continued brushing up on reading the textbooks.

Within two weeks I was posted to the Green Howards, the Yorkshire Regiment, stationed at Stanley Camp, at the farthest west point of Hong Kong Island, while their Regimental Medical Officer was on leave.

One of the evenings, when I was on call, I had to visit a house half-way up the peak on Hong Kong Island, to see an army major who was vomiting blood. The roads were steep, with narrow hairpin bends. The ambulance driver needed to manoeuvre his vehicle adroitly to reach the house, and the stretcher-bearers carried the patient precariously down the stairs, negotiating corners to position him safely in the vehicle.

However, the work at Stanley was pleasant enough and included looking after the mule company on the island. Spring was starting to approach, and the flowers were beginning to bloom but it was still very cold. Moreover, I had a chance to explore a bit more of Hong Kong.

After two weeks, the RMO returned. I think that there must have been an oversupply of army doctors in the colony at the time and the powers-that-be did not know what to do with me, as I was then sent to fill in at the paediatric ward at the British Military Hospital at Bowen Road in Hong Kong.

Thus I spent a week or two with very little to do.

The boredom was relieved by the dentist attached to the hospital who was an Indian – he said he was a Pathan, although a very short one. He was very fond of the night life whilst incurring as little expense as possible. He would work out the timing of the floorshows at the various night clubs in Hong Kong, and we would visit the night clubs in turn just in time to catch the floorshow. He would then make a fuss so that we had a table at front with the best view of the floorshow. Then we would have one beer apiece, watch the performance, and then move on to the next night club. That way we saw two or three floorshows during the evening for the price of two or three beers!

Then the next posting was back to the Field Ambulance at Sek Kong.

Again the work was boring, relieved only when the clerk at reception thought he would make himself useful by putting all the mercury thermometers in the heat sterilizer to sterilize!

The weather was beginning to warm up, and I went for walks, exploring the surrounding hills and taking photographs. Castle Peak, a sea inlet at the western side of the Kowloon peninsula was a pleasant place to visit, with places to walk, up to the Chinese Temple, and the Dragon Inn Restaurant, where a decent meal could be obtained.

On the sick parade, cases of otitis externa, nicknamed "Hong Kong ear", began to appear. The most effective treatment was found to be packing the ear with gauze impregnated with Ichthammol Glycerin (BPC), which was immediately soothing, repacking the ear the next day with the same substance, then repacking, using Aluminium Acetate instead of the Ichthammol Glycerin, on the following day and the day after.

The day came when a soldier reported sick, both ears affected. Impishly, I took the chance. The rooms had a reception room, a consulting room and a treatment room. I packed both the patient's ears with Ichthammol Glycerin, and saw the patient next day. In the consulting room I removed the pack from one ear, and then we went into the treatment room to put in a new pack. After putting the pack in one ear, I went to the soldier's other side and removed the pack from the other ear. There were soldiers sitting all round the treatment room. There was a buzz of talking until that moment. Suddenly all went quiet!

Summer had brought the hot weather, which I enjoy. The seasons in Hong Kong are very variable. As already mentioned, early in the year is cold, damp and miserable. During spring, warm days begin. Summer is hot and humid with the advent of storms and typhoons. In autumn, there are long spells of beautiful warm days, with clear blue skies. It begins to get cold at night but late autumn and early winter are the most pleasant times of the year.

Drug companies were beginning invite me to functions, usually a dinner, consisting of as many as fifteen courses of Chinese food, exquisitely cooked. At these, I met various people and made new friends.

At weekends I explored the Hong Kong hills by foot. I grew to enjoy Hong Kong after about six months and then I really grew to like the place very much.

During that summer I had also become involved with a small group of doctors who went out with the Hong Kong Red Cross to do immunizations and other small matters of hygiene on the outlying islands off Hong Kong. We were taken to these islands by the Hong Kong Harbour Police. On the islands, we would set up a baize-covered card table under a tree, do some elementary consultations, and give medical samples by way of treatment. It is unlikely that any of these treatments were of help, but it seemed to satisfy a need. From our point of view, we had the opportunity to see some of the less often visited and more primitive areas in and around Hong Kong.

I learned that the people in the cities that comprise Hong Kong are mainly Cantonese, with Cantonese as their language. The people in the country are mostly Hakka and speak their own Hakka dialect. Mandarin was very rarely spoken.

*Sek Kong walled village in the Hong Kong New Territories,
with Hakka women dressed in traditional garb.*

Life in the army continued to be uninteresting. I heard that the Regimental
Medical Officer of one of the local Gurkha battalions was due to end his short
service commission in the near future and I put in an application for a transfer to replace him. It seemed that it would be preferable to the current existence. Besides which, the Gurkha battalion was due to return to Malaya the
following year.

A week or so later, I received an invitation to attend a mess dinner with
the 1st Battalion of the 6th Gurkha Rifles at Tan Mei Camp. It was not as lurid
as the guest dinner David Niven describes in his biography, *The Moon's a
Balloon*, but it was a full-dress affair. The Commanding Officer, Lt. Col. N. E.
V. Short, was on leave and I was sat at the right of the Second-in-Command,
Major Iain Brebner. As the spelling of his name suggested, he was a Scot and
was from Edinburgh. Despite the formality and the protocol, it was a pleasant evening. There was wine with the dinner, and port, Madeira and whisky
circulated with the coffee. At the same time, a piper marched round the table,
playing. After the dinner, we all moved outside and watched and listened to
the pipes and drums. Then it was all over, and I returned to Sek Kong.

I must have behaved myself because my request for a transfer was accepted.

So I waited, reading, appropriately enough, James Hilton's *Lost Horizon*,
which I found later was set in an imaginary land, Shangri La, situated in what
would have been Nepal, at a time before that country had been opened up.

However, before I started as RMO to the Gurkhas, some of us decided that we would have the long weekend of August Bank Holiday at the Buddhist monastery on Lan Tau Island.

We travelled on a junk to the island. We were on the top deck and from below us came the rattle-rattle of the Chinese playing Mah Jong. Looking down on them, each game lasted only a matter of minutes. We landed on the island and walked up to the river where we crossed by ferry, the trip costing us three Hong Kong cents each. As five cents was the smallest coin, two one-cent notes were given by way of change. As, at that time, one Hong Kong cent was equivalent to 0.15 British pennies, and as one or even two cents can buy nothing, I have theses notes to this day.

A Hong Kong one cent note.

Disembarking on the other side, we started on the eight-mile walk up to the monastery. It was a good path, broad steps made of granite slabs. By evening, we reached the moon gate entrance to the monastery. It was a beautiful sunset, silhouetting the pagoda on the pass between two hill peaks.

The meal was vegetarian, the best vegetarian meal I have ever tasted.

And so to bed. The bed was a platform of hard boards, softened by a thin rush mat. There was a mosquito net with some holes in it, big enough to let mosquitoes in but acting as a trap to prevent them escaping again! Finally, to make sure that we did not have a night's undisturbed sleep, the loud temple gang rang every hour of the night! In his book, *Juan in China*, Eric Linklater describes a similar stay at a monastery in China.

In the morning, we rose, showered and brushed our teeth in the pond with goldfish swimming in it. Then we had breakfast and had the morning to explore. In the courtyard of the monastery, we met three middle-aged Chinese ladies, who introduced themselves. One was the widow of Dr Sun Yat-sen.

After lunch, we made our way down the hill by a shorter but steeper path to another village on the island, where we boarded another junk home.

Ferry across the river on Lan Tau Island.

A street in Hong Kong.

Hong Kong harbour scene, a study of the traditional and the modern

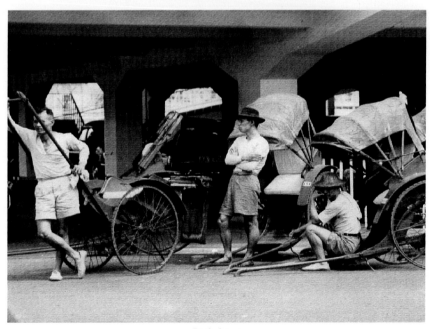

Rickshaws

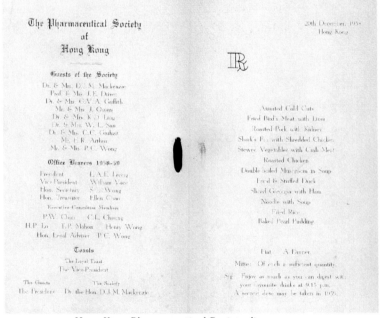

Hong Kong Pharmaceutical Society dinner menu.

Chapter 10

The Gurkhas

Surrounded by hills with shade trees and green grassy slopes, the Gurkha Camp, Tan Mei, was quite beautiful. The officers' mess was attractive, neat, the entrance shaded by flame trees (*Delonix* or *Poinciana gloriana flamboyanta*). There was a bell and a couple of cannon to add colour. Our rooms were pleasant, neat and tidy, without the dust and mustiness prevalent at Sek Kong.

The British officers were very welcoming. The outgoing Regimental Medical Officer was Captain Young. He was meticulous in showing me the work to be done and initiating me in learning Gurkhali, a language not unlike Hindustani. The language had a grammar somewhat similar to Latin, although, of course, the vocabulary was different.

There was also a separate mess where resided the Queen's Gurkha Officers, who were Gurkhas who had been promoted in the ranks to a position of officer status where they looked after the ethnic as well as the military side of the men of the battalion.

The Sick Room was a nissen hut divided into a reception and waiting room with a cast-iron stove, and a consulting room. The Family Hospital was a modern building, well equipped, with a labour room and wards and a consulting room.

There was a medical corporal, who had a limp sustained when he had damaged his ankle by taking over a Japanese trench during the war, a deed for which he was awarded the Military Medal. There was a receptionist who also took over the duty of teaching me Gurkhali. At the Family Hospital were two midwives and Phyllis Castle, the social welfare sister.

The sick parade was at 7.00 am. It lasted about two hours, after which we went for breakfast. Breakfast began with fruit juice, followed by cereal, fish, eggs cooked in whatever way we wished, followed by toast or bread with butter and jam, and tea. After the initial shock, I learned to cut down on the number of courses, and tended to skip lunch. Sunday breakfast was different. It consisted of mulligatawny soup, followed by kippers, then bacon and egg.

After breakfast came the family sick parade. Many of the children suffered from chronically perforated ear drums which required regular toilet.

The Gurkhali language has one peculiarity in that there is no word for anaesthesia or numbness. If the Gurkha has a patch of numbness, he uses the word *dukh*, which means "pain"! As can be imagined, this could be totally confusing if not borne in mind. A patient may point to a skin lesion and state *dukh chha* ("it is painful"). If he means "it is numb", the lesion could be leprosy.

In a regiment, there was quite a lot of administrative work to do. Pulmonary tuberculosis is common among Gurkhas and regular chest x-rays had to be kept up to date. Most of the soldiers were recruited on a three-year contract basis and they had to be medically inspected to see if they were fit to be re-employed after their three-month leave. There were regular health inspections of the camp. This was quite enjoyable as it gave some exercise, and the aroma in the cookhouse where the curry was being cooked was quite delightful. Gordon Camp was another, secondary, camp on the coast beyond Castle Peak, which also had to be visited regularly and inspected.

There were about five hundred in the battalion and about the same number of dependents, wives and children. We all got to know each other and it was like a very large family.

Life had really become much more pleasant. In the mess library was a book about *Gurkha* which was an account of Gurkha history describing how, like many countries, Nepal was divided into a region of small families until Prithvi Narayan Shah and his successors established a unified state in the central Himalayas.

At regular intervals there were formal dinners, which, despite the formality, were quite pleasant. Some of these were attended by the officers only, to others, guests had been invited. The evening would begin with drinks in the anteroom, everyone correctly dressed, then the dinner would start: soup, main course and desserts, accompanied by sherries, wine and port, Madeira or whisky. While we drank the coffee, pipers would entertain us by marching round the table playing a medley of tunes, ending always with "The Black Bear". This battalion did not have the somewhat juvenile mess games after these dinners as often happen in military regiments.

Even more fun were the Sunday curry lunches. These were occasionally accompanied by recitals by the pipe band or the silver band of the neighbouring 1st Battalion of the 2nd Gurkha Regiment. On one occasion the daughter of the Hong Kong Governor was a guest and some of the younger subalterns pulled her leg about Gurkha customs.

Regimental dress was immaculate. From the native garb of the tribes in the hills, the men adapted to the neat, clean, spotless uniforms of the Battalion. Likewise, the officers had to be attired as well. Each of us had a Gurkha orderly. Dressing the first morning, I was completely taken by surprise when he put his hand up my shorts to ensure that my shirt was arranged without an unnecessary crease.

I had not been long with the battalion when the first of the real Gurkha customs occurred, Dashera.

The 1st and 2nd Gurkha Regiments were recruited from West Nepal, and consisted of Gurungs and Magars, with Puns, Ranas and a few other clans. They tended to be stocky with broad Mongolian faces. The 7th and 10th Gurkha Regiments were recruited from East Nepal and consisted mainly of Rais and Limbus. They tended to be thinner with rather narrower features.

Most of our Gurkhas were Hindus, with a caste system. There were one or two Buddhists and one or two Presbyterian Christians.

Dashera is a Hindu festival, a combination of two separate commemorative ceremonies, celebrating the victory of right over wrong, and involving the sacrifice of goats and buffaloes. In the hills of Nepal, it should last for ten days, but in the Regiment only the four main days were observed.

Leading up to the main ceremonies, parties were held. Tables and chairs faced the main stage and a clear area in the centre of a large marquee. The officers and wives, the Gurkha families, wives and children, took their seats facing the stage. Gurkhas, bearing two buckets, one containing beer and the other rum, came round the tables and asked if we want rum or beer. It was wiser to choose beer as a second Gurkha dipped a pint glass into the fluid and served us!

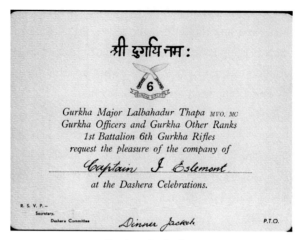

Dashera invitation.

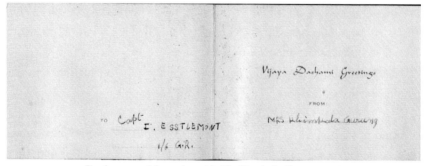

Dashera card from the midwife, Kemkala Gurungseni.

When all were seated and served, the performers on the stage began. The Gurkha women seldom danced, although I have seen one or two of the wives, particularly later on in the evening, joining in the dancing. Some of the men dressed up as women, painted their faces and pirouetted and glided about in the set dance formations.

There was an all-night ceremony called *Kalratri*, when a jet black goat was decapitated exactly at midnight. The following day, a buffalo was held by its head to a post and a Gurkha, with a large kukri, cut off the head with a single, slicing blow. A successfully clean head-cutting signifies good luck for the following year.

Dancers at Dashera. The Gurkha in a suit is Asbahadur Gurung, later mentioned on page 85 when he visited me in Aberdeen. The "girls" at the other end of the line are, in fact, men, taking the girls' roles for the dancing.

More dancing.

A successful beheading of the bull.

The first full moon after Dashera was the festival of Diwali, when myriad candles and lights are placed outside houses at night to guide the goddess Laxmi back after one of her victories. During Diwali, gambling was allowed for three days. Gurkhas are serious gamblers and, to keep this habit within bounds, in the course of a year, gambling was confined to these three days.

It was now September and October.

One long weekend, I visited Macao. The ferry was a two-decked steamer, the type of ship featured in *Ferry to Hong Kong*, which was filmed in Hong Kong at about the time I was there. The voyage took many hours, past Lan Tau Island and Castle Peak, in the beautiful coastal scenery of that part of the world, with perfect weather.

Arriving in Macao, I found that my remaining Latin was useful in reading the public notices. I stayed at an inexpensive hotel, noticing in the hotel rooms the rules for guests in the hotel which included, among other things, the fact that, if there was another occupant of the room, three dollars would be added to the bill. It was a fine evening and I managed to take a number of good photographs.

Next day, I explored Macao, which is not very large, visiting the fort on the hill, the remains of the Cathedral, and the old colonial cemetery in which an ancestor of Winston Churchill is buried.

The following day, I took the small ferry to Coloane, the farthest of the small islands forming part of the Macao territory. The small ferry landed at the jetty on the beach. There was a dirt track road, some small wooden Chinese houses, and that was all. There was a Land Rover with a European, who spoke to me and asked me, "What are you doing here? No-one ever visits the island!" He said that he was the District Officer, offered to drive me to a beach on the other side of the island where there was nice swimming, and said that he would join me for lunch and a beer later. We crossed the island and he left me at the beach, where I swam and lazed. There was a small shop/café and at midday the District Officer returned and we had a beer and some Chinese lunch. He was Portuguese and had been stationed in West Africa prior to his present job on the island.

I returned to Macao for the night and, next day, made the long voyage back to Hong Kong.

By this time I had come to know the British Gurkha officers. Major Iain Brebner, being a Scot as mentioned previously, was always a good friend. He was also a musician and trained the pipe band. In Edinburgh, his next-door neighbour was Compton Mackenzie, the author.

Major Henry Hayward-Surry was somewhat acid, with a quick-witted but rather sarcastic sense of humour which often got him into trouble. Like many of that ilk, he responded favourably to ripostes of a similar nature and we were friends for many years. Captain Gray was another Scot, from Dundee; Captain Woolley was the Quartermaster, a Yorkshireman who had come up through the ranks. There were a number of lieutenants, National Servicemen like myself, Ted Ayres-Hill, David Hill and Roger Garside. Majors Gil Hickey and Colin Fisher were married officers and lived in the army village in Sek Kong.

The Commanding Officer, Colonel Short, finished his tour of duty and was replaced by Colonel Wynne Amoore.

One of the British officers was married late in the year. We attended the wedding, and then afterwards some of the British and Gurkha officers went for a meal at the Golden Phoenix restaurant and night club.

One of the Gurkha officers present, who had been with us on the previous tour of duty in Malaya, had become separated from the rest of the men in the jungle. He was missing for weeks and had been presumed dead, when he re-emerged from the jungle, bringing with him, in a sack, the heads of six Communist terrorists. While lost in the jungle, he had obviously not been idle and had put his time to good use. This Gurkha had a particularly impassive face. His lack of expression would put Buster Keaton to shame. While we were having our meal at the restaurant, however, a very attractive Chinese girl entered. The expressionless look became replaced by a gaze of intense interest as he watched the girl cross the floor!

In Hong Kong, the last four months of the year usually has spectacular weather, bright sunny days, not too hot, with blue skies, and nights which are cool. An "exercise" was held in a peninsula at the east side of the New Territories, a part of the training for wars. As there was no actual fighting and the "exercise" mainly consisted of walking, it was very pleasant.

At night it was time to eat, and the orderlies prepared the meal. I had chosen Gurkha rations, which turned out to be curried sardines with rice. It tasted very good. After eating, tea was made. In making the tea (*chyar*), the tea leaves were boiled in a mess tin, sweetened condensed milk was added, with some sugar, and about a fifth of a bottle of rum! After tea, the rest of the bottle of rum was shared around. As I had the medical Land Rover, I had the stretcher as a bed. It was very comfortable.

Life settled back to normal. Sick parade was enlivened by the pipe band practising on their chanters nearby. Christmas came and there were the usual rounds of parties. At New Year we were told that the Regiment had become "Queen Elizabeth's Own 6th Gurkha Rifles".

On New Year's Day, the Commanding Officer had booked a box at the horse races at the Happy Valley racecourse. I invited along, as my guests, the local army dentist and his wife. I planned for us to have lunch at the Sky Restaurant in Hong Kong, which had been recommended to me as the place where the local Chinese businessmen went for lunch.

The Sky Restaurant was well named, as it was on the top floor of one of the Hong Kong skyscrapers. We had a very pleasant lunch of dim sum, bits and pieces of Chinese food picked out from baskets carried round by the waitresses. When I received the bill, I said to my guests that I would settle the bill while they made their way outside. It amounted to only about eleven dollars! It was a splendid meal but I was afraid that the couple might have thought that I had taken them out on the cheap.

The afternoon at the races was quite pleasant – I am not a horseracing fan – and champagne was served. I put twenty dollars on a horse and recovered four hundred. I then decided that such an event was unlikely to repeat itself and I have never again bet on a horse!

Gurkhas are traditionally wary of the sea, the *kali pani*, (*kali,* black; *pani*, water). In Hong Kong, using Gordon Camp, near the sea, all the men in the Battalion were taught how to swim, as were their wives and children. As the wives were too embarrassed to undress, they learned how to swim in their saris. However, the time was approaching for the voyage to Malaya, when the Battalion, wives and children would have to cross the *kali pani*. Gurkhas notoriously become seasick. I began to save up as many as possible of the anti-vomiting tablets used in pregnancy.

However, we still had a few more months to go in Hong Kong.

The Hill Race was a race up one of the nearby hills, about 1,800 feet high. The winner ran up in about eighteen minutes, and then ran down again in about three minutes, running in long, bounding steps. I was curious to know how they ran up and down the hills so easily and noted that their feet could flex up to the shin almost completely. We are born with this ability, but Westerners learn to sit on chairs while people from Asia tend to squat rather than use seats, and retain the flexibility at the ankle that we lose.

Furthermore, when we squat, the position is uncomfortable because the bones of the lower legs tend to squeeze the calf muscles against the muscles at the backs of our thighs. Gurkhas have notoriously bandy legs, and now, my curiosity fired, I looked at what happens in the squatting position, and it seemed to me that, while squatting, the bones of the lower leg tended to curve round the bones of the upper leg, thus reducing the compressing action of one bone against another. Some years later, when looking at prehistoric skeletons, it was seen that the vertebrae of the spine were more wedge-shaped than cylindrical as a result of the use of the squatting position, but I do not know if Gurkhas' spines are likewise formed.

The stoicism of Gurkhas is famous. One Wednesday afternoon, while the men were playing football, I was called to see one who had injured his ankle. On examination, it was apparent that he had fractured the distal end of his fibula. All that this soldier wanted to do was go back onto the football field! While we waited for the ambulance, I sketched his portrait in pencil and it was later framed and is hanging with the rest of my pictures.

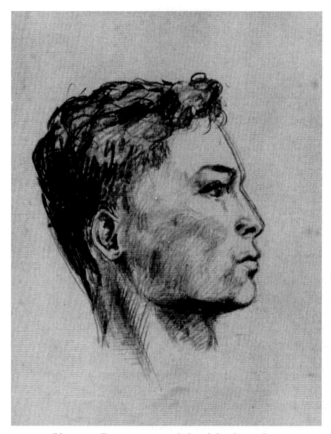

Pharesor Gurung, a pencil sketch by the author.

One of the Gurkha children had needed to have one leg amputated after it had been trapped under a falling tree. In Hong Kong in those days there was no way that an artificial limb could be found for him. The bootsmaker (he made more than one boot!) fashioned a cup which was fastened to the stump of the leg and a broom handle was fitted into a socket underneath. The last time I saw this boy, he was running around playing football with the rest of the children, kicking the football with either foot.

The wives were very simple, in the kindest sense. One was pregnant but had begun to have some bleeding, starting to have a miscarriage. The maternity hospital was two to three hours away, the ambulance having to cross on the ferry to Hong Kong Island. Gurkha women especially are notoriously averse to having operative treatment, but it was explained that this pregnancy was unlikely to produce a live child and that the sooner the womb was cleaned out, the sooner would she be able to try for another.

She went off and I thought little more about it until, a week later, there was a telephone call from the maternity sister at the hospital. Both of the obstetricians were Roman Catholic and, in their wisdom, they had decided to delay any dilatation and curettage, just in case the pregnancy could be saved. During this time, the woman had lain comfortably in bed, and had decided that, after all, no operation was going to be necessary. By this time, she was bleeding more heavily and the obstetricians were becoming quite worried by the patient's refusal to have anything done.

Again, it was Wednesday afternoon and her husband was on the football field. He was contacted and arrived in the medical centre after about half an hour. The position was explained to him and he was asked if he would speak to his wife on the telephone. He was agreeable to try to help but mentioned that his wife had never ever used a telephone!

I telephoned back to the sister, told her that the husband was now available to speak and explained the situation that his wife knew nothing about telephones. The sister told me later that the patient had looked at the telephone receiver very doubtfully, had tentatively held it in front of her with her hands between the mouthpiece and the earpiece, and then, when she heard her husband's voice, would not stop talking, then hung up! It is a credit to her faith that she recognised his voice without seeing him. After about half an hour, she agreed to the operation and it went ahead successfully without any further hassles.

Minbahadur, another pencil drawing by the author.

Gurkhas are very prone to pulmonary tuberculosis and the time had come for all the members of the Battalion to have their chest x-rays taken by Mass Miniature Radiography. The MMR machine was in Kowloon so an attempt was made to arrange for it to visit the Battalion to take this vast number of x-rays. At first the request was refused, then a decision was taken for the machine to go to the Field Ambulance at Sek Kong, which would mean that one and a half thousand men, women and children would have to be taken the three miles to the x-ray unit. This was logistically impossible in terms of trucks and petrol, and when this was put to the Lieutenant Colonel at Sek Kong, he facetiously said that the Battalion, the wives and children could march along for their x-rays. When this decision was put to my Commanding Officer, he blew his stack, and telephoned the Brigadier, who was an ex-Gurkha officer. I did not hear the various conversations but it would have been nice to have been a fly on the wall! The final result was that the MMR unit was stationed at our camp, and those needing x-rays at Sek Kong had to visit us for the procedure to be done!

One night, there was an emergency at the medical centre and, without thinking, I hurriedly dressed and started running down to the centre. The next thing I knew, I felt the point of a kukri on my chest. I had not seen anyone and the Gurkha guard had just materialized out of the darkness. On another occasion, the military police had decided to test out the security of the camp and found themselves in the guardhouse until the morning, when they were checked by their Commanding Officer and allowed to go free.

In Hong Kong, one of our British officers was involved in an accident. He was fond of rock climbing and had gone for the weekend. Iain Brebner, Henry Hayward-Surry and I had remained in the mess after a very satisfying curry lunch. That evening, an orderly brought the news that the officer who had gone climbing was dead. He had been on his way home on his motorbike, having completed his climb, when he had an accident and was killed. Some of the Gurkhas who had been in Hong Kong for the weekend had seen a body lying at the side of the road on their way home but had not thought anything about it.

The funeral was held and interment was at the Happy Valley cemetery. We all had to be in full uniform, complete with sword. I had never been taught sword drill so found it somewhat cumbersome.

In February 1959, the Battalion held a display of the pipes and drums on the football pitch, together with the silver band of the 2nd Gurkha Rifles, to celebrate our leaving Hong Kong two months later. I had bought a tape recorder, and recorded the event. I still have the record and have had it transferred to CD as a more permanent record.

In the meantime, the stocking of anti-sickness tablets was not progressing very well. When the time came for the Battalion to embark, there were enough tablets to supply one each to one third of the number of people who were to undertake the four-day voyage to Singapore. What we did was to give one tablet, whether an anti-vomiting tablet or an aspirin tablet, to each man and wife as they boarded the ship, and explain that it would prevent them being sick on the journey. It worked! There were no cases of sea-sickness during the entire voyage. The four days on board ship was pleasant, sunny, but boring.

Retreat Invitation and programme.

Combined bands of Military Band and Bugles of 2nd King Edward VII's Own Gurkha Rifles (Silver Band) and Pipes, Drums and Bugles of Queen Elizabeth's Own Gurkha Rifles

Sir Robert Black, the Governor of Hong Kong, signing the Regimental Visitor's Book.

The Governor of Hong Kong being introduced to the Gurkha Pipe Major by Lieutenant Colonel Wynne-Amoore, the commanding officer of the battalion.

Major Henry Hayward-Surry replenishing the glass of the Adjutant, Captain Tim Beillers.

Chapter 11

Back to Malaya

From the ship, the Battalion travelled by train to Kluang, to the new camp, which was set in an old rubber plantation and was not as attractive as Tan Mei Camp in Hong Kong.

Regimental life went on. Troops went on detachment to the jungle farther north where they were mopping up the Communist terrorists in the still-existent Malayan Emergency.

As well as my own battalion, I had to look after the Gurkha soldiers of the Garrison, which was across the airstrip from our own camp.

Despite the rather more shabby state of our new camp, I enjoyed being back in warm, steamy, colourful Malaya again.

There was sick parade, family sick parade, prenatal parade, deliveries, and the routine of army medical work. A new medical centre was built, very comfortable, except that the floors were highly polished, which made it dangerous for the men in their army boots. A squad of men was employed scrubbing the floors with sand to make the surface safe to walk on!

At the mess, Captain Robin Adshead had returned from leave and was billeted in the room next to mine. We got on well and shared musical evenings over a beer.

With my tape recorder, I recorded one of the Company nautches and later edited it from four hours to a more manageable size. It has now been transferred to CD.

Looking after the Garrison brought about one unfortunate mishap. A

Garrison Gurkha wife had gone into labour; I was notified and ordered the Garrison ambulance to transfer her to the camp hospital for delivery. A couple of hours later, there was a frantic telephone call to say that she was delivering her baby but was still in her quarter as the ambulance had never arrived. I went to the quarter with the midwife, completed the delivery and then transferred the mother and child to the hospital. There was a complaint from the Garrison that a child had been delivered at home. The 2I/C, Major Iain Brebner, when he heard what had actually happened, wrote a blistering letter to the Garrison about the delay in supplying the ambulance. He was a good person to have on side.

On another occasion, we had been keeping a graph of tinea pedis (foot ringworm) picked up at the monthly foot inspection. The figures were usually low, in the order of one to two percent, but once they had shot up to nearly thirty percent. The 2I/C came in that evening, his face like thunder. He asked: "What the hell were you doing excusing the entire pipe band from wearing boots?"

"Oh, it was the band," I answered, then the story evolved. The band had just been to Singapore and had been quartered in revolting barracks. We both enjoyed writing the letter to the Singapore Garrison.

Treatment of the foot condition was simple – application of Castellani's paint twice daily for four days, then application of Whitfield's ointment for four days, then a further week's treatment with Castellani's paint. It worked every time. The bright Castellani's paint had the added advantage that it was immediately obvious whether or not the treatment was being applied.

During the year, there was a celebration of the presentation of the title of "Queen Elizabeth's Own" at Ipoh in north Malaya, with a four-day party, and the Colonel of the Regiment, Field Marshal Lord Harding, attended.

The main dinner in the evening consisted of a barrel of oysters, with champagne. I was conversing with Colonel Shaw, the colonel of the Gurkha depot in Sungei Patani, who asked if I knew his medical officer, which I did. He said that this medical officer wanted to leave, and asked me if I knew of any reason for his dissatisfaction. I postulated that it might be due to the fact that he had a short-service commission and might want to make the army his career, in which case service with the Gurkhas, having to learn Gurkhali, would have only limited application. I pointed out that, at that time, there were eight Gurkha battalions, the depot, and various Gurkha corps, and so it would make sense for there to be a cadre of Gurkha medical officers who could learn Gurkhali well and serve their army service in the Brigade of Gurkhas. With the number of battalions, they could do their three-year stint with a battalion, and then have their six months' leave before their next three years with another battalion.

Colonel Shaw asked me to wait a minute, and then brought over Lord Harding so that I could repeat my suggestion, which I did. Lord Harding then asked how this would affect such a medical officer's seniority, to which I replied that the medical officer was the advisor to the commanding officer of the battalion, so that his actual rank was not really material. Lord Harding seemed interested and said that he would discuss my idea with the Director General of the RAMC. It was interesting to learn later that my suggestion had been implemented and that there were medical officers who had led a continuous career with the Gurkhas.

Next morning, our breakfast consisted of more oysters and champagne.

During the four days in Ipoh, some of us explored one of the neighbouring iron mines and went up a limestone cliff face to look at some recently discovered aboriginal cave paintings.

Then, back to Kluang.

I was in my second year of National Service. If I had wanted to stay on with the Gurkhas, I would have been welcomed with open arms; especially as I would have had Field Marshal Lord Harding's recommendation.

I was thoroughly enjoying my tour with the Gurkhas but had other thoughts on my professional career. I had applied for, and had been promised, a job in obstetrics at Ayrshire Central Hospital, starting on 1st January, 1960. I wanted to return to Malaya to practice. My tour with the Battalion would normally have ended in July or August 1959, which would have meant that I would have had about five months with nothing to do until the end of the year.

The Director General of the RAMC had visited Hong Kong at the end of 1958. We had been invited to attend a cocktail party in his honour and, in the course of the party, I approached him and asked if I could extend my stay with the army for another four or five months until the end of 1959. I said that, as most medical officers joined the RAMC in August and there were two months of training, there was a hiatus of medical officers during the months of August to October. There would then be a month during November so that a proper hand-over to the next Regimental Medical Officer could take place.

The Director General seemed interested and, some months later, I received word that my application for extension had been approved.

I wanted to return to Malaya if I could, but how was I to find a job?

Some of the local British Military Hospital doctors had been helping out at a clinic in Cha'ah, a village about forty miles from Kluang, where there was no doctor, and gave me the name of someone whom I could contact to find out about it. This was a Mr Trevor Senton, the security officer on Chan Wing Estate, near Cha'ah.

I contacted him and he asked me to visit him. I had no car so how was I to do so? He suggested that I use a "run-around" taxi, a taxi that takes passengers and "runs around" until it has the full compliment of four passengers who want to do the journey, an inexpensive method of transport. It certainly worked, although some of the passengers had bags of rice they were carrying, and others had live chickens.

I met Trevor in his bungalow, a two-storey colonial building set among the serried ranks of the rubber trees, and he, in turn, introduced me to Mr D'Silva, the owner of the clinic.

We discussed the possibilities and we agreed that I would work in the clinic on my eventual return to Malaya, after my obstetric post and sitting the examination for a diploma in obstetrics.

In the meantime, work went on in the Regiment.

There were glad times and sad times. In Malaya a disease affecting Gurkha babies was encountered from time to time. The child might be seen in the morning with what appeared to be a mild cold, which would rapidly become a raging fever with death occurring within a few hours. I encountered one such case, but had suspected what it might be, and sent the child into the British Military Hospital when I first saw the baby. I went with the child to the hospital and held him while a lumbar puncture was done. It was to no avail and I can still see in my mind's eye this unfortunate infant lying in ice with a temperature of 108° F (42° C). The baby died during the night and I occasionally visited his grave in the Gurkha graveyard adjacent to the camp, with the sad toys lying on the small mound.

I was visiting the family medical centre one day and walked past where a bulldozer had been used to level an area for a football field. I noticed some of the Gurkhas looking down at the bank where the earth had been cut, but thought they had probably seen a snake and thought no more about it. During the sick parade, one of the British officers came in and asked if I would take a look. He, too, had thought that the men had found a snake, but, more curious than I, had gone to take a look. Where the bank had been sliced, there were what appeared to be the ends of two bones. Further along, there was another pair. They looked like human femora.

I went to the adjutant's office and told him that I thought there were some bodies in the camp. He came to take a look and then telephoned military officials in London. The instructions came back that I was to exhume a body for examination.

My Saturday afternoon was spent carefully exposing the skeletons, which were obviously now human. The bones were very soft and crumbled away to the touch but I managed to get a few bits together, with another of the bodies for good measure. Where was I to put them? The obvious place was the hospital mortuary, so I took them up to the hospital in two crates and presented myself at admissions to say that I had a couple of patients for them. I showed the bones to the sergeant, who commented: "Cor; they're dead, aren't they!"

It was many weeks before we received any further instructions. Apparently, as the camp had been a Japanese civilian concentration camp during the war, the bodies were to be left where they are. The bank was later concreted over to hide any further traces.

At a later date, another body was exposed when a trench was dug. As the top had been neatly lifted off, it was obviously a human skeleton.

Dashera came again, and Dewali. I had a new personal orderly, who could do a perfect swallow dive into the swimming pool but could not swim! He swam by doggy-paddling to the side of the pool after the dive.

By this time, I had four midwives. Old Kemkala Gurungseni had been the midwife with the Battalion since time immemorial. She was the widow of one of the men of the Regiment, and had so much experience that she could pick up abnormal pregnancies easily. Iain Brebner put her name in for a decoration but I gather that nothing came of it. There was another, younger Gurkha midwife, an Indian and a very attractive Malay girl. It was of interest that pethidine to relieve pain was used only once in the time I was with the Battalion, such was the stoicism of the women who were in labour.

About a month before the end of my tour of duty, there was another job for me to do. Traditionally, regimental bandsmen were also the stretcher-bearers of the battalion. A competition in stretcher-bearing had been organised for all the regiments in Malaya. I now had to institute training to ensure that our stretcher-bearers were up to scratch. I set up a course including all aspects of stretcher-bearing and we spent some weeks on this. I completed this but had returned to the UK when the competition took place.

The time for me to leave the Battalion had arrived. As was the custom, the soldiers and their families garlanded me with multiple fragrant floral favours. I went by train to Singapore, then I flew in one of the new Comet-4s by way of Tobruk to an airfield in the south of England. Interestingly enough, I found Tobruk to be intensely cold, but then, it was the first of December.

I did a dash to the RAMC depot at Crookham, achieved my discharge, and then did another dash to Kings Cross railway station, where I managed to catch the night train to Aberdeen. Because of the speed of reaching the train, I was still in officer's uniform, so I was given a first class railway ticket, most regrettably as the first class compartments were empty except for me and it was bitterly cold.

So I was back at home. I was twenty-seven years of age and another chapter in my life was over – well, perhaps not quite.

Gurkha wives.

Gurkha wives.

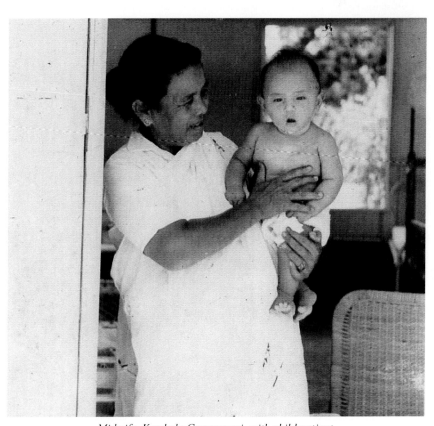

Midwife, Kemkala Gurungseni, with child patient.

The second midwife with child patient.

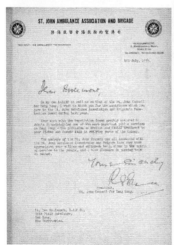

Letter of thanks from St. John Ambulance, Hong Kong.

Myself, taken outside the medical centre at Kluang.

Chapter 12

Aberdeen Interlude

I was back in Aberdeen for a month and met up with old friends whom I had not seen for three to four years.

It was one of those times that realization came that people whom I had known well and with whom I had had close relations, had their own lives to lead and that we had grown apart.

At some point, perhaps before I had left the Regiment, but more probably during the month of December, I learned that a plea had been made for Gurkhas stationed in England to be invited to homes over Christmas. Many of officers at the barracks understandably wanted to spend Christmas with their families and had requested those who could, to provide hospitality to one or more of the Gurkhas.

One of the Gurkhas involved was a Gurkha lieutenant whom I knew, Asbahadur Gurung, and I was delighted that he could come to Aberdeen and share Christmas with us. I remember meeting him at the station and showing him round Aberdeen. One early morning we visited the fish market. Half way down Market Street, he asked if sahib wanted a drink. I had to explain that, in Britain, drinking establishments did not open until later in the day. However, his question was understandable as it is common practice to have a spirituous drink before starting work in the morning, in Nepal.

On Christmas Eve we decided to attend the Christmas Eve church service. My grandfather was somewhat concerned and asked if it was proper for our guest, a Hindu, to attend a Christian church service. As the Gurkhas attend services at weddings, funerals in other parts of the world, there seemed to be no reason why he should not.

It was a beautiful night, the snow was just starting to fall, and there was a thin, unspoiled blanket of snow over everything. Our guest seemed to enjoy the service. Of course, being a Gurkha, he was very polite.

Two days later he was due to leave and I took him into Union Street for some last-minute shopping. I asked if there was anything he particularly wanted and he answered that he wanted a scarf for his wife, presumably a tartan scarf.

We went to the first clothier's store and the girl produced some tartan scarves. However, Asbahadur said they were too small. Could it be a stole that he wanted, except that stoles were not usually tartan? We tried other shops but the result was the same. We had almost completed the length of Union Street and there were only three more shops that we could try when he stopped and said that there was what he wanted. There was a roll of tartan material in the window – he wanted tartan cloth to make into a sari!

We entered the shop and asked for enough tartan material for a sari. We had to judge the length as, of course, the girl did not have a clue how much material went into making a sari. Having seen my maternity patients don their saris, I knew how they were worn and had some idea how much was needed.

Nepal is cold in winter and woolen tartan material is sensible and quite popular in that country.

Asbahadur went off, back to Aldershot, and only a few days remained before I went back to Ayrshire for my obstetric job.

Chapter 13

Midwifery

It was New Year's Eve when I arrived at Ayrshire Central Hospital and dusk was gathering. I made my way to the hospital and then to a building behind the hospital which appeared to be the staff quarters. On entering, I was accosted by the matron, who informed me that this was the nurses' home, but showed me how to reach the medical staff mess.

The consultants were Dr Richard de Soldenhoff and Dr Gilbert Forsyth. The former was quite a character, known as "the Russian doctor" or "Bolshie" in Ayr, and as "the Chief" at Irvine. He had first qualified as a Fellow of the Royal College of Surgeons, then as an obstetrician, at the Royal College of Obstetricians and Gynaecologists. During the war, he had been incarcerated in Singapore by the Japanese. After the war, he became a house surgeon again and had the pleasure of having a name-plate made, displaying his qualifications of FRCS and MRCOG, on the door of his room!

There were four registrars, of whom I knew two. I had met Alex Ross previously at Ayr County Hospital. John Gill had been a year ahead of me at university.

There were also three other obstetrical house surgeons.

I settled in and started work on the following day, 1st January, 1960.

For the house surgeons, there was a four-day roster. The first day was on the labour room, and this could be quite arduous and might involve no sleep in the twenty-four hours if the labour ward was busy. The second day was spent doing routine ward work, taking blood pressures, assisting operations, and being on call for flying squad visits. The third day was being on call for anaesthetics and this day could also be busy. The fourth day was a half day, clerking routine admissions until 1.00 pm, after which one was off duty until 8.00 am next morning. This meant that each house surgeon was on call for 77 hours out of 96, or, to put it into weekly terms, for 134.75 hours a week.

If a doctor was on leave, days two and three were merged. There were occasions when I was awake, working, for over 40 hours at a stretch.

I soon discovered that what was in the textbooks, in form, bore little resemblance to real life, when translated. However, it was a period of intense learning, repairing episiotomies, forceps deliveries, breech deliveries, removal of retained placentas, emptying wombs of retained pieces of conception in inevitable miscarriages, and a hundred and one other procedures. I learned that, after a delivery, if the placenta looked as if it would be retained, then, if one was quick, before the cervix closed, it could be immediately manually extracted, without too much pain. After all, it was pointed out, a hand was smaller than the baby's head, and it would save the mother a general anaesthetic.

The nearest anaesthetists were at Kilmarnock, ten miles away, so we performed our own anaesthetics – gas (nitrous oxide), oxygen and ether – and became quite expert at it. Often, Caesarean sections were done under local anaesthetic, a long needle anaesthetizing the skin through which the incision was made. It was very "hands-on" obstetrics. Pudendal block was used to perform forceps deliveries.

Possibly because he had had to work under extreme conditions during the war, the "Chief" was determined that we learn every aspect of our craft, and, once under his instruction, I gave a chloroform anaesthetic. In 1853, Queen Victoria was delivered under light chloroform anaesthesia, by a method which became known as *chloroform à la reine*. The speed and ease of anaesthetizing with chloroform was quite startling but, of course, the dangers, both by giving too much and the more chronic dangers to the system, make it a risky substance to use.

"Flying squad" calls could be exciting, travelling in the ambulance, wondering how I was to manage this emergency, getting there and dealing with it, then the journey back. Most of the calls were for severe pre-eclamptic toxaemia. I can remember going in to the patient, who had become puffed up with retained fluid, checking the blood pressure, which would be in the region of

240/120 mm Hg, and then administering an enema of Bromethol (Avertin), monitoring the falling blood pressure, and accompanying the unconscious patient back to the hospital. The condition can be frightening. It was common in Ayrshire, it could come on very rapidly (with one patient, the general practitioner told us that the blood pressure had been normal two days previously) and we were fortunate that none went on to actual eclampsia.

Each house officer usually had four flying squad calls in six months – I somehow managed eight.

Another call was to a patient at Muirkirk, a village in the hills, about thirty miles from Irvine. She was a farmer's wife who was miscarrying. Alex Ross took me there in his car and we did a dilatation and curettage in the farmhouse. I can remember Alex explaining after the procedure that antibiotics would be unnecessary as there were no longer any retained products of conception. On the return journey, he pointed out that his headlights were amber instead of white as, by using amber headlights, dark adaption was not interfered with so that vision was improved.

The most memorable flying squad visit was to a house in Ayr. Dr de Soldenhoff came with us to this one. As I left the hospital in the ambulance at about 2.00 am, I was startled to see headlights approaching us then apparently rising into the air. Then I realized that we were approaching Prestwick airport and that the lights were those of an aeroplane taking off. At the same time, I realized that I was not supposed to be on this call at all as I was not on duty for flying squad but had been too tired to remember that fact! When we reached the house, it was filthy and there were no matching sets of furniture, which were all, in any case, damaged. There were, however, two television sets in the one room, each showing a different programme. The bath was used to hold the coal. The patient, a thin, middle-aged woman, was lying on a bed settee with pints of blood clot between her legs. We had brought blood and the Chief got me to take blood from the patient, manually spin it down on a portable centrifuge, check the blood type, then cross-match it with the blood we had brought. A blood transfusion was then set up and the patient was then transferred by ambulance to the hospital. It was, by this time, dawn.

The registrars who had also come did a checklist to ensure that every eventually had been considered, and then telephoned the Chief, who by this time had returned home. His first question was: "What is the woman's religion?" She had had multiple pregnancies and he was considering preventing any more by sterilizing her, which would have been difficult, had she been Roman Catholic.

Much of Ayrshire was Roman Catholic and large families were the norm. By the time that the thirteenth child was born, the elder siblings were old enough to look after the younger members of the family. On one occasion, when I was on labour ward, a mother and daughter were in adjacent rooms, both delivering.

The tiredness resulting from the work was mind-numbing. There were occasions, if one of the house officers was on leave and I had been up all night and the following day, that, administering an anaesthetic, I was almost as asleep as the patient.

I had just managed to get to sleep one night, when the telephone rang, requesting me to attend a multiple delivery, in case an anaesthetic was needed. I went over to the labour ward and took up my place at the head of the bed. The anaesthetic was not required and I was about to give the intravenous ergometrine. The operator asked me to wait a minute as he had not quite finished. When the babies were delivered, I sought the patient's hand under the sheet. A Chinese nurse at the side of the bed looked at me. It was her hand I was holding! Eventually all was done and I returned to bed.

Next morning I went for breakfast and, reading the morning paper, remarked that triplets had been delivered at the hospital. I was then informed that I had been there! I must have lost count in my sleepiness.

There were some amusing moments. I was preparing to do a vaginal examination on a girl who was being admitted. She was lying there wide-eyed, watching me put on the gloves. She asked: "Are ye goin' tae pit yer hail haun' in?" I said that I did not think that would be necessary. She replied that would be a pity, "It wou'd hae gie'n me a thrill!"

Dr de Soldenhoff occasional used hypnoses to relieve the labour pains of deliveries he was conducting. He was once demonstrating to us the induction of hypnosis, passing his hand over the patient's abdomen, when he was called away to the telephone. We started chatting, when the patient's head came up and she told us to shut up – she was hypnotized!

We had just completed a ward round one morning and one of the patients was going to have a Caesarean Section. The Chief then decided that, as I was returning to the Far East, it was time I started doing the Caesarean sections instead of merely assisting. He instructed me to go up to the operating theatre and get started and he would come to assist as soon as he could. Until he came, one of the registrars, Dr Campbell, would assist. The baby was safely delivered and I was sewing up the patient's abdomen by the time the boss arrived.

Half-way through the six months, one of the house officer's tours of duty ended and she was replaced by another girl.

John Gill could be fairly outspoken at times. He had had a remarkable career, having left school at the age of fourteen to join the merchant navy, having sailed round the world, including round the Horn, for a couple of years. He then decided that he wanted to do more with his life and began saving and studying for the university preliminary examinations. Thus he had entered the faculty of medicine.

He was a staunch socialist, which was logical from his beginnings. One day, in the doctors' common room, where our new house officer was sitting, he was expounding about how immoral entrepreneurs, such as Hugh Fraser, were. Our new doctor said: "Excuse me but he is my uncle!" then went on to say that this particular entrepreneur was not approved of by her family, as he was "jumped up". It transpired that her family was that of John Lewis, the big ship-building company of Aberdeen, and Hugh Fraser was an interloper.

One night, I was on the labour ward when I was called to admissions. There was a young girl there suffering from vaginal bleeding. The story came out. She had become pregnant, still unmarried. Her boyfriend and she had gone to Glasgow and visited a well-known abortionist, a discredited midwife. The abortionist had run out of witch hazel twigs and had simply chopped off a sliver of wood from her chopping block, using this to procure the abortion.

She was bleeding quite a bit and, in view of the circumstances I phoned the registrar, who suggested that I check the state of things by examining her vaginally. This I did and found the vagina full of foetal bones, which I removed. The bones were put in a bottle with preservative, and the patient was admitted. Worse was to come because the vaginal discharge grew both tetanus spores and those of gas gangrene. Appropriate antibiotic treatment was instituted, but the situation was such that removal of the womb was probable.

The police had been trying to catch the abortionist for many years. I was conscious that I could be called to court at some time but, as I contacted the relevant authorities some months later to find out what the state of affairs was, I was told that the abortionist had died. In the end she had cheated justice. The unfortunate girl who had suffered from her ministrations was criticized in some quarters for having exposed the woman.

Poor girl; I lost sight of her from there. I think she survived but her future looked bleak. What humanity puts up with because of society's mores.

Two patients I particularly remember during my term at Irvine. One was the sister of Alistair Cook, the American correspondent. The other was a lady of fifty-three. The couple had been unable to conceive and, at fifty-three, her periods had come to an end. She understood that she had reached the menopause and, as so often happens, she started to put on weight. She was well into the pregnancy – her first – when it was found that she was pregnant. The couple was beside themselves with joy. For the baby, it would be like being brought up by grandparents.

During the six months at the hospital, a particular type of research was being undertaken. The Megaloblastic Anaemia of Pregnancy is a form of anaemia that is rare compared with iron deficiency anaemia, but it was thought that its frequency had been underestimated because of incomplete examination of the blood and marrow.

Accordingly it was decided to do a random examination of bone marrows of a hundred patients. The finding was that bone marrow changes were evident before the changes appeared in the blood and that it was found to be indeed the case that the condition was going unrecognized.

It would be impractical for every maternity patient to have a bone marrow examination, although the team that was performing the procedure became expert at it and the patients were not subjected to much pain. It was thought more reasonable to give all pregnancy patients prophylactic folic acid as well as iron.

This measure was a success and it was discovered that there was a second beneficial result in that there was a marked reduction in the number of Accidental Haemorrhages of Pregnancy, a condition which often ended in death.

Much more recently, it has been found that prophylactic folic acid also helps prevent spina bifida in the babies.

At the end of my position as house officer at Ayrshire Central Hospital, I was asked to stay on as a locum registrar while the other registrars had some leave. As I had time to kill until the diploma examination, I agreed to this, but first had a few days' holiday with my parents in the west of Scotland.

On my return from the holiday, one of the registrars wanted to know why I had cross-matched blood for a certain patient. I remembered the patient. While taking the history, on enquiring if she had experienced any bleeding, she had mentioned that she only once had noticed one spot of blood. This had prompted me to automatically set aside two bottles of blood for her in case it was necessary. It transpired that, when this girl had gone into labour, she had started to bleed heavily because of a placenta praevia and that the ready-to-hand blood had saved her life. The lesson to be learned was to listen to the patient and ignore nothing, no matter how trivial it might appear.

My job as registrar included running the prenatal clinics in the various small towns in Ayrshire, assisting at operations at Ballochmyle, doing repair operations at Kilmarnock, being on call for complications occurring at the small maternity hospitals in the district, such as breech or forceps deliveries.

At the end of August, I visited the Edinburgh Festival with a girlfriend from Yorkshire. We saw Stravinsky's *Petrushka*, and later visited the Tattoo, where the 1/6th QEO Gurkha band was taking part. At the end of the performance, I delayed leaving and had the pleasure of renewing acquaintances with the band members at the top of Edinburgh's High Street. It was strange, in such a locality, to be greeted by *"huzoor"* ("presence") from the Gurkhas' smiling faces.

A party at Redhill barracks in Edinburgh had been arranged for the visiting Gurkhas, which I attended. It went on until four in the morning, and, in the course of it I met a cousin of Sherpa Tensing, who invited me to visit Nepal where he would take me up Mount Everest!

Another invitation at the time was to attend a garden party at Buckingham Palace where the presentation of the new Queen Elisabeth's Own regimental banners by the Queen was to take place. Unfortunately, I could neither afford the fare to London nor the cost of the stay there.

Eventually I sat the diploma examination in Glasgow, then had a holiday at home in Aberdeen, until the time of the oral part of the diploma examination, which would take place in London, at the College of Obstetricians and Gynaecologists.

I had timed my flight back to Malaya to take place on the day after the oral examination. The fare was about £100, which was about all I had at the time.

Chapter 14

Cha'ah

On the flight to Malaya there was only one stop this time, at Karachi. A group of people in the plane, drinking, were very noisy. At Karachi, they made straight for the bar. I kept quiet. They ordered a round of drinks. The drinks were supplied. The price was astronomical! This was a Muslim country. I could have warned them but in view of their behaviour, I considered that they got what they deserved.

I was seated beside a manager of Rolls Royce on his way to the Far East. The weather was good and the view of the Himalayas spectacular.

We landed at Kuala Lumpur at the original tin airport terminal, still in existence at that time, and I was met by Mr D'Silva and Trevor Senton, who had left Chan Wing Estate and was now manager at K. C. Dat in Kuala Lumpur.

Mr D'Silva drove me south that night. There were patches of low-lying fog on the way.

Cha'ah was a "new village", one of the new villages created by Sir Gerald Templer, during the Emergency, to keep the population under some sort of control. The main part of the village was double-storey wooden shop-houses with open frontages and living quarters upstairs, at the opposite sides of a *padang*, an open field, on which games could be played, much like the idea of the village common in England, with a periphery of dwelling houses, built by the villagers themselves. This main commercial area was enclosed by a barbed wire fence, starting to disintegrate by 1960.

The people were very poor and the situation was that the doctor had one of the few cars in the village. The main income was from rubber tapping and working in the oil palm industry. The villagers were Malay, Tamil Indians and Chinese. The Chinese were Hakka in Cha'ah, and Hokkein in Labis and Bekok, speaking different dialects. Hakka are sometimes known as "Ke" which means "the outsiders", as they mainly work outside the towns, doing agricultural work.

The Chinese were the shopkeepers and lived in the village, Malays lived in houses on stilts on the outskirts of the villages, and the Indians lived in the village and in estate housing, known as "lines".

My residence was a small bungalow on Factory Road, a laterite road which ran up to the factory of Johore Labis Estate, an estate of the French Socfin group, outside Cha'ah. It was quite an attractive bungalow, sparsely furnished with wicker chairs, a wicker glass-topped table, a simple dining table and refrigerator in the dining room, and a simple bed and wardrobe in the bedroom. There was a bathroom with a washbasin, a Shanghai jar, and an Asian toilet. There was a servant's quarter and kitchen and a well, with the water hand pumped to an overhead water reservoir. Mr D'Silva's house was next door.

The clinic faced the main road in Cha'ah. Next door was occupied by a repair shop and next to that was a *kedai kopi*, a coffee shop.

Cha'ah - residence, 2 Factory Road.

Inside the clinic, the front office/waiting room had a glass-faced counter with shelves holding bottles of basic ingredients for medications. The consulting room was further in; there was a back kitchen and an upstairs.

I had very little equipment: a table, chairs, a wooden bed, a kerosene steriliser, stethoscope, tendon hammer, torch and a few glass syringes and basic surgical instruments.

Each morning, going to work, I crossed a bridge over the river, in which the women of the village stood, washing the clothes.

Cha'ah was in the state of Johore, which had its day of prayer on Friday.

I started work from the very first day and worked every day of the week, to be available for patients and because it was easier to see them in the clinic than being called out to see people in emergency.

There was no chemist so I had to dispense medications for the patients and I was back to student days, making cough mixtures, stomach medicines and various ointments. An injection was an expected treatment so the injection given would be a vitamin injection as diets were poor.

Shortly after beginning work, I visited the Chief Medical Officer of Johore to pay my respects. He was a pleasant Malay gentleman, who had been an obstetrician. When he learned that I had the diploma in obstetrics, he asked if I knew Professor Ian Donald, with whom he had worked. The CMO had studied in Edinburgh and described how he had been studying on New Year's Eve, when fellow students had called in, demanded to know why he was studying and had persuaded him to accompany them, first footing. He said that it was wonderful, visiting people that he had never previously met. He said that it was the best night he had ever had!

A car was now a necessity and I managed to buy an old second-hand Mercedes Benz 170 from one of the doctors at the BMH in Kluang as his tour of duty was finished and he was returning to the UK. It was the first car I ever owned, at the age of twenty-seven.

I was soon introduced to Yunos, the former *Penghulu* (headman of the village). He was Javanese by birth, elderly and small in stature, who had in his time been a merchant seaman, visiting countries all over the world. His son, Ali bin Yunos, became my *che'gu* (teacher), from whom I started learning Malay.

Mr D'Silva had also rented a shop-house in Bekok, a village about ten miles east of Cha'ah, and I began to see patients there also.

Car, Mercedes-Benz 170.

Cha'ah Clinic, Labis.

The officer in charge of the Public Works Department was also Malay, very dark. He had three wives. The eldest was in charge of the house, the second looked after the house, the third wife, who was very attractive, was, presumably, for wifely duties. The husband spent all his time in the coffee shop!

Another friend I made was Mr Pang Voon Lait, the local Member of Parliament. He was Chinese, Hakka, and owned the local general grocery store. He described how, during the Second World War, the Japanese occupying soldiers would take the babies from their mothers, throw them in the air, and bayonet the babies as they fell.

What sort of illnesses did I see? There were plenty of coughs and colds, intestinal worms and the common run of day-to-day illnesses. Vigilance was necessary as tuberculosis was common and, as there was no x-ray facilities nearer than forty miles away in Kluang, the people were poor, a very careful

99

clinical examination was necessary to avoid the patient spending an unnecessary fare to have an x-ray that showed nothing.

The diseases were not all mundane. In Bekok, an elderly patient was an opium smoker, and had been since he was very young. I asked him about it and he explained that, as a young lad, when he first went out to work in the fields, he would return home at night aching all over. An older friend had suggested a pipe of opium and he found it helped. He had continued to smoke two pipes of opium, no more, no less, every evening for the next sixty years, just as another fellow might have a couple of beers.

In the same village, there was a young boy, in his teens, who suffered from epilepsy. He was kept chained up under his house.

After a week or two, Mr D'Silva decided to open a clinic in Labis, another, slightly larger village, ten miles away in another direction. The clinic was in a Chinese two-storey house, well built and rather nice.

I had worked daily for almost two months and Christmas was approaching. We went to Malacca to spend Christmas Day, Yunos coming with us. A week later was New Year's Day and Trevor Senton visited from Kuala Lumpur. We did the rounds, seeing our friends, and then Trevor wanted to see an old friend of his, Harry Thomson, who was on an estate at the far side of Bekok. From there we took a very pretty laterite road through the jungle to see another friend, Freddy Thom, who was the manager of a rubber estate in Paloh, over the hills. The road through the jungle, although pretty, could be risky as there were elephants in the vicinity, and they could be dangerous if frightened.

The festive season over, it was back to work.

Malay, Hakka (Ke), Hokkien, a little Cantonese, and Tamil were the languages spoken. Practically none of the patients knew any English. Although Malay was the official language in Malaya, the local people could not see why they should learn it. As they explained, they could speak to their neighbours in their own language. In Cha'ah, most Chinese spoke Hakka, in Bekok and Labis, most were Hokkein. In the clinic were young girl helpers who spoke Malay, Hakka, Hokkein, Cantonese, and Tamil. In the evenings, I went over with them the questions that would be asked so that there should be no mistake.

One of the most satisfying diseases to treat was beriberi. I would be called to the patient's house because the patient would be too weak to walk and, more often than not, would be in heart failure. The family would often be too poor to eat meat and would subsist on white rice. The patient would be lying on the bed, swollen, bloated, and breathless. Diagnosis was clinical and confirmed by a clinical trial of a vitamin B1 injection. Next day, the patient was much better and in two or three days was back to normal health. Once the diagnosis was confirmed the injection given might be changed to vitamin B complex, as the patient would probably have been lacking in other vitamins also.

The living conditions were very primitive. I visited a Chinese house made of railway sleepers set upright and embedded in the ground. The roof was thatch and the floor was the bare earth. The patient was lying on a rough board bed. I was examining the patient when there was a noise under the bed and a pig crawled out.

The Malay houses were much more civilized. They were built on stilts, with a smooth wooden floor, on which mats were laid. The walls were intricately carved. The kitchen was at the back, with a stone or concrete stove.

There were aboriginals on the far side of Bekok, whose houses had thatched walls and the floors, on stilts, were of split bamboo.

In the gardens of all types of houses would be banana trees and there would be chickens running around. Hibiscus, with bright red flowers, was predominant in most gardens.

Very little could be done by way of treatment except to let nature take her course. The patient usually did not come for follow-up, so there was little point in starting a course of penicillin. If a series of injections was very important, as, for example, streptomycin for tuberculosis, it was better to have the patient pay up front for a month's treatment, or, more if possible. Consultation and treatment cost only three to five dollars a time.

The diseases were diverse and sometimes dramatic.

A poor Chinese woman committed suicide by swallowing caustic soda, a painful death.

Twice I was presented with babies, only days old, usually Indian, who seemed to be having fits. They were suffering from neo-natal tetanus, as cow manure had been used as an umbilical dressing.

Cancers were incurable and my job was to make death as easy and pain-free as possible. A useful aid was egg-nog, made with brandy, eggs, sugar and milk, which gave some ease of mind as well as supplying food.

One such patient had peacefully died. The Chinese let the patient lie "in state" for an odd number of days before burial – three, five or seven. It was with some consternation that, two days later, a relative came to say that he had come to life again. I visited but the patient was truly dead. What had happened was that, when rigor mortis had worn off, the chest had relaxed and air had been released from the lungs, simulating breathing out.

In the early part of the year, I received an invitation to the 1/6th Gurkhas' "Beating of the Retreat", leaving from Kluang to the battalion's next posting. It poured with rain, rendering the Retreat a washout but we continued with the cocktail party in the mess, and the few of us remaining played poker afterwards.

A problem with the clinic was that rubber prices were very low and patients' incomes were extremely limited. Years previously, when there was a boom in rubber, clinics were crowded with people seeking treatments. Now patients only visited the doctors when they considered they absolutely had to. Thus I was obviously not seeing as many as I might. I was asked by another village, Tenang Kampong ("Peaceful village"), also known as Ayer Panas ("Hot water" as there was a hot spring there), if I would also have a clinic in that village.

Tenang Kampong was a beautiful little village, set at the edge of the jungle with a background of the central mountain range, and populated almost entirely by Malays.

One of the Malays, Che Idris, had a party one evening, by way of introduction. The food consisted entirely of Keladi, a root which had to be boiled three times in preparation, as it was full of oxalic acid, which is poisonous. The beer also flowed copiously and great care had to be taken as the host was very generous in supplying it.

I can vividly remember a night call to that village. It was dark and warm. The girl interpreters were in the back of the car. As we drove up the long road to Ayer Panas, the singing of the cicadas, "buzz bombs" as we named them, was a continual monotone. At one point, there was a commotion in the back seat – a flying fox had flown in, and as quickly, flew out. We went on and reached the patient's house, which was just inside the edge of the jungle. From examination, the diagnosis was scrub typhus, as far as I can remember. As I was about to give the mandatory injection, the syringe slipped through the split bamboo which comprised the floor of the house, to the ground below. Such were the hazards of country practice in Malaya.

An Indian male's description of an encounter was that he had "paradise" with a girl.

Such was the poverty of the people that I can remember the expression on the face of a young Indian girl whom one of the helpers was trying to undress. The helper pulled too hard, breaking the bra strap. The girl had worked to make her clothes and was going to have to stitch it all over again. Life can be hard.

A young Chinese man attended me with prolific penile warts. Treatment with podophylin paint was painful and unsuccessful, the warts returning and multiplying from contact. Eventually it became obvious that a circumcision would need to be done to prevent the contact. The young man could not afford going to hospital so it was left to me to undertake an adult circumcision under local anaesthetic. The conditions were primitive and certainly not ideal for surgery, but the operation went ahead. The treatment worked, with little infection.

It was at this time that one of the local European planters came into the clinic. An estate assistant had been attacked, hit on the side of the head with a *changkol*, a pick-like digging implement, had been rendered unconscious, and the payroll had been stolen from him. To make matters worse, the assistant was the nephew of Tunku Abdul Rahman, the Prime Minister. The estate doctor was away, could I please see him?

We went to the estate hospital, where the patient was lying. I asked the estate dresser what he had done so far. The dresser stated that he had given the patient an injection of anti-tetanus serum, a shot of penicillin, and an injection of morphine. I asked why the dresser had given morphine to an unconscious man. The answer was to prevent pain! I made no comment. Here I was with an unconscious man who had been rendered more unconscious with morphine, and I did not know if he was allergic to anti-tetanus serum or penicillin.

Obviously hospitalization was necessary. The estate manager wanted this important patient to go to Gleneagles Hospital in Singapore, 86 miles south. The estate ambulance was out of commission, and the only vehicle that could take a stretcher was the estate postal van, which was not licensed to travel on public roads. However, there was no alternative and I would have to travel with the patient. The manager arranged for his own car, a Chevrolet, to follow the post van in case there was any trouble.

So we set off south in the gathering dusk.

To my relief, the patient began to show signs of consciousness, so I spent the journey rousing him from time to time.

We reached the Singapore border and the immigration officers came on board. They were not going to allow the van to enter Singapore as it was not registered to travel on Singapore roads. I said that the patient on the stretcher was Tunku Abdul Rahman's nephew, that he could be transferred to the manager's Chevrolet, but that it was risky and that, if anything happened as a result, then they, the immigration officers, would be entirely responsible. The van was waved through!

Next came customs with an identical scenario.

We reached Gleneagles hospital at about 1.00 am and the patient was handed over to the medical care there.

I was able to travel back to Cha'ah in the comfort of the manager's Chevrolet, and slept most of the way.

The evenings in Cha'ah were warm and balmy. There was no television and very little radio. I read multitudes of cheap paperback novels and listened to recordings on the tape recorder.

Storms, known as a "Sumatras", sometimes occurred, First of all, all wind or breeze stopped. There would be an eerie silence. Then the coming rain could be *smelled*. Within ten minutes, the gale struck, the rain coming *horizontally*.

Sometimes I went to medical meetings in Johore Bahru, in order to keep up to date. Occasionally there would be a visit to the cinema in Labis, Bekok or Batu Pahat. The films were very varied, sometimes Chinese, but the most memorable were the Marx Brothers' *A Night at the Opera* and *King Kong*, the original version. The showing of *A Night at the Opera* was made more interesting by a flying fox which flew around in the cinema.

There was one evening when I was returning from the clinic, the bridge over the river was blocked after an accident. I stopped to help and was soon joined by the Chinese Police Inspector from Labis. We were hard at work when the Police Superintendent from Segamat arrived, held up by the accident and unable to return home. Eventually, the bridge was cleared and I invited the two policemen to my home, which was nearby, for a drink. We had sat down and were chatting while I poured the drinks. Then our conversation was interrupted by the noise of a car coming down the main road, obviously taking the corner too quickly, and then there was the sound of a crash as the car hit the bridge. We looked at each other then went out to sort out the mess of the next car accident!

Another motor accident I remember was one that happened one day when I was consulting in Labis. The accident occurred a few miles north of the village at a rather dangerous corner. One of the people involved was Lim Yew Hock, who had been the Chief Minister of Singapore a few years previously. His injuries were not too serious but there was a lot of fuss from the local dignitaries that such an important person was involved.

I got to know some of the local planters: Harry Thomson, Frank Fife, Graham Fullerton who was the nephew of my professor of medicine, and others, and we had some pleasant evenings together.

In the latter part of the year, there was a large weekend medical seminar held by the Malayan Medical Association in Kuala Lumpur, which I managed to attend, staying with Trevor Senton. In the course of the first morning I saw a young European doctor wearing a tartan scarf. Just prior to leaving for Malaya, my insurance broker had mentioned that, if I was ever in Penang, to look up Don Ballantyne or Mike Scott, who were also clients of his. At one of the intervals, I approached this doctor and asked if he was either Dr Ballantyne or Dr Scott. He answered that he was, indeed, Mike Scott. We joined each other at lunchtime and got on quite well. I also met the professor of obstetrics at Kuala Lumpur, Professor Derek Llewellyn-Jones.

The weekend over, it was back to Cha'ah and work.

One afternoon, at Bekok, I was asked to do a home visit on a woman in her fifties or sixties who had obviously suffered a stroke. None of the family, including the patient, was interested in going to hospital, so it was a case of daily visits, checking pressure points, doing basic physiotherapy, encouraging movement. Slowly she regained the use of her arms, but the paralyzed leg stayed unusable. However, despite her disability, she was far happier.

One day, at the surgery in Bekok, the husband of this patient appeared, carrying a paper bag. From the bag came the sound of some squawks and this was a present to me of a pair of live hens. At home, some chicken wire was hurriedly put up to form a pen. Christmas was approaching and it was arranged to have a Christmas dinner of one of the chickens. Harry Thomson, Frank Fife and Graham Fullerton came as guests. We chatted, had dinner accompanied by wine and altogether had a very pleasant evening.

It was only a few days later that the second chicken appeared on the table and I was a bit surprised because I had intended to keep it until a later date when I had company. The cookie explained that, since the other had gone, this chicken was pining! Unfortunately, at this suggestion, the chicken I was eating lost all taste and it was all I could do to finish the plate.

There were other parties in the village which were very pleasant. At one Chinese dinner, I had my one opportunity to eat swan, which I found to be somewhat gritty and not very pleasant.

Because of the good recovery of the woman with the stroke, I started to receive calls to many other patients suffering strokes. I visited one elderly woman. She was lying there in her funeral clothes. As she was not dead I asked the reason. The family said that it was easier dressing her while she was still alive than after her death. Another call to a stroke victim was to Kluang, forty miles away. I set off in my little Mercedes Benz car, driving through the rubber plantations to the town, and seeing the patient. Living so far away, daily care was out of the question and I could only advise what to do and drive back.

Practising medicine in that small village of Cha'ah and coming to understand the various cultures was a steep learning curve.

I made many friends from the various races. A party I attended was to celebrate a young Indian girl's first menstruation. There I learned how to eat rice, using the fingers of my right hand.

The Malay Assistant District Officer and I became good friends and I attended the celebration of the fortieth day after the delivery of one of his children, at which event, a lock of the baby's hair is taken.

One afternoon, at the Bekok clinic, a man in late middle age was brought in. I knew him; he was visiting from Cha'ah and had been having a coffee in one of the local *kedais* when he had collapsed. He was extremely ill and died almost immediately, on the table that served as the examination couch. The owner of the shop-house which was rented to be used as a clinic became almost hysterical. She wanted the body removed immediately and everything the body had touched to be burned. The dead man's relatives from Cha'ah were contacted and arrived remarkably quickly from their village ten miles away. The situation was explained to them and they stated that the Bekok people were Hokkein (which I already knew) and had some peculiar ideas! Fortunately, as the body was lying on a plastic sheet, the examination table did not have to be destroyed and only the sheet had to be removed.

A few days later, the local police sergeant, who was Chinese and whom I knew well, came to see me to enquire what the circumstances were. I explained that the reason for the man's sudden death was probably a massive myocardial infarction. He asked what that was and I said that it was the medical name for a heart attack. He said that was fine and put down the cause of death as being due to a "heart attack". Everything was very simple!

The various races normally got on well together but I can remember at one evening party where the *Penghulu* began to complain how the Malay land was being taken over by the Chinese. The local Chinese Member of Parliament responded by pointing out that it was the Chinese who did all the work. The atmosphere became quite heated and an American Peace Corps worker present was somewhat anxious that there might be a fight. There was not and all calmed down.

In Cha'ah there was a lot of learning: Malay, Hakka, Hokkein, and Tamil cultures; the fact that, in general practice, diseases were not always presented as in text-book descriptions. I learned to be largely self-reliant. It was a case of listening to the patient and being meticulous in examination.

A young Chinese man complained of feeling tired. He seemed to have lost weight. As there were no scales, no record of his weight could be taken. Full examination revealed no definite abnormality. The only tests I could do were an erythrocyte sediment rate, which I could do myself, and possibly a VDRL, for which the blood could be sent through the post. The ESR was very high, by recollection, about 80 mm fall in one hour. There was obviously something seriously wrong. The next step was to take a chest x-ray, and with the results so far obtained there was enough reason for the patient to travel to Kluang to have this done. The x-ray showed a tiny spot of TB, too small to be picked up on examination of the chest. Treatment was started with good results.

The account, so far, of my work in Cha'ah has a similarity to a scrap book, bits and pieces all over the place, in no particularly chronological order. Working every day of the week, all through the year, there are no particular milestones to punctuate the periods in time.

By the time I had been working there for about fifteen or so months, my old Mercedes 170 was showing signs of wear and tear, frequently breaking down. I decided that it was about time to purchase a better vehicle. Mercedes cars then, in Malaya and Singapore, were surprisingly inexpensive, and I bought a new Mercedes 190D on hire purchase. It was a diesel model, as diesel fuel was very cheap. As the practice did not supply a car and only paid for running costs, I had to buy my own car.

All this learning had its down-side, however. Although I was employed for $1,200 per month, I did not receive anything like this pay. The reason for this was that, at that time, the price for rubber was very low and the rubber-tappers, on whom the local economy depended, could not afford medical treatment. Shopkeepers and other service provided were similarly affected. This was a very real lesson in social economy. In addition, my employer, Mr D'Silva, was in the habit of buying blocks of land, ostensibly to enlarge the practice.

I was paid a portion of the amount I had been promised, the balance "to be paid later". In a small village such this, there was very little to buy so that, at first, the differential did not appear significant. I was very poorly off. As I had no money, I did not have sufficient to pay for an airfare back to the UK. The situation was illegal and, as the Immigration Department were not told of the state of affairs, I found myself saddled with an income tax bill for the full amount of what I should have been paid in addition to the cost of a new car. I lived very frugally, usually eating bean curds for lunch, and lost quite a bit of weight.

Graham Fullerton had dropped in one evening and we were discussing the predicament. I was unsure how job situations were in the UK. National Service had come to an end at the time of my demobilization from the army, with the result that there were twice as many doctors looking for places of employment. I picked up the latest *British Medical Journal* to find out what situations were vacant and saw that there was an advertisement for a doctor required as an assistant with a view to partnership for the practice of Drs Allen and Gunstensen in Penang! The salary offered was £200 per month. At an exchange rate of $8.50 to the pound that would be $1,700.

Next day, I telephoned Mike Scott, whom I had met in Kuala Lumpur the previous year, and asked if this was the practice in which he worked. He said that indeed it was and asked if I was looking for a job. When I said that I was he asked how soon I could come for an interview. I remember that one of the French planters was on the same train as I went north and that it was the 14th of July, Bastille Day.

In Penang, I met Mike Scott and Alasdair Wilson, two of the doctors in the practice. Drs Allen and Gunstensen had retired some years previously but their names had been retained as the title of the group. I was shown the consulting rooms. They were spacious and the waiting room was in wood panelling. After the surgeries in Cha'ah, Labis, Bekok and Ayer Panas, they were like heaven. There was a much overdue visit to the dentist, where I met Ian Bennett for the first time. I was introduced to the Penang Swimming Club, where I spent the rest of the afternoon. At Dr Wilson's house in the evening I was quizzed about my career until then. At one point it was mentioned that the salary would be $1,600, to which I answered that the advertisement had stated £200, which, at the current exchange rate, was equivalent to $1,700. My accommodation, that night, was at the E & O Hotel and I returned to Cha'ah on the following day.

About a month later, I was asked to come for a second interview to meet the third partner, Don Ballantyne, in his office, and that evening we dined at the E & O Hotel. I can recall that, at some point in the evening, I asked what cost would be incurred if I were invited to become a partner and was told that Dr Scott had paid about $6,000. Towards the end of the dinner, Don Ballantyne said that I was offered the job and could I start as soon as possible, as Dr Wilson was on leave and they were short staffed? I said that three months was the usual professional notice but Don said that he thought that six weeks would be adequate. According to the contract drawn up with Mr D'Silva, notice had not even been mentioned! A lawyer with whom I checked stated that I could just walk out!

Mr D'Silva was naturally very upset and made life very hard for the next six weeks, which just made it easier for me to leave. The only thing I regretted was leaving the girls who worked in the practice, who were, of course, out of a job. A number of the patients pleaded with me to stay but, as they very seldom attended, they were not really giving me a living.

The evening I left, I had dinner with one of the local planters and, "spiritually fortified", I drove north to spend the night with Graham Fullerton who was then on an estate near Malacca.

Chapter 15

Penang

It was 3rd October, 1962. I had been in Cha'ah two years and changes in occupation and location always seemed to happen in October.

I drove to Penang and arrived at the Penang ferry on a beautiful sunny evening. Penang was originally an almost uninhabited island, first settled by the British in 1786. The main city, George Town, was founded in the same year. It had become a city of nearly a million people when I practised there, in contrast to the small Malayan village where I practised previously.

It had been arranged that I rented one of the houses owned by Mansfield's, a shipping company in Penang.

The medical group I joined serviced, as well as the local population, many of the industries on the island and neighbouring mainland – a tin and lead smelter, the Port Commission, rubber and oil palm estates, shipping. The patients were Malay, Chinese (mainly Hokkien), Indian and expatriate Europeans.

The practice was well equipped, with our own x-ray unit, and there were local laboratory facilities. There was a nearby pharmacist but there were no services such as physiotherapists.

I was shown my consulting room and my work initially was to help Dr Scott with the sick parade at Penang Port Commission first thing in the morning, after which I would consult at the main rooms in Beach Street.

That weekend, I bought two cakes of chocolate as a treat after my privations at Cha'ah. I ate them and felt quite sick.

Following the stress of the previous two years, life was peaceful and uneventful.

The central street in Penang is Penang Road. It was a street that jostled. The shops jostled to fill up every space, the goods in the shop jostled to fill up every shelf, the Chinese, Malay and Indian shoppers jostled, looking at goods, bargaining, buying. It was pleasant to wander down this street with the hustle and bustle of the shoppers. From some of the shops emanated the fragrance of sandalwood. The buildings were of brick with a cement facing. The shop-houses were of the typical Southeast Asia variety, two-storey, with an open front, and offices and living quarters upstairs jutting out over the pavement and giving shelter to the shoppers on the pavement underneath. Between the pavement and the vehicular road was the monsoon drain, deep and with the typical smell of fermenting debris. On the pavement, vendors erected card tables on which they displayed wares – the Indian cook skillfully flipping the pancakes he was cooking; another Indian selling spectacles.

There were advertising signs everywhere – "the eyes and piles clinic", "pleated skirts at rock bottom prices", "tooth extraction – Western patients get the needle".

I settled in to work. I now saw Caucasians as well as the local population; diseases were not as florid or dramatic as in Cha'ah but there were enough to keep me occupied. As the practice covered local businesses and shipping, there was plenty to do.

One of the assistants of Mansfield's, the firm that owned the house I was temporarily renting, came to see me one day. He asked me if I remembered him. He had been my drill corporal at Aldershot during my basic training four years previously! It would be tempting to think that I made sure that he received an injection but I do not think that this was necessary and it would have been unprofessional to have invented an excuse to do so. As it happened, we became quite good friends.

Dr Wilson returned from his leave in the UK and there were four doctors in the practice now.

About a month after arriving in Penang I received a letter from my relative, Dr Mary, to say that she was visiting Penang. Obviously I was delighted to be a host to her. With the building of the new Penang airport, Butterworth was being used for civilian as well as military planes. I approached Dr Wilson to ask if I could meet my aunt at the airport. He demurred and then said that, as it was an elderly lady travelling alone, he would permit it.

On Sunday, we went for lunch at the swimming club. We were sitting after lunch when Dr Wilson came over, taking up a pose with one leg on a neighbouring chair, and asked how Dr Mary was enjoying her trip. He asked where she was going to next, and Aunt Mary said that she was going to Kuala Lumpur. He asked where she would be staying and she replied with Sir James Thomson. The leg came off the stool. He asked if that was the Chief Justice and Aunt Mary said that it was. He then asked who else she was seeing and she mentioned a leading industrialist who owned Malayan Airways. The next question was where she was heading after that, to which the answer was Hong Kong. And where was she staying there? Aunt Mary replied, with the Haw Par family. This was the family who owned the Tiger Balm Gardens. Dr Wilson sat down. At the end of the conversation, he invited us to dinner with him at the Penang Club. Dr Mary at that time was President of the world Soroptimist society and, as such, came to know these people.

On Christmas Day, there were no close friends with whom to celebrate, but in the evening we had been invited to cocktails at Dr Wilson's house.

That year, to the best of recollection, I attended the New Year's Eve Party at the E & O Hotel. I had met and become friends with George Gauron, an assistant with one of the shipping firms in Penang. He had found for me a partner, a Chinese girl. The next working day, I was accosted by Dr Wilson about whom I had taken as a partner. Apparently it was not "proper" to be associating socially with the local races!

The lease of the house I was renting was coming to an end and I was able to rent the house formerly occupied by the vet for the racecourse. It was small, of very manageable size, on a corner of Scotland Road overlooking the racecourse. Every Sunday there were races so I had a good view of the horses running except for the finish, which was hidden by the totalizer board. I timed the races and discovered that, in an afternoon of racing, only ten minutes was spent with the horses actually running! To me, it seemed a tremendous waste of time.

I began to attend the St Andrew's Presbyterian Church on Sunday mornings and became a member of the committee. After church, I would go to the Penang Swimming Club and soon started to crew on the "GP 14" yachts in the race on Sunday afternoons.

Thus I settled into a routine.

Dr Wilson sponsored me to become a member of the Penang Club. As the Club was looking for new members, I managed to join at a very low entrance fee. I also inherited Dr Allen's billiard cue, the number of which was A1 but, as I was not interested in billiards, I played only one game.

I was introduced to Mr J. G. Brown, an old resident who had joined the stock broking company of A. A. Anthony in the 1920s. His wife, from Aberdeen, had died just before I came to Penang. He had a wealth of information about the history of the island.

The practice of Drs Allen & Gunstensen had gone back many years, probably to nearly the start of the twentieth century. Prior to the Second World War, the partners were Drs McKern, Allen and Gunstensen, who had qualified around 1930. They would have started practice in Penang in the early thirties. When the Japanese invaded, Drs Allen and Gunstensen were interned in Changi Gaol. Dr McKern, however, hid in the cellar of his large house at Batu Ferringhi, near the Penang Swimming Club. There he successfully hid, being looked after by his amah and her husband. Eventually, two years later, he was betrayed by his Malay driver and interned in a prison camp in Sumatra, where he died.

At the end of the war, the two doctors, Allen and Gunstensen, returned to Penang. As there was limited accommodation available, they set up residence, together with J. G. Brown, in St Andrew's Church manse, in McAlister Road. Strangely enough, when they went into the manse, they found, in the middle of the dining room table, the minute book of Penang St Andrew Society.

Dr Ballantyne, who had qualified in Glasgow in 1948, had been a ship's doctor on one of the City ships which had called into Penang in about 1950. The two doctors asked him to join the practice, which he did.

Dr Wilson had qualified in Edinburgh two years later, in 1950. He had avoided National Service, but gave varying accounts as to the reason, at one time saying it was a hernia, at another time saying it was a perforated eardrum.

They would have joined the practice in about 1950 and 1952 respectively.

Dr Scott had qualified in Glasgow in 1951, but had been called up and had served in the war in Korea. He would have joined the practice in the mid-fifties.

My work was with the Penang Port Commission in the consulting rooms and visiting the two rubber estates, Bertam Estate at Kepala Batas and Malakoff Estate, not far away. The estates were visited weekly.

One of my early patients was Heather McLeod, who attended Upland School, and who was brought to see me by her father, Captain Len McLeod, the chief harbour pilot. Another was Madam Lee, an elderly Chinese lady who lived at 11 Logan Road. Both patients were to appear in my life for many years.

About six months after I had started with the Penang practice, Don Ballantyne left. Before he was due to leave, and, as after that the number of doctors in the practice would be less for the foreseeable future, I was given a holiday, the first in three years. I drove south through Malaya, visiting places and people I had met. One night I stayed at the village house of a Chinese friend in Cha'ah.

Seeing how other races live is always of interest. The sleeping arrangement was a fairly large single room for the family. The mattress was wood. The toilet facility was a corrugated iron enclosure outside, with a Shanghai jar, from which water was scooped to pour over oneself. Urinating was done in the corner of this metal outhouse, and there was a bucket latrine for other purposes.

From there I drove north to Gemas, over the laterite road through the jungle by Bahau, to hit the east-west road leading to Kuantan; then north again to the beautiful, unspoiled beaches at Kampong Kuala Kemaman, where I met up again with the Malay Assistant District Officer whom I had known at Labis.

I returned over the central range by Raub. The view was spectacular, the jungle being covered in a veritable canopy of bright orange jungle creepers.

I had two nights at the Cameron Highlands Hotel, from where I walked up to the tops of the hills. The lower slopes were deep jungle and occasionally there was the sweet smell of native orchids. At the tops, the trees became stunted until there was nothing but low shrub.

I went back to Malacca, staying with Graham Fullerton. While there, an outbreak of cholera began in the town. When I arrived back in Penang, we began immunizing all the staff of the companies with whom we dealt. Bertam Estate had about 750 workers and about an equal number of dependants who were immunized at the estate family hospital. By co-operating the lining-up of labourers and the swabbing of arms, Mike Scott and I injected one and a half thousand individuals in the course of half an hour.

After Dr Ballantyne had left, I moved into Dr Scott's consulting room, which was somewhat larger than the one I had been using until then.

Mike Scott was interested in walking, which I also enjoyed, so on a number of Sundays we walked in the jungle which covered the Penang Hill. On one Sunday, while out walking, Mike seemed in a bad mood. Soon it all came out. Dr Wilson had decided that the shares in the practice should be divided 55 percent to himself and 45 percent to Mike, who considered that shares should have been equal, or at least more equal. He said that he had not realized that, in medicine, it was "dog eat dog".

After that, he did not broach the subject again and I concluded that Dr Wilson had got his way.

We were again functioning with three doctors. One day Dr Wilson asked how we would feel if we had a Chinese doctor. I certainly had no objections and Dr Teh Ewe Wah joined the practice. Shortly after, he married an Irish girl.

Apart from the above, the first year in Penang must have passed quite uneventfully, for the next significant event happened on 22nd November 1963. It would have been the following morning in Penang when I was working in the Penang Port Commission in an adjoining consulting room to Mike Scott, who knocked on my door and entered to say that the American President John F. Kennedy had been shot. There would be few people who did not know where they were when the news of President Kennedy's death was announced.

I was still in debt to the Income Tax Department and to the car hire-purchase firm. Trevor Senton had told me what to do about the income tax debt. I gather he had worked there at one time. He said that when a demand came in, to send them a thousand dollars. My file would then go to the bottom of the heap until the next time. I do not know how accurate he was but it worked!

A few days before Christmas, I received a phone call from Mrs Dorothy McLeod to ask what I was doing for Christmas. I had made no plans and she invited me to join them for Christmas Dinner in the evening. Christmas was going to be an empty affair for me so I accepted this unexpected and kind invitation.

The party was made up of Len and Dorothy McLeod, Heather and Selwyn Buckwell, who was Dorothy's brother. We had an excellent dinner, photographs were taken and there were party games. We all thoroughly enjoyed ourselves and this high note ended the year.

At that time I did not realize that I my life would intertwine with those of the McLeods for many years.

Chapter 16

Settling In

B y then, life was fairly routine: to the Port Commission first thing in the morning, to the office, calls in the morning, lunchtime and in the evening, to the estates on Wednesday afternoon; gardening on Saturday afternoon, to church on Sunday morning, to the swimming club for lunch, then crewing for one of the participants in the "GP14" sailing race in the afternoon, finally home. The evenings were spent reading.

The work varied when on duty on weekends. On Saturday afternoon we would see patients in the office. On Sunday mornings patients would request home visits, so that we were generally on the road for most of the morning. Sunday afternoons were usually quiet and I would sit and read in case any calls came in.

One Sunday afternoon was an exception. I received a telephone call that the manager of the Hong Kong and Shanghai Bank had fallen down the stairs and hurt his back. I picked up my medical bags and was just going out the door when the telephone rang again. The daughter of one of the company managers had swallowed something poisonous. I had just put the bags in the car, when a shipping company car drove in to the driveway. A seaman had accidentally cut off the fingers of one hand.

I applied a pressure dressing to the bleeding fingers, then went to the child who had swallowed the poison, gave Syrup of Ipecacuana and instructed the parents what to do, then went to the bank manager and ascertained that he was reasonably alright. Then I returned to the house and arranged for the consultant surgeon to get the mariner to hospital, went back to the poisoned child who was now successfully vomiting and arranged further care with the paediatrician, and finally returned to the bank manager for a fuller examination and treatment.

There were practice meetings once a month, rotating in each other's houses. I can remember one such meeting, in Dr Wilson's house. The telephone rang and Dr Wilson answered it. It was for me. The caller was John Gill, who had been a year ahead of me at University and whom I had met again as a registrar at Ayrshire Central Hospital. He was now with the World Health Organisation and was visiting Penang on his tour of duty. We arranged to meet. When I returned to the room where the doctors were sitting, Dr Wilson was very suspicious. There was a Dr Gill, an Indian, in one of the practices in Kuala Lumpur.

One of my main jobs was looking after shipping. This entailed seeing crewmember patients in the rooms and visiting ships at the dockside, in the harbour and at sea.

If a Japanese crewmember came in who knew no English and had no interpreter, I would call in one of the Chinese clerks and would ask him to write my question in Chinese. The Japanese crewmember would then look at what had been written, and then write the answer. Although spoken Japanese and Chinese are different, the written language is the same. Japanese written language has been simplified now, which makes such means of communication more difficult.

The Indonesian seamen were easy to speak to, as the Johore dialect is very much closer to Indonesian than is the Penang dialect. Also, I had learned to speak Malay very grammatically, which was much closer to the manner of speaking in Indonesia.

I can recall being asked to come aboard one of the American "Steel" ships, which were made entirely of steel, as the name implies. I went down the steel passageway which was painted a uniform green-grey, and entered the steel cabin, the inside of a large steel box, painted in the same green-grey. The sound of the footsteps resounded from the reverberating steel walls. On examination, the sailor was obviously severely depressed. During the process of taking his history and elucidating how he passed his spare time, I enquired if he had any hobbies. He replied that his hobby was playing the trumpet!

I was at home, at lunch, one day, when there was a phone-call asking me to come down to the rooms right away. One of the tanker captains had fallen into the sea but had been rescued; could I please examine him to ensure he was alright? I checked him over and indeed he was fit and healthy. I asked him how it had happened. He stated that they were coming into the harbour with the pilot at the helm. When the captain saw that all was well, he decided that he would go below for a rest. On the way along the deck, a rat crossed his path and he kicked at it. The ship's rails were down at that point as there was painting being done, and he slipped and fell overboard, unseen by anyone. The current carried him away out to Muka Head into the Straits of Malacca, a distance of about twenty miles, when an incoming Guthrie's ship spotted him and he was rescued.

I remarked that it was a good job that he could swim, to which he replied that he was a Shetlander and had never been taught to swim (the old Shetland belief was that anyone falling into the sea was a sacrifice to the sea god). I asked him how then he had managed, and he stated that he had sort of "doggie-paddled" and kept himself afloat. The tide did the rest. He added that he was getting a bit anxious as there were signs of sharks beginning to appear.

On one Japanese ship, I was accompanied to the patient by the captain, who was very courteous. Having taken the patient's temperature, the captain took my mercury thermometer and plunged it into boiling water "to sterilize it"!

There was a call one day to the E & O Hotel, to a very pretty Chinese film star. She was examined, the condition was diagnosed, a prescription was given and I gave the customary injection into her rather attractive buttock. To my consternation, she burst into tears. Nonplussed, I had started to pack my bags when, looking round, I saw she was grinning. She was an actress, after all.

Another actor I treated about that time was the Chinese "Elvis Presley" of the Far East. He was first seen at the theatre where he was playing, with the symptoms of an acute peptic ulcer. Appropriate treatment was given and he was asked to come in to the surgery next day, for follow-up. This he did, entering the waiting room with a great flourish, wearing a brightly coloured Chinese brocade silk jacket, much to the delight of the other waiting patients.

There were sadnesses also. There was the young Malay girl, barely out of her teens, with the early symptoms and signs of pregnancy. Her boyfriend, a

British "other rank", was due to return to the UK. However, he had promised to come back and marry her. She was very naive.

Another Malay girl became a frequent attender. She learned that I was studying to speak better Malay, and gave me books. Then, one day, when I was checking her, she put her arm round me. She was a nice girl but I was not going to become involved amorously with one of my patients.

Meanwhile, a new minister was arriving to take over the church. This was James Aitken Muir, who was until that time chaplain to Scotch College in Perth, Australia. This was the same James Aitken Muir who had been the minister in the Presbyterian Church in Sek Kong in the New Territories in Hong Kong and who had gone on to administer a boys' home elsewhere in the Territories. I had visited him at the boys' home with the two Gurkha midwives, and we all paid a visit to a leper colony. Lady Baden-Powell, on her visit to the Guide and Brownie Company of that colony, described it as "the most important Guide Company in the world".

I became even more closely involved with the church.

When Mike Scott was on leave, I would do the visits to Uplands School. On one such visit, there was a relieving headmaster, a Mr Gerald Hawkins. After the school inspection, I went to make my report. After I had done so, he said that he had found a "rather good" Hunting Port, and insisted I try it. Eventually, I managed to break away and made my way to the hill cable railway, somewhat inebriated.

By now, I had paid off my car hire-purchase and paid off my income tax debt, and was also due my annual local leave, and had saved up enough for a visit to Hong Kong.

On the flight there, I was sitting beside a Chinese gentleman, who introduced himself as David Sung. We chatted. He was the owner of flour and sugar mills in China, and, I discovered later, the brother of Soong Ch'ingling, the widow of Dr Sun Yat-sen, whom I had met years ago in the monastery on Lan Tau Island. Many years later, putting together forgotten facts, I recalled that, when I was about ten, I had been introduced to an attractive Chinese lady in Aberdeen, Scotland. I had been told that she was the wife of Chiang Kai-shek, but could not then understand why she was called by another name. It was not until my experiences in Hong Kong and Malaya that I realized that Chinese ladies, when marrying, often retained their own name. Mrs Chiang Kai-shek was also known as Soong Mei-ling and was sister to David Sung and Soong Ch'ing-ling. Thus, I had met two of the three Soong sisters and their brother, all powers of force in China.

In Hong Kong, I spent two weeks, with a trip to Macao, where I had lunch at the Macao Inn, recommended as one of the best restaurants in the world.

The minister, Jim Muir, had given me a contact, an ex-army officer, who had been stationed at Sek Kong when I was there.

One day on that visit to Hong Kong, when I was walking along Nathan Road in Kowloon, I happened to glance up to a new shop on a mezzanine floor. My parents had, some time previously, asked if I could find for them a gong, not the little dinner variety, but a large one. Outside this new shop, which was named the Temple Bell, was a large gong, between three and four feet in diameter, hanging on a wooden stand. I went up and enquired the cost and was able to purchase it for three hundred Hong Kong dollars. The shop, being newly opened, wanted to make a quick sale, to bring good luck. The shipping to Aberdeen was going to cost as much as my purchase

However, it was time to fly back to "Malaysia", as it had now become. This time, I was sitting beside a broad fellow, a planter by the name of Mike Cole, who had been visiting his fiancée in Hong Kong.

My holiday finished, I was back to work.

On a visit to one of the Ben Line ships, I had become friendly with the ship's mate, a man by the name of Ian Mackay. I remember that he "dunked" ginger biscuits in his tea. The ship was visiting Penang shortly after this leave and I caught up with him again. He mentioned that the ship was on the way to Hong Kong and asked if there was anything he could get for me. A thought came to mind and I asked if it was possible for him to deliver the gong from Hong Kong to Aberdeen, explaining that it was very large. He was very happy to do so.

When we met some months later, it came out that he had not visualized how large the gong was until, in Hong Kong Harbour, a lighter with some smiling Chinese men and this huge object came out to the ship. However, he managed to store the object in the hold and he delivered it to Aberdeen. He telephoned my father and said that he had the gong for him. My father replied that he would get the estate wagon and pick it up. Ian Mackay said that he would need more than an estate van! A truck went to Aberdeen Harbour to collect the present.

My father at that time, and for many years after, was very involved with the Scout Gang Show. Every year thereafter, the gong would be taken to His Majesty's Theatre for a diminutive scout to bang the gong in J. Arthur Rank fashion, to open the show.

I was getting to know the young European planter assistants from the estates in neighbouring Kedah. One weekend, a number of us were staying at an estate near Baling. One of the assistants was clearly very worried. He had just received a letter from Singapore, purporting to be from a girl he had met on the ship out from Britain. The letter stated that she had a problem. The worry went on until it eventuated that one of the other planters had seen him creeping back from her cabin early one morning and had arranged the hoax.

The fate of some of these young men that I knew was not all that happy. One was drowned when his car "left the road" and landed upside down in a deep, flooded monsoon ditch. Another died of typhoid fever.

At Christmas 1964, there were no definite arrangements for the festive season and a group of us made up a party to have Christmas dinner at one of the hotels in Penang.

So another year came to a close.

Chapter 17

1965

I had been with the practice of Drs Allen and Gunstensen by then for over two and a half years. The advertisement to which I had replied in 1962 had stated that an assistant was required for three years with a view to partnership. To date nothing further had been said. Was I going to be offered a partnership? If not, then the practice would presumably need to pay a passage for me to return to the UK.

By this time, Sundays had fallen into a pattern when I was not on call: church in the morning, out to the swimming club for curry lunch, then sailing in the afternoon. I crewed for the manager of the Dutch Bank of the Netherlands, Rolf Veltema, and we must have made a good team as we invariably won the Sunday afternoon race.

There was one Sunday afternoon when the weather was a bit wild. As usual our little "GP14" yacht was away ahead of the rest. Because of the distance, the wind and the rain, we failed to hear the gun signalling that the race had been cancelled. We had just rounded the first buoy when the rudder broke. I was sitting on the windward side. When a yacht is blown over, it usually goes right over on to the lee side so that this position is very safe, with the crew sitting up, well out of the water. This time, however, the boat keeled over the opposite way, towards me, and I went down into the water. I swam round the stern and Rolf was in the water, next to the bow. He called out to me and asked if I could swim! Shortly after, the rescue launch came out and towed us ashore.

On another occasion, Jean Paul Galibour, a French planter connected with Socfin, whom I had known in Johore, asked me to crew for him on a little pleasure trip round Pulau Tikus, a small island in the bay. He steered too close to the island, a gust of wind hit us and we ran into the rocks. The boat was undamaged but we were overboard. Fortunately, the water only came up to our chests and we managed to manoeuvre the boat round to the lee of the island. I then became conscious that my left wrist felt peculiar and I realized that my watch was no longer there. I felt around with my toes; felt an object that could be the watch and picked it up with one foot, rescuing it.

Once again, the rescue launch was employed to pick us up.

In Penang, I was also interested in acquiring some good hi-fi equipment and had just bought a Leak amplifier. A local wood carver, Wah Dah, had made a cutlery cabinet for me and I designed a similar cabinet to hold the new equipment, with large speakers, set in the room to get the best stereophonic effect. Some of the officers from the Gurkha Regiment in which I served used to visit me when they were holidaying in Penang and I can recall that the new equipment was a good source of entertainment.

One Sunday evening, on or about the 24th April, when I was sitting at home, some friends telephoned and suggested that we go along to the Sports Club for a drink. We were sitting and standing around, having a drink, when some people came into the club. One was a young girl. I thought that she looked a wonderful person. She was an inch or two shorter than I, blonde, and wearing a simple green dress. The thoughts went through my mind: What a lovely person; if I do not make a move, someone else will get there first and I will have lost my chance to get to know her. We were taken over to be introduced.

When the girl spoke, it was with a beautiful Southwest of Scotland accent. I did not want to say bluntly what I wanted to say, so I prefaced it with, "I've always wanted to marry a Scots girl," and followed it with what I really wanted to say: "Will you marry me?" I had never before proposed to a girl, and she is the only person to whom I have ever proposed.

She replied, "I am engaged," and showed me the ring on her finger, which I had not noticed. Her name was Mary Mars, and the story was that she had just arrived in Penang as an army teacher, to teach at Minden Barracks.

As a student, she had spent her holidays touring Europe so, now in the army, was hoping to see more of the world, in the Far East. Just before leaving Scotland, her then boyfriend had persuaded her to become engaged. I can remember not putting into words my thoughts that, if she was just engaged, what was she doing out here, in Penang?

Two weeks later, I was at church as usual and there was Mary. After the service, I went through to the church hall for a cup of tea. She was sitting there and, looking round, she asked me to join her. She had seen a Chinese funeral with all its noise and so I explained what happened in this culture. We were the last to leave; she on her trishaw and me in my Mercedes Benz car.

However, as she was engaged, it was not for me to interfere with another man's fiancée.

Life went on. About two weeks later, Helen Metcalfe, another Minden Barracks teacher, suggested dinner at the Penang Club. The Club was not doing too well at the time. The annex, which had been the restaurant, was being pulled down, the breakfast room had become the dining room, and the Men's Bar had become the general bar.

We met at the Club, Helen Metcalfe, myself, and Mary Mars. We had a couple of drinks and then had dinner. I smoked at that time and, that evening, I smoked a lot. However, I did not pursue what seemed to me would only end in disappointment.

In July or August, a practice meeting was being held in my house, when a car drove in to the driveway. I went out to see who it was. It was Helen, who had come to tell me that Mary had broken off her engagement. She suggested I might give her a telephone call.

Later, I heard from Mary her story.

Having qualified as a teacher, she had gained further qualifications in elocution from the London College of Music, and a Diploma of Licentiateship in Speech and Drama (Teaching) from the Guildhall School of Music and Drama. She started teaching at the local primary school in Bishopbriggs near Glasgow, but wanted to see more of the world. She applied for a job as an air hostess. Ability to speak other languages was one of the necessities of such employment and she could speak German and French. However, her mother put her off being a "waitress in the sky". She then applied for a post as an army teacher, preferably in the Far East, and so landed in Singapore and was posted to Penang.

It had been suggested to her that, if she did come to the Far East, she might enquire about a David Ellis, also from her part off the world. Almost immediately, at a gathering, she had enquired of David Ellis. One of the people present said that he was the David Ellis she was looking for. He suggested that, on the following day, which was a Sunday, he would show her round the island. He started the tour round the island, but this involved stops at various places for a drink. At one spot he pointed out a lamp-post, which was different from the others as he had knocked down the original one and had to replace it. He called the new one the "David Ellis" lamp-post. Mary was becoming more and more concerned, and they were on the way home when her driver suggested stopping in to the Sports Club for another drink. There she met a group of people and one of them proposed to her. She suddenly realized that all her mother had said was true and that Somerset Maugham's stories were accurate!

And so we met for the first time.

The Sunday after our meeting, she attended the church. The pews were all decorated and she had asked why, to be told that a Scots doctor had been married the previous day. She thought, "The rat!"

However, it was Dr Wilson's wedding.

Now that Mary was free of romantic attachments, my work was to convince her that I would be suitable to be a husband for her. We began meeting, and the Penang Club was the place where I took her for dinners. Penang society was not large and was always intensely interested in what was happening. At the Penang Club, it was at least respectable and there were always waiters around as chaperones. I got many late fees as we often stayed beyond the normal closing time.

One evening we went for dinner at the Swimming Club. The setting was ideal. The moon shone through the gently waving palm trees and was reflected glittering from the sea. The waves broke gently on the beach.

I once again asked Mary to marry me. Again the answer was "No."

My three years as assistant with the practice was almost up and I was offered a partnership. It would cost me $350,000, paid off in monthly instalments over three years. I accepted.

One evening Mary mentioned that Anne Scott, Mike's wife, might know Maureen Lindsay, a friend of hers. I mentioned it to Mike and he said he would ask Anne. A few days later the answer came that Anne did not know this girl.

One evening, we sat down to dinner in the Club. One of the boys asked if we would like to dine in the new Club building, which had been constructed on the seaward side of the old Club. Thus, we were the first to dine in the refurbished Penang Club.

Time went on. I asked Mary a number of times if she would marry me but always the answer came that, if she wanted to marry me, she would let me know.

Late in the year, Mary came on the phone to say that her mother was very ill and that she was going back to Bishopbriggs the next day. She agreed to come to dinner at my house as we had the evening free. It was a sad evening. She had brought over some records and we listened to them, talked and had our dinner. She was obviously very worried.

After dinner, she asked if there was anything she could do for me in Britain while she was there. I answered that she could post my UK Christmas cards as they had been neglected as a result of my other preoccupations. I added that she had better let my mother know otherwise she would be wondering why on earth the cards were being posted in Britain.

We went through the cards, sorting out the local and the overseas ones. She suddenly stopped and asked, "Who is this Rev. Harry Donaldson?" referring to the person to whom one of the cards was addressed. I answered that he was the minister at Alloway Church and that I had got to know him and his family when I was at Ayr. Mary then said, "He was the minister who baptised me." She added that, just before she had left for Malaysia, there had been a function at her local church, that she had been sitting beside him, and that he had remarked that there was a young doctor whom he knew in Malaysia but that he did not know where he was. Mary then added some sentences into the card.

I drove her back to the teachers' mess. I felt very sad.

Tomorrow came. Mary had left her gramophone records with me. Among them were Scottish songs sung by Kenneth McKellar, whose children Mary had taught, and a record by a comparatively new French artiste, Françoise Hardy. I played them over and over again. I did not know what was going to happen in the future. Suppose she remained home and did not come back to Penang?

Christmas was coming and Graham Fullerton was visiting to spend the season with me. There was some talk that some of the Negri Sembilan Tunkus would be arriving as well but that did not eventuate.

So 1965, a year full of event, came to a rather sad end.

Mary Gibb Mars.

Mary Gibb Mars. A better photo-graph but misleadingly not show-ing her clothes.

The talented Miss Mars, highland dancing.

Chapter 18

The Coming Year

So January came. Jim Muir, the minister, was the Chieftain of the Penang St Andrew Society and had asked if I would give the Toast to the Lassies at the Burns Supper, the first time I had ever had to speak in public. Mary was to give the reply; that is, if she was in Penang. If not, someone else would have to do it.

I had been writing to Mary practically every day. At the beginning of January came the news that she was coming. Then there came the news that her mother had suffered a relapse and died. Under normal circumstances, the army will pay for a flight if someone is gravely ill but will not pay for a passage for a funeral. The reasons are not hard to understand. By the time someone dies, it is too late to see them. However, on this occasion, Mary returned home. Possibly someone paid the fare.

More waiting.

The 25th of January, Burns' Birthday, was approaching.

Almost there, Mary returned.

I was ecstatic.

Mary's speech, replying to the Toast to the Lassies, was done at the last moment.

On the night, the speeches seemed to be well received. Someone noticed that we were holding hands under the table.

Apparently, when Mary had returned to Bishopbriggs, her father had telephoned the army to cancel her contract as she would be needed to look after him at home. Her employers had telephoned to her to find out if this was the case and she had replied that, no, she was keeping her job.

After the emotional turmoil of the previous two months, life settled back to Mary at school and me at work plus courting.

At the end of February, we went for a car run to Taiping, visiting the beautiful gardens and exploring the jungle road to the swimming pool. Mary agreed to marry me. I was ecstatic.

We both went to tell the senior partner, Alasdair Wilson, the news. For some reason or another, Mike Scott had become very cold towards me.

My home leave was due and I was taking it from April until July. It was decided that we would not become officially engaged until I returned to Penang, and that the wedding would take place on 3rd September, the day after my thirty-fourth birthday. That leave was bitter-sweet. It was my first leave back to Aberdeen for over five years and here I was, having just met the girl I wanted to marry.

I started my first letter over Penang Harbour, as the plane ascended, describing the ships lying in the roads.

The leave had been arranged so that I could visit, on the way, Yusuf and Marie Kodwavwallah in Nairobi, Kenya. It was a long-standing invitation.

My first stop was Karachi airport. I got into conversation with an elderly Portuguese gentleman, also waiting for the plane. We discovered that I had met his son who had been stationed at Coloane Island, off Macao, when I visited two years previous and who, since then, had been transferred to Portuguese West Africa.

On to Nairobi where I was delighted to catch up again with the Kodwavwallahs, and so the leave began.

After leaving Dewsbury, I had caught up with Yusuf once in 1960, at which time he was married to Marie and working in Sheffield. When I was in Cha'ah, he wrote to me asking about conditions in Singapore, where he was thinking about applying for a job. His story became more interesting. He had been born in Karachi, prior to partition, and so, although he was an Ismaili Muslim, he had Indian nationality. His father was very poor, but when Yusuf had expressed an interest in studying medicine, his father had scraped all his money together and paid for him to go to Bombay University. In turn, after qualifying, Yusuf had paid for his brother to become a lawyer. His father was illiterate. After Yusuf's mother had died in childbirth, when his father had discovered how conception occurred, he was mortified and had expressed that, had he known, he would have stopped getting children.

When partition between India and Pakistan occurred, Yusuf was still at Bombay University. If he had reverted to Pakistani nationality, he would have had to leave. Thus he was still nominally Indian.

After marrying Marie, he had returned to Karachi to practice but had found the state of medicine there so corrupt that he applied for three jobs: in Singapore; in Sheffield; and at the newly opened Aga Khan Jubilee Hospital in Nairobi. He obtained the Sheffield job and had been there for just a fortnight when he received a phone call asking him to come for an interview for the Nairobi job. By this time, he had the Sheffield position with a contract for a year, but he had things to do in London so he went down for the interview. There he explained that he had a year's contract in Sheffield, that the political situation in Africa was too unsettled and that, in any case, as he was really Pakistani with Indian citizenship, he had decided to take out British citizenship, which would make it easier for him to obtain work.

He returned to Sheffield, but two weeks later he received another phone call. The Aga Khan wanted to speak to him! Being an Ismaili Muslin, he had no choice but to comply. At the interview, the Aga Khan explained that the political situation in Africa was, in reality, no different than anywhere else in the world. British nationality? He, the Aga Khan, would fix that for Yusuf. As he had a year's contract with Sheffield, the job in the Nairobi hospital would be held open for him! The Aga Khan went on to explain that Yusuf and his English wife were an ideal couple to work in the Aga Kahn Jubilee Hospital, which was dedicated to the Aga Khan's father and was intended to be entirely cosmopolitan.

Thus, at the end of his work in Sheffield, Yusuf and his wife had motored over the Sahara and begun work in Kenya.

After I arrived in Nairobi, the Kodwavwallahs had arranged a night's stay at Tsavo National Park, half-way between Nairobi and Mombassa, Kenya's port. For a main road between the country's capital and its main port, it was rather remarkable, being a dirt road and deeply rutted. The scenery, however, was spectacular. The flat plains were studded with the flat-topped trees and animals of all varieties. After an evening meal in the restaurant, where there was a notice advising the animals not to disturb the humans at their drinking place, we retired to bed in the chalets. During the night lions were sniffing round the compound.

When I woke next morning at Tsavo, Mount Kilimanjaro stood out clearly, the regular snow-topped peak majestic against the blue sky. In the near distance, a family of lions lazed near a watering hole.

The few days in Nairobi passed quickly. We visited the Rift Valley and I had the experience of enjoying five completely different types of curry with the various friends I met.

Then, on to the UK. I attended a GP refresher course in Edinburgh and met up with Iain Brebner, who had been 2I/C with the Gurkha battalion and was now the Colonel looking after Edinburgh Castle.

My mother, of course, wanted to know about *the girl*. When Harry Donaldson received the card from me at Christmas, with the paragraph Mary had written in, he had immediately telephoned my mother and had told her we were an ideal couple! She had then phoned Mary, who was in Bishopbriggs at that time, and invited her to Aberdeen to see the gong!

Then, of course, I had to go to Bishopbriggs to meet Mary's father and ask her hand in marriage as we were not to be engaged until that had been done. I stayed a week with him and met all the other relatives. On the very last night, I plucked up my courage and said that Mary and I intended to become married and asked for his blessing.

At last I was on the way back to Penang, taking four bottles of malt whisky. This was more than the allowance so I stuffed them into my overcoat and managed to take them through the airport without paying any duty. Alasdair Wilson had sent his car with driver to take Mary out to the airport. What a joyful meeting.

There was only two months until the wedding. I made my formal proposal in church on the 3rd of July. Neither of our families would be out for the wedding, but Mary's father had offered to pay for it. We had to make the arrangements ourselves. The service would be in the church and the reception in the form of a cocktail party in the Penang Club, the first of such celebrations in the new building. There was a wedding dress to be made and we drove up to Hat Yai and Songkhla to buy ivory-coloured Thai silk material, to be made up by the dressmaker.

The wedding, on 3rd September 1966, went according to plan. For the first night of the honeymoon, we stayed at the Mandarin Hotel in Penang, then we had almost a week at the Smokehouse Hotel in the Cameron Highlands. We were highly amused when David Ellis, trying hard not to let us see him, appeared in the restaurant with a Chinese girl.

Then we returned to work and the start of married life.

At Christmas that year the army had special concessional flights for army families and we took advantage of that, Mary's father and my mother coming out to visit during the Christmas time.

*Signing the Wedding Certificates, watched
by the minister, James Aitken Muir.*

The Penang Club, 1966..

The Penang Club, 1966..

Chapter 19

Married Life

Mary was very much the wife that I would desire. She was, in my eyes, beautiful; she was intelligent; we had a number of common interests although each of us had our own involvements.

We had settled in together very comfortably.

It was now 1967.

Early New Year's morning, I received a call from one of the Ben Line ships. Two seamen had fallen down some steel steps. Could I check them over? One of the seamen had cuts and lacerations and it was obvious that he was going to have to go to hospital for surgical repairs. The captain thought that the other one had escaped uninjured. He was lying comfortably in his berth and I asked him what the date was and if he knew where he was? He replied that it was Christmas Eve and that they were in the middle of the Indian Ocean! The captain and I looked at one another. He was obviously going to join his friend on the way to hospital.

Life became more humdrum after this. We managed to persuade the Turf Club, who owned the house I rented, to have it painted. Wah Dah made more pieces of furniture.

Dr Muir, the minister's father, visited Jim in Penang. He had delivered Mary, so now I had met the doctor who had brought her into the world and the minister who had baptised her. Dr Muir, unfortunately, died on his way back to the UK.

Later that year Mary became pregnant.

We became more involved with the Penang St Andrew Society, and Mary took over the job of secretary.

In November, the Malayan currency went off the standard of the pound sterling and there were riots. There was a curfew but the practice doctors obtained passes so that we could do house visits. It was somewhat awesome to drive down the roads, deserted except for empty cars, some lying on their sides, and some burning. Fortunately, during these riots, there was no loss of life.

However, the Penang St Andrew Society Ball had to be postponed until early the following year. We were stuck in our house with all the haggis for the Ball and all the bottles of wine and whisky.

On 5th January, Mary woke with stomach pains. I looked at her and she was having contractions. She was only at thirty-one weeks into her pregnancy. She was booked into the maternity hospital at Minden Barracks, so we drove out there and she was admitted. The obstetrician managed to halt the labour was about a week, but on 12th January, labour started in earnest.

As the baby would be premature, Mary was given no analgesics and I sat with her all night. About five in the morning, she asked if she could have an aspirin. There was not much point in one aspirin but the baby, a boy, Graeme was delivered at about six or seven o'clock.

He was kept in the incubator, but in those days it was thought, erroneously, that breast milk could not be given. It was heartbreaking seeing Mary standing beside the incubator, looking at her baby. Mary was allowed home after a week but Graeme remained in the hospital for a further three weeks.

Eventually the baby came home and the family was united. St Andrew's Ball came and went, and life settled down.

One day I was driving home for lunch. Mary, all smiles, came out of the French window with Graeme in her arms, but I saw a dark shadow cross the driveway and frantically waved for her to keep back. Mary afterwards said that she thought that I had gone mad because I drove the car to the edge of the lawn and started scrunching the wheel. It was a hamadryad; a king cobra, six feet long, and I had managed to get the car wheel onto its head and moved it to and fro until there was no movement from the snake.

I coiled up the snake and deposited it on the bunch of rubbish waiting to be burned. Next day, I suggested to the gardener, Karuppiah, that it was time he put a light to the rubbish. We watched as he approached the pile, looked, and jumped about a foot in the air when he saw the snake.

After that we got some geese, which are good for keeping away snakes. When Graeme was old enough to walk and run, he had great fun herding these geese.

One afternoon, Major Henry Hayward-Surry paid us a visit. He had telephoned but I was delayed at the office. He came to the front door to be greeted by Graeme, stark naked, seated on his potty, quite a welcome for a very correct, somewhat crusty, bachelor army officer!

I was ordained as an Elder of the Church and, shortly after that, Jim Muir's tour of duty ended. He was replaced by a young man, Derek Kingston. We were now due for UK leave, to which we were eagerly looking forward. Mary had still to meet my father and members of the family, and especially my paternal grandmother, who had brought me up in the first year of my life, when my mother was ill. She was now ninety-five years of age.

In May, there was a practice meeting. It had been discovered that Dr Scott had pulmonary tuberculosis. The senior partners had decided that the leave due to us would have to be postponed. I was, of course, intensely disappointed and at one point, Dr Scott said that I and the baby could go to the UK for a short time but that my wife was not to go.

As the problem was that the manpower in the practice was depleted, this did not make sense. It was obvious that Dr Scott had an intense antipathy to Mary. On the other hand, I wanted so much for Mary to meet my family. There was now a division in the practice and feelings ran high.

Things simmered on. Our leave was postponed and my grandmother died later that year.

Christmas came and our guests for Christmas dinner were the new minister and Jim Collier, manager of the Chartered Bank, and his family. He had been an officer of one of the Gurkha regiments during the war so we had a common connection.

Early in 1969, it was decided that Dr Scott would have the lobe of the lung with the tuberculosis removed. He was an atheist but decided to have spiritual ministering by Derek Kingston. Things started to go wrong in the relationship between the minister and my family. There were needling remarks and I began to have less interest in the church.

In the practice agreement no allowance had been made for prolonged leave of absence due to illness; the three remaining doctors were working hard and it became obvious that some action was necessary. Dr Teh and I could ill afford to buy Dr Scott's share in the practice, which went into hundreds of thousands of dollars, but it looked as if this was going to become necessary. We were still paying off our original shares. Dr Wilson managed to get Dr Scott to reduce the amount he was to be paid, so one hurdle was passed.

Feelings in the practice continued to run high and Dr Teh resigned. In the course of a few months, out of a practice of four doctors, only two were left, Dr Wilson and me, to see the patients. I had taken over the sick parade at the Eastern Smelting Company, the tin smelting works. It was hard work, two doctors looking after the work for four. This went on for four months.

Mary, baby Graeme and I had one weekend of respite, a long weekend on Langkawi. On the previous evening we visited George Davidson, an architect, about some St Andrew Society business. George offered to fly us to Langkawi in his small plane. We declined. I said rather flippantly that "what goes up must come down".

We drove to Kedah from where the small launch started, ferrying people the sixty miles to the island. A notice on the boat stated that the passengers were earnestly *solicited* to retain the counterfoils of their tickets because from time to time they would be inspected on the voyage and anyone without the counterfoil would have to get off the boat!

Langkawi was, at that time, completely unspoiled. We stayed at the resthouse, from where we visited what there was to see – Mahsuri's grave; the site where the rice had been burned many hundreds of years ago; the hot springs; Pantai Rusa, a beach at the other side of the island, which we had to ourselves; and, on the next day, the lake of the pregnant princess which was supposed to have a white crocodile. It was an idyllic weekend.

Returning to Penang, I opened the newspaper. George Davidson had been killed in a plane crash during the weekend.

It was about this time that a shipping patient consulted me in the office. He was complained of headache and generalized pains. Symptomatic treatment was prescribed. The next patient came in, from the same ship, with similar complaints. When the third crewmember presented himself, with a similar story, I began to wonder. This third crewmember was the ship's electrician, and I started to ask questions. All worked in the engine room and it was mentioned that one of the fans was not working. I contacted the agent. The ship, the *Bennachie*, was stuck in Penang harbour for ten days until an expert

LIFE IS WHAT YOU MAKE IT

from Singapore rectified the problem. The company was not very happy but the crew was very pleased at this unexpected holiday in Penang.

Eventually, late in the year, two doctors joined the practice. Dr Chris Lawson had recently ended a tour of duty with the Malay Regiment, and wanted to continue working in Malaysia. He and another Chinese doctor, Dr Tham, became assistants.

One evening, there was a telephone call from the British High Commission. I was asked if I had signed an application for a passport of a James Aitken Muir, who was, by this time, resident in Hong Kong. I had, and it was explained that he was in Bangkok on holiday but that he had been involved in an accident and did I know who his next of kin was? As it happened I had visited Jim's brother in Edinburgh the previous year, and had his two brothers' addresses in a small diary which I had not thrown out.

Afterwards, the story came out. Jim had been on leave in Bangkok with Francis Batson, a gynaecologist, to whom we had introduced him originally in Penang, and who was now also living in Hong Kong. One evening, they had been out for dinner and had decided to take a taxi home. It was discovered afterwards that, after midnight, taxis were hired out by anyone keen to make some extra money. As Francis described it, he had become concerned as the taxi was travelling much too fast, when it crashed. He thought that Jim was dead and the taxi driver was certainly dead. However, Jim was taken to hospital and was in coma for a week before he came round. We managed to contact a bank manager who had been transferred to Bangkok, who found the hospital and kept us informed of the progress.

Mary was again pregnant, and since our leave had been postponed, we invited my mother and father to come and stay with us over Christmas. Despite the fact that relations with the minister had altered since Dr Scott's illness, Derek Kingston was a bachelor living on his own and we invited him for the Christmas dinner. On that evening, I recall, he made the statement that marijuana gives a wonderful religious experience.

New Year's Eve was approaching and we made the usual arrangements to be at the New Year's Party at the Penang Club. Early in the morning of New Year's Eve, Mary woke once more with abdominal pains. The baby was not due until 25th February. The journey to Minden Barracks Maternity Hospital was again taken.

Mary was once more given bed rest and pethidine to try to put a halt to the labour. This time it was more successful but she was confined to bed for days and then weeks. I would speak to her by telephone and visit as often as I could. One morning on the telephone she mentioned pain in her left leg. I became somewhat alarmed and phoned the obstetrician, whom I knew, wondering if there was the possibility of a deep vein thrombosis. Apparently, then, all hell broke loose. The obstetrician examined and measured the leg and heparin injections were started. Fortunately there were no complications, the condition settled down over a number of days, but she was in hospital for nearly a month, a very expensive business as we were paying for the treatment. Fortunately we had a health fund which, though they did not normally pay for maternity care, agreed to pay half because of the complication.

Of interest, although the minister had spent so much time with Dr Scott, he never even once visited Mary in hospital.

At the end of January, Mary left hospital and, in fact, had to be induced the day after the baby was due. Seonaid Mairi was born on the 26th February 1970, with her thumb in her mouth. After the trauma of Graeme's delivery, her birth was easy.

The tensions with the church became so unbearable that, one evening, when I drove to the church hall for a Session Meeting, I stopped opposite but was unable to leave the car to attend the meeting. I sat there, watching the session taking place through the open doors, then drove away as the meeting broke up.

I felt too disconsolate to deliver the Communion Cards, and Mary took on this duty for me. One day in the first few months of 1970, the minister came to see me. He wanted me to "resign". I said that I had done nothing wrong and that, if he wanted rid of me he would have to be responsible for that act. Thus I left the church.

No reason was ever given and it was not until some time later that the full story came out. We were all curious to know why Dr Scott had behaved so. As the odd behaviour seemed to start at my question about whether Anne Scott had known Maureen Lindsay, Mary wrote to Maureen to ask. Maureen, however, would not divulge a confidence, but we managed to find a reason. It had been a shotgun wedding. It now became clear that the Scotts were terrified of their secret becoming known in the small community in Penang.

Mary continued to attend church but I began to reconsider the whole subject of faith. Eventually I came to the conclusion that man was not made in the image of God – God was made in the image of man. The Gospel of St Mark states: "Judge not, that ye be not judged" (vii.1) and the Gospel of St Luke: "Judge not, and ye shall not be judged" (vi. 37). I had been judged, and this was the result.

Despite the events that had occurred, my wife and I remained on friendly terms with the minister, and also with the Moderator of the Presbyterian Church in Malaysia, who lived in Kuala Lumpur, and whom we hosted on his visits to Penang.

Because of my senior partner's illness, the leave which was due to me and my family was postponed. My wife and I had wanted my grandmother to meet her first great-grandson, but she died shortly after the cancelled leave would have taken place.

On one of the Moderator's visits I said that I wanted my grandmother alive again so that she could meet her great-grandson, at which the Moderator told me not to be so silly. Thus it became obvious that, not only did miracles not happen, but that the clergy did not believe in them either.

Once more, we were due leave, now delayed by two years. Dr Tham had left and another assistant, Dr Yeoh, had joined the practice.

It crossed my mind that perhaps I could have a shot at the examination of the Royal College of General Practitioners while we were in the UK. Having been in general practice now for nearly ten years, I thought I had a good knowledge of the subject. I wrote to the College and asked the requirements and a copy of the examination paper, if possible. The material arrived and I realized that there was a great deal I did not know! I decided that there was no way of attempting to sit the examination but that I had better catch up on some reading. I again wrote the College and requested a recommended book list. It duly arrived. As there was no medical library in Penang, I had to order the books for purchase from the University Bookshop in Penang.

About this time, there was a warning telephone call from Alasdair Wilson. Dr Lawson wanted to visit his parents in the UK and had asked if perhaps I would delay my holiday so that he could go. He was coming round to see me. We laid our holiday plans on the coffee table inside the front door. It worked. When he saw the plans, he "forgot" to state the reason for his visit.

It was about then that I was asked to visit Gerald Hawkins, who lived out near Batu Ferringhi. It was he who had plied me with the "rather good" Hunting Port on my visit to Uplands School. He was now in his terminal illness, dying of kidney failure. Looking after him entailed frequent visits, at least once a week. At first he was upstairs in his bedroom, a room decorated with the flags of all the Malay States hanging round the walls. He showed me through the house. One room had been laid out as a library with banks upon banks of books and pictures that he had taken in the jungle. There was a fairly close-up photograph of a seladang, a wild jungle cow, rather danger-ous, as it was likely to charge for no reason.

As his condition deteriorated, he was moved downstairs, where he lay on a *charpoi*, facing the garden. His kidney condition did not affect his hor-mones. Every day his driver took him into Georgetown to the hairdresser although he had practically no hair. The staff was composed of young attrac-tive-looking Chinese girls.

A rather buxom Methodist Tamil nurse was hired to look after him. I noticed that, if she had to go to the other side of the *charpoi*, she always took care to go round the head end. Asking her why she did that, she answered that when he died, his soul would go out through his feet and she did not want to be in the way!

One evening she had completed her chores and was preparing to leave. She asked her patient if there was anything else he wanted. His large, pale blue eyes opened and he answered, "Yes, I would like to hold your tits!" She disappeared down the path as fast as her legs would carry her.

The time for us to go on leave arrived. We decided to do all that we had planned for two years previously, but now we had a child and a baby.

Chapter 20

A Full Holiday, 1970

Mary, myself and the two children boarded the plane to go "up 'kye" on the flight to "Bangkok-a-doodle-doo", to use Graeme's words.

We went to our places. One of them, by the window, was occupied by a French woman. She had the window seat and was not prepared to give that up. Mary took the passage seat – there were two in the row – and I had to find another seat in the row in front. In view of the woman's intransigence, Mary held Seonaid, who was then six months old, with her feet on the woman's side. Seonaid did her stuff and lay there kicking all the way from Penang to Bangkok.

In Bangkok, we were staying at the Siam Intercontinental Hotel. We toured the city during the day and had a wonderful Thai curry in the restaurant in the evening. An *amah* had been hired to baby-sit during the evening.

Next day, we travelled by SAS over India, landing at Tashkent. There we saw the bureaucratic effects of Communism, cold and very regular, with lots of propaganda. One passenger was foolish enough to take photographs, despite having being warned against doing such a thing, and his camera was taken and the film removed.

Mary was breastfeeding Seonaid, but no concessions were made for this by the SAS staff, so the baby was fed quite openly.

We flew over the Russian steppes with a head-wind, so that we were an hour late in landing at Copenhagen. We had intended changing our money there, but not only was there no time to do so, we were chivvied to hurry up.

We were told that we were keeping the plane waiting. There were no trolleys – they had all been commandeered by other passengers who were unhampered by children and could move more quickly – and none of the ground staff made any attempt to give help. Our opinion of Copenhagen was not good.

We boarded the next plane, which took us to Hamburg. The German staff there were more helpful and we were taken by a shortcut through the back of the terminal to get to the plane. The next stage of the journey was to Berlin.

We arrived at Tempelhof airport about six o'clock in the evening. No luggage! We had caught the plane but the baggage had not. And we had no money.

Thus we sat for three hours for the next plane to come in with our bags. We retrieved them but the next problem was to get us all to Mary's German friends in Spandau. A very kind customs officer lent us money for a phone call and it was arranged that a taxi would take us there and "uncle" Walter would pay the taxi driver when we arrived there. They were all very trusting.

We were exhausted, but that did not prevent our hosts from opening two bottles of white wine and two bottles of Champagne to greet us. We eventually got to bed at three or four in the morning, Berlin time.

Next morning, our hostess took Mary out for a walk in the park. She could hardly keep her eyes open. I lay unconscious. Next day, Mary and I went for a tour round the city and into East Berlin. Graeme was taken to see the famous Berlin Zoo.

After Berlin we travelled to Stockholm to stay with the Haglunds, Swedish friends we knew in Penang. They had been missionaries in China and interned by the Japanese through the war.

Our next place of call was to visit an architect friend of mine south of Oslo in Norway. From Stockholm, to fly by Aeroflot to Oslo was an experience. The fittings were completely basic, as in wartime planes. Seonaid was slung in a hammock from the rack. The air hostess at the rear of the plane, all sixteen stone of her, yelled out to the other air hostess at the front, "Natasha!" and Natasha lumbered up the passageway like an elephant!

We visited Ibsen's home and saw the diminutive beds, sometimes used by the Norwegians, in which they slept sitting up. In Oslo itself, we visited the maritime museum, with Viking longships and the *Kon Tiki* raft.

Then, after our convoluted journey, we arrived in Britain!

We visited all the relations; then, because we had visited them early in the holiday, we had to visit them again before we left! Part of the time was spent in Aberdeen, part in Bishopbriggs. The two children were baptised. We visited the Edinburgh Festival and had some time in Mull, at Craignure, attending a Ceilidh. I attended a GP refresher course in Aberdeen. There, I learned for the first time about testing for gestational diabetes as part of the regular antenatal screening.

After two months in the UK we had about ten days in Nairobi, staying with the Kodwavwallahs again. This time we visited Mombassa and Malindi, meeting the Aga Khan's sister, going out in a glass-bottomed boat to see the coral reefs and going overboard to swim among the fish. Graeme came into the sea with us, being nibbled by the little fish.

The holiday ended by returning to Bangkok and visiting Chieng Mai, staying with Graham Fullerton at the Thai Celadon Factory.

During that holiday we made up for all the holidays we had missed!

Chapter 21

Back to Work and a Flitting

With the previous tensions no longer present, things were now amicable, peaceful and uneventful.

For some four years now Mary and I had been involved with the Penang St Andrew Society. Mary had been Secretary for about three years and I had been Chieftain in the year 1969-1970.

She had a diploma in teaching Scottish Country Dancing, which was useful in teaching those who wished to learn the dances preparatory to the St Andrew's Ball, and was also an accomplished highland dancer, enabling her to give displays on the night of the event.

We met some interesting people, one of whom had been a reporter for one of the leading British newspapers. He described how he had once interviewed Hitler.

His first attempt had been a non-event as he had been granted an interview, been taken to a seat outside the door of a big room at the far end of which Hitler could be seen behind a big desk. After waiting for a considerable time, he was informed that the interview was cancelled.

The second time was somewhat extraordinary. The reporter was taken into a big hall and asked to take a seat at the side of the hall. He waited, and eventually Hitler came through a door at the end of the hall, striding along its length, expounding his dogma. He marched up and down, finally exiting through the door by which he had entered.

The remainder of 1970 was fairly quiet. I now had my books on general practice and began reading. Graeme was starting to learn how to swim. Mary, who had never learned to swim, also attended swimming classes. On Sundays there was the sailing after the Sunday lunch at the Penang Swimming Club.

One amusing item happened when Mary telephoned Chris Lawson at his home, to be told that Dr Lawson could not answer the phone just now as he was sitting on the toilet!

1970 passed into 1971 and the lease on our house in Scotland Road was coming to its end. The Penang Turf Club required the house for a new vet, which meant that we would have to find new accommodation. It was sad as we were fond of our small home.

A house at 5 Lim Mah Chye Road had been vacant for nearly two years since Dr Teh had left Penang for New Zealand. The owner, who lived at number 3, next door, was desperate for an occupier as he could not bear having a property unoccupied and not producing income. He had made his money during the Second World War, building houses for the Japanese invaders. His residence was huge and the expansive living room looked even bigger as the upper part of the room was panelled with mirror glass.

Thus the house was rented at a very reasonable cost, for three years with promise of tenure in the future.

Moving house was accomplished within twenty-four hours on 1st October 1970. Mary emptied a tank of petrol transferring goods from one house to the other.

Annual leave was due and, almost next day, we set off to Hong Kong for a three-week holiday, two adults and two children. We had arranged to stay at the Presbyterian manse in Kowloon, at the invitation of the minister, Jim Muir, who had married us. Jim had largely recovered from his accident, the only residue being that he could not completely control the movements of one of his little fingers, which hampered his piano and organ playing a little.

The best months in Hong Kong are October and November, when the days are sunny and warm and the nights are cool. We explored the island and the New Territories and ate at the Repulse Bay Hotel and the floating restaurant at Aberdeen. We caught up with Lawrence Pottinger, who had been a major with the 1/6th Gurkha Regiment and was now the Protocol Officer to the Hong Kong Governor.

We spent a day or two in Macao, twice having lunch at the Macao Inn, which is renowned for its cuisine. At all these high-class restaurants, the two children behaved impeccably, although tiredness overcame Graeme at the Macao Inn and he finished the meal asleep with his head in the plate. To finish off the meal there, I suggested that, as we were in a Portuguese colony, we should finish off with a port. Mary said that she could hardly do that – it was an old man's drink! I suggested that she try a white port. She accepted and we finished up with another and bought two bottles to take back with us!

It was such a good holiday that we stayed a further week.

Jim unfortunately caught cold, so we plied him with hot toddy. Next morning he stated that his cold was much better but that it had gone to his head!

Towards the end of our stay in Hong Kong I heard that Colin Scott, whom I had known with the Gurkha Regiment, was with the Battalion in Hong Kong. I was uncertain of his current rank. He must be at least a major, so, to make sure, I asked for Colonel Scott when I telephoned the Battalion – better to err on the upward side than the lower. However I was correct, he was indeed the colonel, the officer commanding the Battalion.

We invited him and Jim to dine at one of the better restaurants and, with the help of a bottle or two of Chateau Margaux, we had a splendid evening.

All too soon it was all over and we returned to Penang. Life became somewhat humdrum again, well almost. Our third child was now incubating. Mary was pregnant.

Mary was deeply involved with her Guide Company. She had the use of the St Andrew's Church Hall. However, the new minister, Dr Yeo Choo Lak, was not pleased that Mary was not converting the Guides to Christianity. The Chinese were mainly Buddhists and the Malays were Muslims. If she had converted any of the Muslims, we would have been out of the country in a shot. The minister became more and more difficult, finding faults with everything. Finally he formally excommunicated Mary. This action summed up all my opinions of the Christian religion: one-sided trial, judgment, and sentencing in one fell swoop.

In the meantime, there was a lot to do in the new house, which was almost bare of fixtures. Some of the furniture, which I had designed and which had been built in teak by the cabinet maker, Wah Dah, had been transported, but we had no dining room table. I had thought out some ideas while we were in Hong Kong and the table was begun.

The work in the practice was as usual, without any highlights. The year went on and passed into the New Year.

According to custom, premature labour threatened but was delayed by one of the newer progestogenic drugs which were by this time available, and the pregnancy progressed to full term.

In July, when I was consulting, I received a telephone from Mary, requesting the use of the driver. This was unusual as she had her own car. She had attended the normal antenatal consultation and had mentioned that she had experienced a pain while turning the corner of Lim Mah Chye Road. The obstetricians, Dr Tharmaratnam, did a quick check and suggested that she return home at once and get the office driver to take her to the Rumah Sakit Bersalin (the maternity hospital) as soon as possible. This was done; I completed the morning's work, had a quick lunch and went on to the estates in the afternoon.

Bill Wilson, the relieving manager on Bertam Estate while Roy Carter was on UK leave, asked how Mary was. I explained that she was in hospital in labour and he suggested that I phone the hospital and find out how she was getting on. I dialled the hospital, the telephone rang, and Mary answered, to state that we had a new Catriona! Evidently, she was being wheeled back from the labour ward when a wall-phone in the corridor began to ring and, without thinking, she had reached over, taken it off the hook, put it to her ear and heard my voice.

Our family was now, in our opinion, complete: Graeme, Seonaid Mairi and Catriona Muireall.

Chapter 22

Holiday and Work

Over the previous two years I had been reading and reading from the booklist that the Royal College of General Practitioners had sent me. UK leave was again due in 1973 and I thought that, having done all that studying, although my original intention was to forget about the College examination, I might as well sit the examination after all.

This time, there was no dallying in the flight to the UK. It was straight back to Britain.

Catriona was christened; we had holidays back in Mull, returning to Aberdeen by Glen Coe and Kingussie. At Glen Coe we had booked a night at the Kings House Inn, a historic old inn at the head of the glen. Before dinner, we had a cocktail in the cocktail lounge, which had a picture window with a spectacular view of Buachaille Etive Mór, Seonaid and Graeme drinking their orange juice.

Dinner was well presented and the two children behaved impeccably. At one point, Seonaid, who was then three, decided that conversation was in order, leaned over and said loudly: "Graeme, what is the boys' toilet like?" It was one of those moments when talking in the restaurant had dulled so that her penetrating voice could be heard in all points of the room. There was a moment's silence then a burst of laughter.

We returned to Aberdeen and the next object of the agenda was the College examination. The written part was in Edinburgh, so we had a couple of nights there, the family all staying in a hotel. The oral was sat only if the written part had been passed, so it was with relief that news came that I was to have the oral, which was to take place in London, at the College headquarters in Princes Gate.

At this examination, I was taken to task for not considering pulmonary embolism in one of my cases. I answered that deep venous thrombosis and pulmonary embolus was practically unknown in the Chinese. It was not until 1994 that the hereditary blood factor V Leiden mutation, leading to thrombotic conditions, was described, present in about five percent of Caucasians but absent in Asian people. Another condition absent in the Chinese population is congenital dislocation of the hip. I had wondered if this was due to the fact that Chinese babies, instead of being conveyed in prams, are carried straddled on their mother's hips. Nowadays, on finding the condition present in a baby, the primary treatment is to have the baby nursed with their hips straddled in a double nappy or a cast.

One of the examiners was Professor Pinsent who, at one point, asked when I found time to read. Without thinking I answered that I read the books when doing house calls. Seeing the expression on his face, I quickly explained that I had a driver and that I sat in the back seat, reading while going from patient to patient!

After the previous UK holiday, this one was comparatively quiet.

Very shortly after, news arrived that I had passed the examination and the certificate came by post.

I was not long back at work when I was faced with a new problem. One of the company managers was due to be repatriated, but his wife suffered from claustrophobia and would not travel in a ship's cabin. Travelling by plane was equally difficult and she would only take a plane journey if I accompanied her.

It was so arranged. We travelled to Kuala Lumpur by car and boarded the aeroplane. I sat in front of the patient and kept up a conversation all the way to London, keeping her mind occupied. She swallowed Valium like lollies, with no apparent effect. I had my medical bag with me, with essential drugs, so I went to the customs officer to explain the position. There were two alternatives, one being for customs to retain the bag until my return and the other to do a drug count, to be repeated on the way back. All this was too hard for the customs officer, who said that I just take the bag through.

In the meantime the manager had arranged a hired car. Having completed the flight, I prepared to go to the hotel where I was to stay in London.

However, the patient wanted me to travel with them to the manager's mother's house in Somerset, in the west of England. As well as her fear of closed spaces, she was afraid of her mother-in-law! So we went. It was the first and only time I ever saw Stonehenge.

The patient eventually delivered, I had to return to London by train. At the station, the queue for taxis was long and it was going to take hours to obtain one. A university student came to my aid and said that the newly opened Tower Hotel was not too far away, that we could walk, and that he would help me with my bags. We reached the hotel and I offered him a drink. As far as I was concerned, it was a well-needed one.

We talked for a while and the student eventually left. I finished my drink and, suddenly, the picture window of the bar was filed with flashing lights. It was the 5th of November and Tower Bridge was silhouetted by the most spectacular fireworks display I have ever seen. I eventually got to bed after sixty hours without sleep.

This trip had been arranged so that I had a day or two's rest before returning. As I was now a Member of the Royal College of General Practitioners I looked in at Princes Gate to explore the College premises, then went to a classical record shop and bought one or two records. I had lunch at the hotel with my uncle, who was Secretary and Director of Heinz foods, and my aunt and his sister, who was visiting London and staying with him. In the evening one of my friends from University days came to dinner.

Next day, it was back onto the plane to Penang, another long journey. Back home, I slept for thirty-six hours.

Dr Wilson had bought the house opposite to ours and, shortly after our return, there was a practice meeting there. One of the items mentioned was that Gerald Hawkins had died.

It was about this time that a Thai woman consulted me. She was obviously extremely depressed. In those days antidepressant drugs had not been invented and I spent many long consultations listening to her story and discussing rational aspects of her thoughts. It is now apparent that I was practising a rudimentary form of cognitive therapy.

Week after week she saw me, then she felt too ill to come into Penang and I had to start doing house calls on her. She lived far out the coast past Batu Ferringhi, so I would drive out after surgery every Thursday evening. One evening she mentioned that she had thought of walking out into the sea until she drowned, which was a bit alarming. The consultations went on, week after week for over a year, then one day she said that she thought she was better. Some months after that, she wanted to take us, the whole family, and her sister with her family, to lunch at the Rasa Sayang Hotel, which had been opened not long previously. We went in and she said that she wanted lunch for twelve. The waiter looked round – there were four adults. He should have looked down – there were eight children!

Our accountant at that time was Fred Weatherly. He telephoned one day and said that he had someone with him who claimed to be Gerald Hawkins' son. We arranged to meet at the deceased patient's house, out along the coast. The story came out. When the Japanese invaded, Mr Hawkins sent his wife and family back to London but he was interned in Changi Jail. At the end of the war he had returned to Malaya, as it was then, with a woman whom everyone thought was his wife. His original wife and family had remained in London. Eventually his current "wife" died and he had lived on until he, himself, died.

When that was all sorted out, Mr Weatherly left. Mr Hawkins' son explained that he had now to sort out his late father's possessions. He took me down to the library and asked what on earth he was going to do with all these books. He asked if I wanted some. There was a whole set of a first edition of Ridley's *Flora of the Malay Peninsula*, published in 1922, other books on Malay orchids, flora and birds, a copy of *The Four Adventures of Richard Hannay* by John Buchan with the author's signature and various other books of interest to me which I was delighted to take off his hands.

Mary and I invited this visitor to dinner one evening. The stories he told were an evening's entertainment. In about 1947, the late Mr Hawkins had been the Minister for War. He had been interviewed by a *Straits Times* reporter who had asked him about his family. The reply was a curt rejoinder that he did not wish to discuss his family!

Chapter 23

1974 and All That

This period was about the most tranquil and event-free of my life. I was happily married, had three small children, we had managed to achieve worthwhile holidays, the practice was running smoothly.

Dr Lawson left the practice and Dr Tham had left the practice two to three years previously. Dr Ng Teng Kok had replaced him in 1972 and become a partner in 1973. Dr Yeo joined as an assistant in 1973 and remained for two-and-a-bit years, after which he migrated to Darwin, Australia.

Mary was deeply involved with the Girl Guide movement. She had been a Guide throughout her youth, and was by then the Training Commissioner for the State.

Both Mary and I were still on the committee of the Penang St Andrew Society. I had been Chieftain for the years 1969 to 1970 and from 1972 to 1973.

There was only one problem during this period. Despite being a part-ner in the practice and therefore, to all intents and purposes, self-employed, I was still on an employment pass. In Cha'ah, I had worked by means of a yearly employment pass on behalf of the Cha'ah Clinic. On joining Drs Allan and Gunstensen, I was granted an employment pass for three years, from October 1962 to September 1965, 1965 to 1968, 1968 to 1971, and 1971 to 1974. In 1974, I was granted an employment pass for one year only. A possibility might be to obtain permanent residency or Malaysian citizen-ship. However, even with the backing of many Malaysians, including three high court judges, this was unsuccessful. There was no surety for the future. I could be asked to leave the country at a moment's notice.

Another problem was going to be the secondary school education of our children. The primary school in Penang was perfectly satisfactory, but later it was going to be a case of sending them to boarding school, either in Singapore or back in Scotland.

A few years previously a lead smelting plant had been started at the tin smelting works and the problem arose as to how to monitor the health of the workers. On one of the holidays, I had been given a trip to Liverpool, paid for by Eastern Smelting, and had learned about the use of δ-amino-laevulinic acid measurements in the urine as an inexpensive and convenient way detecting the early onset of lead poisoning. Over a period of time, kits had been obtained and the smelting laboratory was used to do monthly estimates. Over the years, only one case of chronic lead poisoning was detected.

There was more drama when working with the shipping aspect with the practice. Ships were visited at the wharf, in the Penang roads and out at sea, these visits being facilitated by the use of the harbour pilots' launches. On one occasion the patient had to be slung over the side on a stretcher and lowered down to the launch, a somewhat unnerving experience.

I had to go out to the Straits of Malacca to bring ashore a ship's First Officer who had cleaned out all the drugs in his ship, an oil tanker, including those in the lifeboats. He was suffering from acute pancreatitis and was completely jaundiced.

There was the one night when a ship's junior officer had, with the help of alcohol, gone berserk, smashed up his cabin, including tearing down the curtain rails of his bunk and pulling the wash basin from the wall, smashing it. It was one of the few occasions when I had to use intravenous largactil to bring the patient under control.

On another occasion I had to go on board a ship in the roads. The captain met me and invited me into his cabin. He said that he was worried about his chief engineer. He had noticed that the man was drinking excessively and had started taking notes on his consumption of alcohol. He said that, in the course of the previous week, the engineer had drunk 329 bottles of beer. During the current week, the beer consumption had diminished to 126 bottles, but two bottles of gin a day were also being consumed (it was a Dutch ship). I was taken along to see the patient, who was quite jaundiced. He was hospitalized, but of course this meant that the ship had to remain in Penang harbour until a new chief engineer could be flown out.

It was not only on board ship that I saw some extraordinary things. At almost midnight one night, there was a telephone call from the daughter of one of Penang's Chinese millionaires. Her mother was notorious for often wanting a visit during the night for some reason or other. I went to the house and the daughter met me at the door. Her parents were away for the night. She took me upstairs to one of the bedrooms. She and a European friend had had an evening on drugs and Carlsberg beer. The room was a mess. A four-poster bed was smashed, the telephone was in pieces, a large Chinese jar was in smithereens, a strip of the thick fitted carpet was torn from wall to wall and the telephone directory was torn in two. The friend was sitting on the floor, propped up against the wall, very much under the influence of drugs and alcohol.

I telephoned the consultant, who wanted nothing to do with it, which left me to handle the situation. Fortunately, I got on quite well with the daughter so I instructed her to keep an eye on her friend, let me know if there was any deterioration overnight and I would call in the morning.

Next morning, I called in. Father was, by this time, home. He had very little to say but took me up to the patient, who was awake though somewhat tired. Over the next day or two, things gradually settled down to normal.

On another occasion, a well-known lawyer in Penang sent for me one evening as his girlfriend had attempted to commit suicide by taking an over-dose of medication. The complication was that the lawyer's girlfriend was the wife of a local GP and the suicide attempt was in the marital home. This time there was no alternative to hospitalization. This was arranged and the ambulance had arrived. At the end, as I was descending the staircase, the husband had just arrived home, a thoroughly embarrassing situation. The general practitioner and his wife eventually divorced and the girlfriend and the lawyer were then free to marry.

Penang Island is practically free from malaria, but it was present on the mainland. I often knew when there was a patient with malaria in the estate hospital by the distinctive smell like burning flesh. However, on one occasion, in the estate hospital, there was a middle-aged Malay man whose only complaint was of feeling tired. He was afebrile and the spleen could not be felt. A four-hourly blood film for two days was a routine procedure for all admissions, and the only abnormal sign in this patient was the presence of *plasmodium falciparum* in his blood. Appropriate treatment resulted in resolution of his fatigue. Malaria comes in all guises. This elderly Malay must have built up a remarkable immunity.

With the large shipping trade I used to see many syphilitic primary chancres. The feel of this firm, intracutaneous, painless "button" is unmistakable. It is so unmistakable that I once diagnosed a chancre on the lip. Dark-ground illumination under the microscope invariably confirmed the diagnosis.

Gonorrhea was less common than I used to encounter in the army. One of the more bizarre cases was anal gonorrhea in a Chinese patient, a not unattractive rather effeminate looking young man employed in the local Cold Storage.

At that time, the gonococcus was starting to become resistant to penicillin and I had begun to increase the treatment to penicillin on two successive days instead of the single dose given previously.

A seaman consulted me with a "dose", microscopically confirmed. I gave the first injection, having checked that he was not allergic to the drug. I then explained that it was unwise to take alcohol as the alcohol could interfere with the action of the penicillin, and the penicillin could make the alcohol work too well, with possible unfortunate consequences.

This particular patient had a rebellious streak but, next day he turned up for his second injection, which was duly delivered. Afterwards he told me that, on the previous day, he had known that he would be told not to drink alcohol, that he had no intention of complying with this, but that, because of the way I had put it, instead of going to a bar as he had intended, he had gone to a film instead and had come back on the second day for his next shot.

Another condition seen frequently was the thalassaemia trait. The patient would be mildly anaemic, with a blood count resembling iron-deficiency anaemia. The spleen could not always be felt, although, at some stage in the patient's life, it would become palpable.

The Eurasian child of a Chinese mother was brought frequently because of "measles". This boy would have fever and a rash. On enquiry, I found that when the fever occurred, the mother gave him aspirin and brought him to see me. Apart from the slight fever and the spots, there was never anything to find. I suggested that, on the next occasion, she give no aspirin but bring the child. This time, there was fever but no spots. The boy was having mild episodes of haemolysis from time to time, resulting in mild fevers. The rash was a reaction to the aspirin.

One Muslim family all had the thalassaemia trait. Their great-great-grandparents had come from Yemen and the grandparents had been cousins.

On another night call to a house in a *kampong* (village) on the outskirts of George Town, a Malay wife had impaled her husband's hand to the table with a knife. It needed the infiltration of local anaesthetic to free the husband.

Tuberculosis was common. In those days it was readily responsive to Streptomycin, PAS and INAH and we treated our own patients with the disease.

Late one evening, I was called to see an elderly Chinese man who had been found by his mates to be unconscious. Full examination failed to reveal any stroke or other cause of his loss of consciousness, except the he had pinpoint pupils. These men were bachelors who lived together in this canvas shack since coming to look for work in Penang many years ago. They swore that the patient never smoked opium. Nevertheless I gave an injection of Nalorphine and called in to see him next morning. The patient was cheerfully sitting having breakfast. The story was that, no, he did not smoke opium but he had a cough and a friend had suggested he try some opium. However, instead of smoking it, he had swallowed a pellet, with devastating results. The Chinese often used opium when they had a cough, frequently masking tuberculosis.

Palliative care in Malaysia was entirely the province of the general practitioner. There were no luxuries such as departments of palliative care to assist. If the patient could afford it, nurses could be employed to help, but it was usually the family who looked after the dying patient.

Strangely enough, I never encountered pain to be a problem, even in patients dying with cancer. Perhaps the patients were more stoical than their western counterparts. On the other hand, opium was freely available, and it is possible that the family administered it. A useful aid was eggnog, freely laced with brandy.

The patient liked to die at home. The families were not happy about this, as the ghost might haunt the house. There were "dying-houses", euphemistically called "convalescent hospitals", where the families took their dying relatives.

I remember being called to one. Perhaps the family was having second thoughts about whether or not the patient was indeed dying. It was a night of torrential monsoon rain and I was soaked to the skin, running from the car to the building. The ward, with all the dying patients, was depressing, gray, lit by fluorescent lighting. Despite the fact that I was dripping wet I examined the patient. She had suffered a stroke and certainly did not seem to be dying. I arranged for her to get out of the place and into the general hospital.

This was also the year when we were due to renew our three-year lease on the house. Unfortunately, our landlord wanted the house back as his son was going to be married. He and the son came to see us but, as we had expended quite a bit on the furnishings, we were not keen to have to move out, nor were we keen for another "flitting".

As it was stalemate, I went to see Tom Hepworth, the retired high court judge who was now in private practice as a solicitor. He was rather pessimistic. He said that there used to be leases where there was an extension clause, and legally tenancy could run on, *ad infinitum*, at the same rent. Silently I pointed out the last clause in the deed, which effectively said that we could renew the lease on the same terms. In 1971, our prospective landlord had been very keen that we would be bound in to the agreement – now he was not so sure. Tom said "Good God" or words to that effect! And so the lease went on.

Chapter 24

Moments Educational

About this time, I met Dr Steve Arasu at a medical lunch. He approached me and mentioned that I had an MRCGP. There was a move to create a Malaysian College and it was suggested that I might like to help. A committee was formed.

Professor John Forbes and Dr J. S. Norell came out from Britain to facilitate the formation of the new College and give guidance. I showed them round and they sat in on the Eastern Smelting sick-parade, for which I was able to produce the most interesting illnesses, including one of our leprosy patients. In the afternoon, we visited the estates, where, although nothing had been laid on, other dramatic events happened, including a child brought in with epileptic convulsions.

In another direction, the Universti Sains Malaysia had started in Penang. A problem had arisen in that many of the potential lecturers had families and there was the complication of how to look after and teach these children while the parents were lecturing.

It was known that Mary had a head teacher's qualification in primary education and so she was approached to ask if she would run a kindergarten school. The problem here was that she also had a young child. It was agreed that she would do so provided that Catriona could also attend although Mary was not, strictly speaking, on the University staff. The new kindergarten facility for the children of University staff became the Tadika Sains Malaysia.

The University had, naturally, many professors and lecturers that had come from Britain and America, so that our practice was an obvious choice for these expatriate people.

From the Penang Club library, I had just read an interesting book about a young psychologist who was interested in the Glasgow street gangs and had managed to join one, using his experiences there for research purposes. I mentioned this book to a patient who had come to consult me, whereupon he told me that it was written by him. Indeed, the patient was very young-looking and would easily have passed for a teenager.

Thus we were all very busy with the practice, starting a College, and beginning a kindergarten/primary school at the University. It was also a time when we made new friends with the University staff.

1974 turned into 1975.

One day, Mary was approached by one of the female lecturers, an American, Mrs Sather, who asked if my wife knew who had previously lived in the house that this lecturer had rented in George Town, Penang. We had known the previous two owners of the house, extending over a period of about ten years. The lecturer asked if one of the previous occupants was a little old lady who wore long white gloves and a hat. Her garb was old-fashioned and seemed highly inappropriate in the intensely humid climate. This was indeed the case. The little old lady, Mrs Soutar, was the dignified daughter of a long-established expatriate family who had owned a large department store in George Town. She had been widowed, had become more and more frail and had eventually died in the house only a few years previously. Her dress was in keeping with women's clothing of expatriates in the first half of the twentieth century. Mrs Soutar continued to wear such clothing until the end of her days.

Mrs Sather went on to explain why she was asking. She said that she had awakened from sleep the previous night, and had become aware that there was someone in the room, the little old lady, wearing a hat and long white gloves. Mrs Sather's husband had not been wakened but continued to sleep peacefully in the bed alongside. The old lady said that she was very worried about her jewellery. Her will had stipulated that all of it, in its case, was to be thrown into the sea in the Penang Straits, and she was uncertain if this had been done. The old lady had eventually just disappeared.

As it happened, Alasdair Wilson and his wife were the executors of Mrs Soutar's will, so we invited them round for a drink and recounted the story to them. They were somewhat perturbed and hastened to make it very clear that every detail of Mrs Soutar's will had been fulfilled. The American lady must be told that her description fitted Mrs Soutar perfectly, but the executors were at a total loss to know why her ghost had appeared.

Interestingly, we heard that the executors had shortly afterwards hired a boat and had gone out into the Straits. Coincidentally, Mrs Wilson never again wore the distinctive jewellery which had attracted much admiration over the last few years, and the old lady was not seen again.

Graeme was now seven, Seonaid five and Catriona turning three. Life was running reasonably smoothly, with me at the practice during the week, Mary and Catriona at the Tadika, Graeme and Seonaid at the primary school, St Christopher's.

At weekends we were either out with friends or had gone for a curry lunch at the Penang Club. One Sunday, I had gone early with Graeme to the Club. We were sitting quietly, Graeme reading a book, I looking at a magazine, when another friend, Major Tom Allen, came in and joined us. Tom had served with the 5th Gurkhas during the war. He began to comment about some noisy children who were running about in the restaurant. Typically the army major, he said that children should not be allowed in the Club House. I silently indicated Graeme sitting quietly reading. Said Tom: "But he's disciplined!"

In 1975, we took our holiday at the Plantation Agencies bungalow in the Cameron Highlands. It was to be the last of our holidays for a long time.

The St Andrew Society was running well, although it was gradually becoming smaller, due to the repatriation of Scots businessmen in the community to make way for local managers.

The new Chieftain was Alistair McBoyle, an electrician managing one of the companies. He was very personable but prone to overindulge in alcohol and make mistakes. He tended to be the "clumsy guest" in the Eric Berne game "Schlemiel" (*Games People Play*), breaking something, becoming profusely apologetic, and then being forgiven. He had the pleasure of messing and avoiding punishment.

The committee decided that, as Society numbers were becoming so low, the Society funds would be used to subsidize the Ball. Unfortunately, at the Ball, Alistair managed to insult the Penang State Governor, Tan Sri Datuk Sardon. Furthermore, at the first committee meeting after the event, the Chieftain gleefully announced that the Ball had made a profit. As, in the event of the society closing, any remaining funds would go to the government, this was the last thing we wanted! It was therefore decided by the committee to persevere for another year. I was again elected to be Chieftain, with the unenviable mandate of supervising the demise of the Penang St Andrew Society, a society which had been running since prior to 1912.

The next question was whom to invite as official guests. For years, the guest list had included the Governor of Penang, The Chief Minister, The High Court Judge, the President of the Royal Society of St George. The minister of St Andrews Church had not been invited for a number of years. In the light of the behaviour of the Governor of Penang in the preceding year, he was no longer a welcome guest. How were we to drop him from the guest list without offending him?

Then I had an idea. There would be only three official guests. The President of the St George's Society was necessary as the representative of the rival national society. What we would do would be to invite Tunku Abdul Rahman, "Bapa Malaysia", who now resided in Penang, and also the British High Commissioner. Because of the seniority of these latter two guests, the Governor could hardly object.

Thus, 1975 drew to a close.

Chapter 25

The Calm Before the Storm

Life, at this point, seemed reasonably smooth. The only problem was the tenure of continuing to stay and work in Malaysia. The three-year employment pass had been reduced to one year, so that application had to be made yearly.

The two older children attended St Christopher's Primary School and the youngest, Catriona, accompanied Mary, who was running the Tadika.

On some evenings Mary went out to teach Scottish Country Dancing to members of the St Andrew Society. One time she returned after dark and said that there was a strange man in the street in front of the house. I took the car and drove slowly down the road. Indeed there was a young Malay sitting on the road verge, plucking the grass and eating it. We went back in to the house and telephoned the police, who said they would come right away. Within five minutes a police car entered the street and slowly drove along. By this time the young man had got up and was walking further along the street, which was L-shaped and a *cul-de-sac*. As we watched, the car slowly passed the wanderer, turned at the end of the *cul-de-sac*, and slowly returned. As it passed the stranger, the car door opened, an arm came out, grabbed the man and pulled him into the car. The door closed. As the car passed, the policeman gave a cheery wave.

Weekends were usually spent on the beach, or we would be invited out by Mike and Enid Lloyd on their motor boat to one of the nearby islands, where we would spend the day, with a picnic on the island.

On other Sundays, we would have lunch with Joan and Frank McKenna at the Penang Club, and the children would play in the splash pool there.

Then, from time to time, there might be curry lunches, often held by Jack McKeown. At one, we met Cearbhall O'Dalaigh, who was then the President of Ireland. I can recall sitting and drinking Irish coffee with him!

Every Sunday a quiet Indian couple would have lunch at the Penang Club. One day, it was reported in the newspaper that the husband had been found murdered in a ditch. The story slowly unfolded that he had been hired by the government to investigate a rich Indian entrepreneur on the mainland. This entrepreneur was evidently completely ruthless. The story went that he had an Indian driver who was employed at a pitifully low salary. The salary was such that the driver could not afford a dowry and so was unable to marry. He approached his employer who gave him a wedding gift so that the marriage could take place. After the wedding the driver's boss said that the gift was a loan which would have to be paid back, at such a rate of interest that the driver would be completely unable to pay it off and leave his job.

On the work side, patients came in with the usual ailments.

There was the home visit to the Chinese old lady with a cough. In order to examine her chest, I asked her to remove her *baju*. She was very reluctant. Her family explained that, if she did so, then the "winds" would enter. I was acquainted with the "winds". At the Kek Lok Si Temple at Ayer Itam, there were huge statues of the four winds trampling the unfortunate humans underfoot. If the "winds" entered, the old lady would suffer (rheumatic) pains all over. After some persuasion, she reluctantly bared her chest. An accumulation of skin cells came off her chest like a breastplate, revealing new pink skin underneath. She had not removed her clothes for months! Strangely, there was not much smell, only a faint musty odour. It was clearly demonstrated to me how the skin of the body grows from the inside, and the old, dead skin cells form a protective covering. Normally, on washing, we wash off the surface layer of dead cells, together with any dirt gathered on them.

There was the other home visit to another old Chinese lady who had developed an ulcer on the top of her foot. In spite of all I could do, the ulcer became deeper and larger, exposing, then eroding through the tendons. With much patient effort, the ulcer eventually healed.

Above: *Kek Lok Si Temple, Penang.*
Right: *Statue of one of the four "winds" trampling humans underfoot.*

One Friday evening I was in the surgery, packing up and preparing to go, when one of the Malay employees of Eastern Smelting came in with an acute attack of diarrhoea. Examination disclosed nothing unusual apart from the expected slightly tender abdomen. He was advised to keep up his fluids and avoid solids, and was asked to come to the Company sick parade next day.

However, there was a phone call early next morning requesting a house visit on him. Going in to see him, I found that he was extremely ill and the whites of his eyes were a yellow coppery colour. He was so ill I immediately sent him in to hospital. After the sick parade and normal consultation times in the surgery, just before lunch-time, I telephoned the consultant in the hospital to enquire after the patient. The consultant told me that the patient had died about two hours after admission!

I went home for lunch with this disturbing information. I could not stop mulling over it. Early in the afternoon, a thought struck me, and I telephoned the consultant, asking him if any blood samples had been taken. Yes, he said, a blood test had been ordered but no results had yet arrived. I telephoned the laboratory and asked if they had received blood from the patient. They said that blood had been received for a blood count but that it was useless as it had haemolised and that they were going to throw it out.

I said not to throw it out but to test it for arsine and arsenic. The result eventually arrived to the effect that there were large amounts of arsine present and also hydrogen sulphide. Next Monday morning, at Eastern Smelting, I made enquiries and discovered that, when the tin ingots had been put into sheds to cool, some of the workers had asked the crane drivers to pour on buckets of water to speed the cooling, which was, in fact, a forbidden practice. Furthermore some of the workers stated that, when they entered the cooling sheds, there was a smell like garlic. The diagnosis of arsine poisoning was obvious.

It also struck me that there had been an epidemic of patients in the sick parade with symptoms of abdominal pains and passing blood in the urine. It had been the month of Ramadan, during which Muslims fast during the day, even in a tropical climate. In an industry where workers were subjected to the heat of the furnaces, kidney stones were not uncommon. Subsequent x-ray examinations had not shown kidney stones, but it was presumed that there had been stones which had been passed.

The urine testing was the normal side room method. If I had also examined the urine under the microscope I might have detected that there were no blood cells and therefore realized that the blood passed had been haemolised.

Snakes in the Snake Temple, Penang. These snakes are Pit Vipers and are poisonous.

Chapter 26

Storm Clouds Gather

O n the practice side, the situation was changing. Dr Ng wanted to increase his share in the practice, which was, at that time 20 percent, Dr Wilson's being 45 percent and mine 35 percent. Dr Wilson asked my thoughts on the matter. Dr Ng had been with the practice four years by then, and I, fourteen years.

My copy of the *Encyclopaedia of General Practice* (Butterworth, 1965) states: "The new partner must reach equality with the others within ten years with some increases in the intervening time, and no partner may have an initial share less than one third that of the largest share in the practice. Nowadays parity is often reached before a ten year period." I showed this to Dr Wilson, who said nothing.

Later in the year, Dr Wilson again broached the subject of Dr Ng's increase in his share of the practice, and asked what I thought his share should be. I stated between 25 and 33⅓ percent. He asked me if I would be prepared to state so, and I said that I would. Nothing was said or discussed further, but a practice meeting was called on the last Sunday of October 1976. At this meeting, Dr Wilson declared that he was prepared to make a package deal.

My Employment Pass was due to expire at the end of September 1977 and Dr Wilson was a permanent resident. I had made applications for permanent residency but had heard nothing. At the practice meeting, Dr Wilson stated that he would sell Dr Ng five percent share of the practice then, and that he would expect me, if I got my permanent residency, to sell five percent of my share in October 1977.

I was completely taken by surprise that this had been sprung on me in such a way, and also very disappointed that I was still considered a junior partner, on a par with Dr Ng, after so many years and after my support during the very difficult period when there were only two doctors in the practice. I felt that the situation had been stage-managed, as indeed it had, and it would it would have appeared to be churlish not to accept – as Dr Wilson had said, it was a package deal, "take it or leave it".

Thereafter, things became very difficult. Relations within the practice were strained, to say the least, the future was uncertain, not knowing whether or not I would be able to remain in the country. Dr Wilson became even more dictatorial. There were no practice meetings, Mary and I were excluded from all social functions which he and his wife ran, and he did not communicate in any way except to criticize for faults real or imagined. He was sarcastic, disparaging. He objected to guests we invited to our home on the grounds that they were not friends of his.

I was also in the situation where, if I did not get my entry permit, I would lose all the capital I had invested in the practice by the terms of the practice agreement.

Many years later I discovered that Dr Wilson had commanded Dr Ng not to talk to me, an order to which he objected, replying that, in his eyes, I had done nothing wrong. However it confirmed the fact that I was being deliberately excluded.

One Saturday morning, I had occasion to visit a patient with acute sciatica on a ship in harbour. He was in such agony that I told the captain that he would have to be hospitalized in Penang. The captain refused to allow him to leave the ship. Back in the office, I telephoned the shipping agent and explained the problem.

Shortly after, Dr Wilson came through to my room and ordered me to write a report to state that the patient was fit to go on with the ship. After thinking about it a little, I wrote a report to the effect that the patient had acute sciatica, that preferably he should be hospitalized in Penang, that the captain had ordered him to continue with the ship, and that, accordingly, if the seaman came to any harm, all responsibility lay with the captain. Within twenty minutes, the seaman was ashore, on his way to hospital.

The situation was now very difficult. I wanted to continue working in Malaysia but the odds seemed to be piled high against me. There was the possibility that Mary and I would lose all our money if my employment pass was not renewed. The tensions in the practice were stretched to breaking-point. I enjoyed meeting patients, the intellectual stimulation occasioned by diagnosing their problems, and trying to help them. Now I was being dictated to about how to do my work.

My feelings had reached a nadir. It is impossible to fully express feelings or emotions into words with meaning. If this is what life was going to be, telling lies to please the people who paid us, it was not worthwhile. My perception of the medical profession was to try to help people who were suffering. Profit was a secondary consideration. Although I no longer believed in God, the phrase *"You cannot serve God and Mammon"* (Proverbs) seemed appropriate.

I had successfully defused the current problem but it was going to be an uphill struggle if Dr Wilson was going to negate all that I was trying to do. I could only see that life in that practice was going to be hellish. I could see no way forward. If treated in the office at all, it was obviously as a lackey. There seemed to be no point in going on living.

That Saturday afternoon, I ordered all the morphine ampoules stocked by the Georgetown Dispensary, with the intension of injecting them intravenously when all the consultations were completed. When stress becomes unbearable, suicide seems an easy option.

A Malay patient was sitting with me when the injections arrived. He saw them, realized my intensions and told me not to do it. The present-day perception that Muslims are aggressive and uncompassionate was put to the lie.

There was only one consideration. I had a wife and family whom I loved and who, I hoped, loved me. I telephoned Mary to express my intentions and she came straightaway, saving my life.

Even now, as I write this, I can still feel the almost unbearable distress. It was an object lesson on the powerful impact of interpersonal relations.

I then consulted Dr Subramaniam, the consultant psychiatrist, who helped to steer me through this most difficult period in my life. I avoided Dr Wilson as much as possible and went on seeing patients as a routine, which helped to pass the time. That way I avoided being ordered how to conduct my consultations.

Chapter 27

Interlude

The day of the Penang St Andrew's Ball arrived. This time, all ran according to plan. Tunku Abdul Rahman was seated on my left, between Mary and me, and his wife was on my right. As she spoke only Raja Malay, conversation with her was somewhat limited. Tunku Abdul Rahman was a delightful guest. In the course of the evening, costumed Girl Guides whom Mary had trained gave exhibitions of Scottish Country Dancing and Mary was able to introduce Tunku to one of them, a daughter of one of his school friends.

The British High Commissioner and his wife were also guests.

The evening went well and the surplus Society funds were successfully used to subsidize the occasion. As an aside, I was able to introduce Tunku to Scotch malt whisky.

Christmas was approaching, and one Saturday afternoon, we went into De Silva's, the jewellers, to have a look. We looked at some Waterford cut-crystal, a bowl, a couple of decanters and a water jug. They were very expensive and we decided not to buy. The following week, I came home for lunch and there were the four crystal objects sitting on the dining room table.

I went to Mary and said that I thought we had decided not to buy them. She said she had thought that I had bought them.

We went down to De Silva's. It transpired that my Thai patient had gone into the shop and said that she was looking for a present for Dr Esslemont. The astute assistant had said that we had been in and admired these four objects and she had bought them all for us!

169

The finale to the Penang St Andrew Society took place on the following 25th January 1977, when the Burns Supper, celebrating the poet's birthday, was held. Each year, haggis was shipped by the Ben Line for the ball, and some was reserved for the Burns supper, two months later. The ball was held at the E & O Hotel, the staff of which were supposed to retain the surplus in their refrigerator. When Mary went to the hotel to transfer what was left to the Penang Club where the supper was held, she was told that it had been all used up for the ball. She knew that this was untrue as she had checked how much was left after the ball. Unfortunately for us, however, the Chinese are very fond of haggis! We tried to obtain replacements from all over Malaysia and Singapore, with little success.

In desperation, Mary hunted her cookery books and, for a week, I had various "wersh" (insipid) concoctions of "mince and tatties". She eventually found a palatable recipe in a book by Mary Baxter, and also discovered that she had made the error of using chicken liver whereas the much coarser ox liver was much better. Thus, the main course of the Burns Supper was saved. The meal ended with drambuie cream, which would have put an end to any lingering doubts.

One of the William Thompson & Co. owners of Ben Line visited Penang at this point and the shipping agent and his wife, Mike and Enid Lloyd, invited us to dinner with him at the Merlin Hotel. After the dinner, Mary entertained us all with a demonstration of Highland Dancing, the *Seann Triubhas*.

In the meantime, the relentless, pressurized unpleasantness from Dr Wilson continued. A picture was becoming clearer. Many years previously, Dr Scott had said that Dr Ballantyne had been pushed out of the practice by Dr Wilson. Dr Scott had himself gone. None of the Chinese doctors – Dr Teh, Dr Tham, Dr Yeo – had stayed long. Dr Lawson had wanted to leave within a year of joining but had been persuaded to stay on for two years. Within a year of leaving to the UK, he had returned to a practice in Kuala Lumpur. When Mary and I were in Kuala Lumpur or Chris Lawson was in Penang, we met from time to time, and on one occasion I had asked him his real reason for leaving our practice. He replied that he had found Dr Wilson "too much" and that he could not put up with him any more. He stated that he found his current practice much more relaxed and congenial.

I could see a picture emerging. Dr Wilson was paranoid and brooked no rivalry. He was perfectly pleasant provided he was "top dog". I had had the temerity to suggest equality. It was also obvious that he had enriched himself at the expense of Mike Scott, myself, Wah Teh, and Ng Teng Kok, who had all bought into the practice; by the fact that Dr Scott's share had been diminished by persuasive talk, and that Dr Teh, by his leaving contrary to the practice agreement, had forfeited his share. Another Freudian clue showed in the fact that his wife had taken up painting and copper tooling, and there were several pictures of fighting cocks, which was not too subtle, as the history was that Dr Wilson had had an affair with, and eventually married, another man's wife! This had evidently led to blows.

Eventually, as things were not improving, Dr Subramaniam asked if I had considered resigning from the practice. This required a certain amount of thought. My love of Malaysia had in no way diminished and I did not want to leave, as would have to be the case if I left the practice. And where to? Also, the practice agreement stipulated that the six-month notice to retire could not be given within three months after a holiday. Our last leave had been in 1975, so that was no problem provided that we forewent any more leave.

We went to see Tom Hepworth again and I submitted my resignation a few days before the end of March 1977, to leave the practice on 30th September. All that had to be done was to sit it out for the next six months.

At one point, Dr Wilson said that I was due leave and that taking leave would not jeopardize anything – he may have hoped I would change my mind, as my departure was liable to damage the practice – but I did not trust him.

I applied for immigration to Australia and South Africa, where some close friends were going.

In May, there was a Monday holiday, which applied to Penang but not to Kuala Lumpur. We spent the weekend in KL, went to the Australian Consulate and applied for immigration. The positive response came through in three weeks. Perhaps the fact that I was the medical examiner to the Australian Consulate helped.

The Penang St Andrew Society closed up and the committee presented me with the Chieftain's badge and the little silver Quaich. The last month in Penang was spent in farewell parties. Everyone was very kind, except, of course, Dr Wilson.

On our last day in Lim Mah Chye Road, Mary supervised the packing by the expert Chinese packers. We had five days to leave the country so we spent about three days in rooms in the Penang Club. On the first evening a party was going on. Dave Hastie, the manager of Malakoff Estate, was there. He confided to me that he was going to terminate the contract with the practice after I was gone.

Prior to our departure from the Penang Club rooms, Ng Teng Kok and his wife called in with a present. It had to be a clandestine visit as, if Dr Wilson had found out, Teng Kok would have been in trouble. As it was, I warned Dr Ng that, now I was out of the way, his turn would be next, the next "rival".

Hazel Weatherly lent us her estate car for our last days in Penang.

Then we boarded the express train for Kuala Lumpur. Dave Hastie joined us on the train and accompanied us as far as Ipoh. My Thai patient had given us a bottle of champagne, with the instructions that we were to drink it on the train. I popped the cork through the open carriage window and it just missed a passing postman on his bicycle.

In Kuala Lumpur, we took the poor children, who had not had much of a life over the previous year, to the zoo.

I had spent nearly twenty years in Malaya/Malaysia, Mary had been there twelve and a half years. Now this was all over.

Then on to Singapore and on to the Qantas plane to Australia for the next stage of our adventure.

Tunku Abdul Rahman.

Tunku Abdul Rahman making his speech at Penang St. Andrew's Society Ball, 1976.

A slightly different version of the same photograph.

Chapter 28

Starting Afresh

The first Australians I had met, at Kamunting, had not favourably impressed me. They had seemed to me to be undisciplined and disrespectful. We had met others, who had given a more favourable impression, later on in our stay in Penang. First impressions make the most impact so I looked forward to Australia with some misgivings. The crew on the Qantas flight were pleasant, fortunately.

The weather during the flight was bright and sunny and we got our first ever sighting of Australia at the very recognizable Shark Bay.

At Perth, we were met by Max Keys, the former headmaster of Scotch College, whom we had entertained with his wife two years previously at the suggestion of Jim Muir, who had been chaplain to the school prior to his stint in Penang. Max had visited again after our decision to migrate to Australia, so had made arrangements for our arrival.

As we were "Asian immigrants" we did not merit the "£10 passage" and the hostel accommodation provided for immigrants from Britain, so Max had booked us into the Forrest House Motor Lodge, which was considered reasonably inexpensive.

Unfortunately, Max had developed a tenosynovitis affecting his wrist, so, next day, we were picked up by Peter Hunt, a Perth-based architect whom we had shown round Penang in the previous year at the suggestion of his friend Max Keys.

My primary object was to find a job, so Peter took us to the Australian

Medical Association offices which were then in West Perth. There, news was not good. Jobs were not easy to find. We were given some contacts but they were not what we were seeking. The next stop was the Royal Australian College of General Practitioners where I met Dr Hugh Cook, the President of the Western Australian Faculty, who warned me to watch out for one of the names I had been given at AMA House, again not very promising.

Peter then took us for a tour of Perth and Fremantle, with a stop at Cicerello's, the fish and chip place there.

The next few days were spent following various leads, not very productively. We went to the equivalent of the labour exchange. Again there was little to offer. By this time we were becoming worried about our money and asked if there was a cheap hotel where we could stay. We were offered the Forrest House Motor Lodge! Obviously the cost of living in Australia was many times greater than in Malaysia.

We enquired about the dole, for the first time in our lives. The government under the then Prime Minister, Malcolm Fraser, had just passed a law whereby the dole was not available until the applicant had been out of work for six weeks.

In the course of the second week, we had a message from AMA House that a Dr Blair Malcolm in Wickham was looking for a doctor to act as a locum for two to three weeks as the other medico in the practice was ill with jaundice. As Wickham was in the Pilbara, about a thousand kilometres north of Perth, air fares, a house and a car would be provided. He wanted someone as soon as possible and it was decided that we would go there on Friday.

On Thursday, the airline employees went out on strike. There would be no flights until Monday. In the two days' delay and the extra two days in the hotel, our remaining bank balance was reduced by half.

As the height of the plane on which we flew was considerably less than the international flight, there was much more to see and it was more interesting. We arrived at Karratha and were met by a vehicle which conveyed us and our belongings to Wickham. The landscape was dry and bare, a red moon landscape. What struck me even more was the trash of empty cans and bottles at the sides of the road, obviously chucked from trucks.

We arrived at our new domicile, a small brick-built bungalow, air-conditioned. The village of Wickham was a Company village built by Cliffs Robe River Company for the workers at their mine-site. There was a small store and even a church. The house was adequately furnished and the garden was practically bare, the soil consisting of red, packed, dry laterite.

I met the doctor, Blair Malcolm, and he showed me the hospital. Next day I started work and encountered Australian medicine for the first time. He later asked how I found it and I answered that it is the same all over the world.

The time in Wickham was not long, only two weeks. However, on the days off, we visited Cossack, a deserted village begun many years ago; and the nearby "hundred miles beach", a stretch of sand, absolutely clear of footprints, stretching as far as the eye could see, backed by the blue ocean and the cloudless sky.

At the weekend, Blair suggested that we went through the Chichester National Park to Millstream. It was a dirt road, and we travelled through the sparse ghost gums, past the remains of what looked like old volcanic cores with the split red rock boulders round the bases, stopping at Python Pool with its surrounding ring of precipice, and so to Millstream, an oasis of green, with the palms, and the pool in the river growing water lilies. On the return journey, we saw our first kangaroo in the wild.

Twice I visited the mine site at Pannawonica, taking off from Karratha in a plane that was so small that it felt like being in a taxi. It was time for blasting so the pilot took me over the top of a small plateau just as the top was being blown off.

One day, Blair told me that I was to be visiting one of the ore ships coming in to Point Sampson. Next day, he asked if I knew a Captain Len McLeod. I said that he was our next-door neighbour in Penang. He was the captain of the ore carrier. The next we knew, we were all invited to lunch on board the ship, Mary, the three children, Blair and his wife, and me.

There is a cliché about the world being a small place.

At Wickham we were introduced to the Melbourne Cup, the day in Australia when everything stops.

There was news of another locum job, at Kununurra, another thousand kilometres north at the top of Western Australia. This time it would be for three months. We returned to Perth, where I was interviewed for this new job. The interviewer was obviously trying to find out if I was up to the mark for the position. First he stated that it was very hot. I reminded him that I had spent twenty years in Malaya/Malaysia. Then he said there was no television. I replied that we had not had television in Penang. He then asked if I had ever seen leprosy. I told him that I had treated leprosy patients in my last practice.

And so it was another plane journey up north again. The crew complained that our baggage was overweight – it was all our possessions in Australia – and we had to redistribute baggage. They must have sensed that I had not been altogether happy at the problem because on the last sector of the journey I was invited into the pilot's cabin. I had marvellous views of the barren countryside, the "magnetic" termite mounds (all pointing north), watched the "failsafe" manoeuvres of the pilot and experienced the landing of the plane in Kununurra.

So, on to the next job.

Kununurra was a small outback town in the very north of Western Australia in a region known as the Kimberley. We were taken to our new home, one of the few brick-built buildings in the town. It was fairly spacious but was filthy dirty. I mentioned this at the hospital and a young woman came to help clean the house. Mary introduced herself and the girl exclaimed, "You delivered me!" She was originally from near Aberdeen and had been delivered by Dr Mary.

Australia - "outback", North-West Australia.

Iain Esslemont

More "outback"

Another "outback" scene, a waterhole.

178

A common sight in Australia, a dead tree standing alone.

I set about cleaning the bathroom, which was covered in mould. I had to dismantle some of the plumbing, clean it and put it back again.

I had not started work in the hospital yet but must have been on call for the weekend because first thing on Saturday afternoon I had to go down to the hospital.

One of the airline hostesses had been on a motorboat on the Kununurra diversion dam, had fallen overboard and been run over by the boat. The propeller had sliced her left arm and leg. There was no anaesthetist in the hospital. I had to sit down, mentally revise my anatomy, infiltrate local anaesthetic, and then suture the muscles and then the skin. I cannot remember if she returned to Perth that day or the next, but I referred her to Royal Perth Hospital. I later enquired what the outcome was. The suturing must have been satisfactory for they had just left everything in place and removed the stitches later.

Mary, the three children and I settled down to life in Kununurra for the next three months. The town was so far east of Perth that the sun rose at about four or five in the morning, Western Australia time, and the first sick parade started about six. This led to a certain problem as, if we had to contact the hospitals in Perth, no one was around until about three hours later.

Life in Kununurra was very free and easy. The children thoroughly enjoyed it. Graeme went fossicking and soon gathered an orange box full of a collection of stones and fossils. Having been brought up in the warmth of Malaysia, they delighted in the sunshine and the wild countryside.

On the weekends, we went out as a family to the diversion dam, to Lake Argylle, and to the various water holes round and about. The red countryside, with its proliferation of gum trees, was very beautiful, spectacular and dramatic.

However, shopping was about three times the price of goods in Perth – Wickham had been dear but here was more so.

The other doctor was Dr Fred McConnell. We got on well together and took weekend-about on roster.

Much of the population was aboriginal. Diabetes was very common among them. For centuries, they had lived in the semi-desert, eating whatever they could find: goannas, kangaroos, emus, grubs, and the various edible vegetable matter. Now they had an ample supply of food from the shops, not all of it particularly healthy eating, so that they had an intake oversupply resulting in obesity. Their genetic background, pruned by the frugal lifestyle, had left alive those best able to store fat. Those less fortunate had died off. Now the hormonal makeup of those who were the descendants of the survivors could not cope with the more than generous food supply. Perhaps this also accounted for their problems with alcohol.

Their way of living had an effect on their health. Giardia lamblia was prevalent so that diarrhoeas were common. Their abscesses were spectacular. I can remember a quite attractive young woman with a large abscess in the front of her thigh. Under local anaesthetic, the abscess was opened and flushed out with sterile saline. With daily treatments, the leg was eventually brought back to normal. One day when I was walking down the street with Mary, this young lady gave me a wave and a big smile – my wife said sharply: "Who's your friend?"

I found the aborigines to be very friendly and good-humoured. Unfortunately they had little sense of consequences. They often failed to attend for follow-up. Some of them would go to the bottle shop and drink a cask of wine at a time. Women would be seen outside the grocery store feeding their babies with milk in a not-too-clean beer bottle with a teat attached.

There were elements of the white population who seemed to be somewhat feral also. One young lady had six children by the same man. I asked her if she had thought of getting married. She replied that she would never get married because "marriage is so uncertain"!

One weekend, I was called down to the hospital where there was an aboriginal man and wife who had been fighting and both had considerable lacerations. They were accompanied by a white man who had driven them to the hospital. He asked if I would be long. There was quite a bit of work to be done and

South-West Australia, the Boranup Forest, composed of Karri trees, the third tallest type of tree in the world.

I thought that I would be about an hour. He said that in that case he would come back later. The woman had the more severe lacerations, so I decided that I would deal with her first. That completed, I started on the man. All finished, I was just about to leave the hospital when there was a phone message asking if I would call in at the police station on the way back to take a blood sample to test for alcohol. After the telephone call, I noticed the woman sitting there holding a large piece of four-by-four wood. I asked her what she had that for. She answered that she was waiting for her man to come out. I said that I did not want to do another stitching session. She grinned and said, "OK." On the way back, in the police station, there was the white man who had accompanied them, waiting to have his blood taken.

The hospital employee who looked after the hospital car we were using was an aborigine. One day, when we had returned from a trip, he asked me if the car was running alright. I said that it was whereupon he asked, "Are you sure it's running alright?" Again I said that it was and said, "Why are you asking?" He replied that he had forgotten to put the cap on the petrol tank the last time he filled it.

At Kununurra, we became friendly with the hospital phlebotomist, a middle-aged woman. We invited her for Christmas dinner and, although she was a

Mormon, she came.

She told the story that she was the daughter of an English vicar. One Christmas, she had opened her stocking. There was only an orange in it and a note saying that, as she had been so bad that year, that was all she was getting.

In the conversation, it came out that one of her Mormon friends was a Heather McHours, the daughter of Captain McLeod, who had entertained us on board ship at Wickham and with whom she would now have nothing to do. The very first time I had seen Heather was as a patient in Penang in 1962, so our paths had continued to cross over many years.

There was an interesting incident at the hospital Christmas party. At one point in the evening, two invited French geologists came in late. They stated that they had found diamonds and thought that it was going to be bigger than South Africa!

For one period, Fred McConnell took a couple of weeks' leave, and a doctor from Perth came to stand in for him. One patient he was confronted with had lacerations similar to the young air hostess who had been my first patient in Kununurra. The young doctor looked at the lacerations in dismay and said that we would have to get a specialist surgeon. I asked him, "Where from?" It was going to take hours to get the patient to a specialist surgeon for a job he could easily do himself. In the end, the doctor got down to revising his anatomy, instilling the anaesthetic, and started stitching.

All this time I was still looking for work that was more permanent. Max Key's doctor had mentioned that they were considering taking on another doctor for their practice so I telephoned him. However, they had not yet decided.

Towards the end of our three months in Kununurra, a diabetic aboriginal woman consulted me. On her back was an abscess the size of a dinner plate. There was a slight problem. There was no anaesthetist and it would not be prudent to infiltrate local anaesthetic into a potentially infected area. Looking at the abscess, I found that the overlying skin was gangrenous and I thought that I could probably, if I was very careful, cut away the gangrenous skin without hurting the woman. The patient lay on her abdomen on the operating table and I started cutting away the dead skin. It seemed to be proceeding well, when the patient's shoulders began to heave. One of the nursing sisters, who was sitting on a table in front of the woman's head, became concerned and asked if it was hurting. The patient said "No, it tickles!" She was laughing!

I had managed to find my next work. It was again another locum job, but this time with a view to assistantship, in Port Macquarie, in New South Wales, on the other side of Australia. We also had sleepers booked on the Indian Pacific train to take us across to the Eastern States. The Director of Medical Services telephoned and asked if I would like to take a permanent position with the hospital in Kununurra. To me it was tempting, but one of our problems was that there was no secondary school, and we had three children who would require secondary education in the near future.

There was another consideration. Although I had settled in nicely, Mary was more doubtful. We used the public library a lot, and at one point the librarian had asked her to fill in for her while she had some leave. Mary was happy to be usefully employed but there were objections from the local inhabitants as we were "incomers". Thus the family was never really made to feel "at home".

We returned to Perth and boarded the train.

The train was different from any we had been on before. We were given two sleeping compartments, a two-bedded one for us and a three-bedded one for the children. Our compartment had a miniscule toilet and shower, and, as far as I remember, the children shared ours. There was a carriage which was furnished as a sitting room, with a bar and piano provided, and another two carriages which were dining rooms.

The first day and night took us as far as Kalgoorlie, which we reached at 6.00 am. We were given a guided coach tour, giving us our first sight of the famous "starting boxes" in Hay Street, a row of tiny cabins used as brothels. The train continued on, across the Nullarbor Plain, a flat, vast expanse of a sort of moorland. The carriages were transferred to different bogies at Port Augusta as the gauge of the railway lines was different in New South Wales from those of Western and South Australia.

In all, it took four days and the intervening nights to reach Sydney, where we stayed at the Manhattan Hotel. Then we went by bus to Port Macquarie, which was 423 kilometres north of Sydney, up the coast, a day's journey.

This practice was an entirely different kettle of fish. The rooms had been renovated by a designer and the practice ran as an "efficiency" business, with six-minute appointments instead of the fifteen-minute consultations of the practices in which I had worked in Western Australia. This was my introduction to the money-minded practices of the Eastern States of Australia. I ran horrendously late as there was no allowance made for different styles of practice.

The rooms in which the family lived were also miniscule, with every effort taken to squeeze as much into as little space as possible. It was possible to sit at the breakfast table and wash the dishes as they were used in the sink behind us.

There was no way that this practice and I were going to work together. We looked at other practices up and down the coast, but they were equally money-minded.

It was at this point that Mary put forward the proposal that we had little option but to set up our own practice. After my experience of trying to start a practice from scratch in Cha'ah, there was nothing I wanted less.

Chapter 29

The Long Haul

We returned to Sydney.

The lady who ran the locum firm, who had arranged the latest job in Port Macquarie, very kindly let us occupy her holiday house in Newport, north of Sydney, free of charge. This was just as well as we had very little money. The money that I was due for my share of the practice in Penang was beginning to come through, but even there, there was a hold-up. The latest accounts from the practice had been sent to me for signing. However, it was very obvious that Dr Wilson had been spending large amounts of money on new equipment without my knowledge. The equipment would then be immediately devalued by 20 percent on purchase, so that I would be paid less. I refused to sign the accounts, whereupon Dr Wilson dictated that he was not going to pay my share without the documents being signed, and withheld the instalments due. It was only after pressure from the lawyer Tom Hepworth that payments restarted again.

From Newport, by telephone, I contacted the Director of Therapeutics, who knew a pharmacist in a locality named Huntingdale on the outskirts of Perth in Western Australia, where a doctor was wanted. From there I contacted the Council of the City of Gosnells, in which Huntingdale was situated, to seek more details. Apparently, Huntingdale was a new building project, with a supermarket, a chemist, and a few houses. A medical centre was planned. Eventually it was agreed that I would have first option to start a practice in the new medical centre. There was a proviso – that I live in Huntingdale. We kept account of the phone calls, which mounted to over $100, which we paid back to the house owner.

In Port Macquarie, we had leased a Toyota station wagon. We fitted roof bars to which our suitcases were secured with ropes. The remainder of our goods was packed inside. We set off to drive over the Nullarbor Plain to Perth.

The night before, we had been entertained to dinner by some friends, George Drysdale and his wife, who advised us to check that hotel rooms were available on the way as it was the Easter Weekend. We checked with the NRMA, the New South Wales equivalent of the RAC, who assured us that we would have no problem.

We set off over the Blue Mountains, the three children sitting in the back, enjoying the scenery. The hilly road was bordered by trees and there were notices advising that the road could be treacherous in icy conditions, although this did not apply when we were driving, as it was late summer.

Arriving in Canberra, we had problems finding accommodation. Our main impediment was finding a place within our means. The Drysdales had advised us that, if we found difficulty, to go on to Queanbeyan, which we did. At Queanbeyan, the only available place was the Queanbeyan Hotel, an old-fashioned Australian pub. There was a farmers' party and they had only one room left, but very kindly and strictly outside the law, they put down mattresses on the floor for the children, so that all five of us had a bed in which to sleep, all in the same room.

During the night, Seonaid needed to visit the toilet, along the corridor. Mary set off with her, but, on the way there, there was a bedroom door standing open. Inside, beer cans were all over the place and a man was lying on the bed, flat on his back, stark naked. Duties done, on the way back, the door was shut and the cans were neatly stacked in a pyramid outside the door.

Next morning, we went down for breakfast. It was one of the best breakfasts I have eaten, nicely cooked bacon and eggs, large sausages, and all the trimmings. While we were eating, the farmers began to trickle in, distinctly hung-over, trailing with them bottles of soft drink.

We set off again, taking the Alpine Way through Thredbo, and this time resolved that we would try booking ahead early. First Albury, then Wodonga, then Echucha, no rooms were available.

We went on driving. Darkness fell. We made enquiries at a police station with no success. The road traffic authorities advise drivers not to drive tired, but they had no advice what to do in this situation.

By midnight, we were tired but decided not to go on looking. We would have to keep on driving all through the night. We had been warned that it was not safe to try camping at the side of the road. By this time I was almost asleep and Mary took a stint of driving. There were obstacles in the form of kangaroos and wombats crossing the road. As the night went on, our shifts at driving became shorter and shorter until we were only managing half an hour behind the wheel before handing over.

Our original intention had been to drive down the valley of the Murray River, to enjoy the scenery – the only scenery we saw was darkness, the view of the road lit by the car headlights, and the various animals crossing the road! The night became lighter and eventually dawn broke. We crossed the South Australia border and breakfasted at a petrol station. As we wanted to have a look at Adelaide, we drove south and found a motel at Two Wells, where we managed to book a room.

We took a tour through the Barossa Valley and went into Adelaide, having a very sleepy look around before returning to Two Wells. A beer made a very welcome break and helped to ease the fatigue. There was no problem sleeping that night.

The next day's driving took us to Ceduna. By this time, booking motel rooms had become easy. In the room there we found a chocolate Easter egg under the bed, so the children saw something of Easter.

The following day was along the dead straight road over the Nullarbor Plain. At first there was some farm land but the soil was dry and dusty and banks of sand drifting over the road supplied the evidence of the drought conditions. Further along, the fields came to an end and, on either side of the narrow tarmacadam, low shrubby heath stretched as far as the eye could see. From time to time, large trucks and road trains came in the opposite direction and whoever was driving needed to take care as the draught and tail-wind would catch the suitcases on the roof and cause some instability.

Petrol stations were spaced so that one appeared just as we were nearing the end of the tank. Mary was keeping a record of the petrol and where we had to stop to buy it. At one place she said that we had been here before. This seemed highly improbable. It was a place called "Deli". Later we discovered that "Deli" was a contraction for "delicatessen"!

The three children in the back seat were remarkably tolerant but had the occasional display of bickering. We had taken the precaution of purchasing a book of car games to lessen their boredom.

The road approached the sea and, at one point, to break the journey, we went down a side road to the cliffs overlooking the Great Australian Bight. On the slopes down to the cliffs the winds created an ideal draught for some people hang-gliding.

On to Eucla, where the showers were salt water and the living conditions basic, to say the least.

For the next day's journey, we went on to Norseman, where we had to decide whether to travel to Perth by Kalgoorlie or by Esperance and Albany. We chose the former and had no difficulty in finding a motel in which to stay. As there was only one more day's travel ahead of us, we stayed an extra day and spent it exploring Kalgoorlie, including a tour below ground through the Hainault gold mine. It was the first day of April, 1978.

On the last day, we stopped to see Coolgardie and took a walk through the cemetery, where adventurers who had walked all the way from Perth with all their belongings on a wheelbarrow to seek their fortune by finding gold, had ended up, many dying of dysentery and other diseases of poverty.

Then we reached Perth, to start plans of how we were again going to start a working life.

Chapter 30

Beginning a New Practice

After our initial stay at Forrest House Motor Lodge, on subsequent sojourns in Perth, we had been unable to get accommodation at that hotel and found another, equally inexpensive. It was called the Terminal Motor Lodge. I do not know how it been given this name as it was nowhere near the airport, or the rail or bus terminals. It had one advantage as it had a television set, which interested the children.

There were a number of things to do. First we went out to take a look at the locality of Huntingdale and introduced ourselves to the pharmacist. The proposed medical centre was to be an extension to the existing shopping centre, and would occupy a space roughly equal to the shops already there. The district was made up of small brick bungalows.

I had to find a job until the practice started and Dr Cameron of Armadale introduced us to Dr Roger Nicoll, who ran the Southside Medical Service, which catered for after-hours duties and also locums for doctors who wanted holidays. On the day that he interviewed me, in the Terminal Motor Lodge, it was very windy. Mary and the children were in the garden but soon had to go under cover, as bits of tile and chimney pots began falling around them. If any of the debris had hit anyone, it might indeed have been "terminal"! However, we had been told that Perth was the third windiest city in the world so we did not worry too much about it.

A house to live in was the next objective. We were driven around looking at places. The weather was as wild as ever and we later discovered that a cyclone, named Alby, had hit Perth.

On looking at available houses in Huntingdale there were none that would take our furniture. This was a problem that we would have to look at on another day. Next, we needed to find a place to rent. It would be too expensive to continue living in motels or hotels. An estate agent found us a small house for which we had a lease for a year.

The after-hours job began. I was to work from about 6.00 pm until midnight.

The first call came in. It was to a house in Tuart Hill, away up in the northern parts of Perth. I was half-way there when there was another call. The first call was to a man who was so intoxicated that he could not stand. He was an alcoholic who at first refused to be admitted for treatment but eventually agreed.

That night I drove round in this strange city, with the aid of a map. At one point I found myself driving on the wrong side of one of the highways. There were many calls and, although I was supposed to finish at midnight, I did not reach the last call until six o'clock in the morning.

And so this sort of work went on. The day was for sleeping but there were still many things to do.

It had become obvious that, in order to live in Huntingdale, none of the houses in the locality would accommodate our furniture and we would need to build our own house.

We went along to see our architect friend, Peter Hunt, then went out touring the locality to see if there were any suitable sites. Peter spotted an empty area at the top of a small rise. Fortunately he was a friend of the developer and managed to get us the first option on it. As we had no funds, we would require an interview with the bank manager to negotiate a loan. There was a somewhat nervous wait but we succeeded in obtaining two mortgages, one for the land and one for the building. The manager also advised us to have a Financial Manager to look after our insurance and money matters generally. He gave us a name and we took his advice.

The children were introduced to the local primary school in Huntingdale. As it was some distance from our rented house, Mary had to walk there every day with them, a distance of about a mile each way.

From time to time we went round to watch the progress on the building of the house, and, eventually, nearly a year later, it was built, ready for occupation.

In the meantime, I continued with the night work and also managed to obtain a number of locum jobs, acting for doctors on holiday. During one period it became very arduous as other doctors had left the Service and Roger Nicoll and I were doing all the work between us.

On Christmas Day, Roger and his wife had asked us for Christmas dinner, but of course I was on call. Roger had said that Christmas was usually quiet but that particular year it was different and I was called from house to house all over Perth, a city which is forty kilometres across. At one house, when I knocked, the person who answered said that there was no one ill there. When I then asked why I had been called, it was found that there was indeed someone lying on a bed in a back room.

Shortly after I had started with the Southside Medical Service, I came across Blair Malcolm again, as he had moved into Perth to work. He said that the aluminium mining company, Alcoa, was looking for a doctor. As I had previous industrial medical experience I managed to obtain the work, which involved visiting the company on two afternoons each week.

It was tiring work and sometimes during the night I was finding myself almost falling asleep at the wheel of the car. Mary then decided that she would come with me and help with the map reading. But what then were we to do with the children? We fitted up three plastic mattresses in the back of the station wagon, on which they slept as we did the calls. It became known as going out on the "Razzle-dazzle"!

A year after we had leased the rented house our own new home was completed and the furniture, which had been stored in Penang, arrived by ship. It was transported to the house and all the packing cases were moved into the house, under cover.

We knew that when the new practice started we would be fully occupied, so we took a short three-week duty trip to the UK to see the various families, not knowing when we might have a chance of doing so in the future.

We arrived in London at Easter and caught up with my Uncle Gordon and cousins Peter and John. For once, as it was Easter, the London streets were deserted and I dared to drive the family round the famous sights: Buckingham Palace, the Houses of Parliament, Trafalgar Square, and out to see the *Cutty Sark*.

Next, we drove to Bishopbriggs to see Mary's father. As we crossed Beatock there was snow, which the children had never seen. More fell that night at Bishopbriggs, and the kids found it very exciting, building a snow-man and throwing snowballs.

Finally we travelled to Aberdeen and my own parents.

After what was a very fleeting visit, we returned to Huntingdale. We passed the site of where the new medical centre was to be but there was no sign of it being started. Mary went down to the offices of the City Council of Gosnells to enquire about it. She was told, "Didn't you know, but the Council has cancelled all plans for a medical centre."

What were we going to do now?

We had gone into considerable debt building a new house in the area on a promise that had not materialized. I would not be happy continuing the after-hours work indefinitely.

There was one possibility. We would build a new medical centre.

In the meantime we could start practising from our own home. We enquired of the Council but were told that the house "was not zoned" for such an operation. However, they agreed that we could do so for six months only. About this time, the owner of the building site next to our new house came to tell us that he had decided to sell his block of land and asked if we wished to buy it. This might be feasible, and the Council was again approached. They reluctantly agreed, provided that the premises we built could be converted back to a dwelling.

A further loan had to be negotiated with the bank manager – a third mort-gage: one for the land on which our house was built, one for the house itself and one for the new building and set-plan house that was to be built on it.

Thus our new practice started on 1st July 1979. It was a propitious start, as it was the first day of the new financial year.

We had been allowed to advertise for three days and opened the doors and waited. Although Mary was a qualified teacher, she became the medical receptionist. We wheeled a typing table into the vestibule of the house and this became the waiting room. After over an hour, the first patient, a lady, came in. The consultation took place and there was plenty of time for a chat.

She left and we continued to wait. However there were no further patients that day. At least we had seen one and my fledgling practice had begun.

Chapter 31

Growth

After-hours work was supplying our income during this period, but the new practice slowly grew. A drawback was that our consulting room was situated away from the main traffic of the locality.

Originally I had intended to be on call for the practice during the night as well as seeing patients during the day. However, very shortly after the start of the practice, one of the patients began calling me at eleven o'clock *every* night. She kept this up for a week, by which time I had had enough and henceforth the calls went through to the after-hours service. I remained available at night for maternity calls and patients who turned up at the hospital.

Mary had taken over the books, the appointments and the accounts, running on a minimum of staff to economise. We continued to work from the house and watched the new surgery premises being built next door. Within the six months, the building was completed and we moved in and continued consulting without a break. With much more room to move, it was comfortable.

From now on, we worked five and a half days a week in the consulting rooms, Wednesday and Thursday afternoons with Alcoa, alternate nights, Saturday afternoons and Sundays on call for the after-hours practice, and this was to be life for the next period of time.

Naturally I had to be careful with the after-hours work, so as not to attract patients to my own new practice, particularly when seeing patients of nearby practices. However, some patients who had no regular GP came to see me at the surgery as a new patient to the practice. One in particular, James Frost, a somewhat rough-looking man whose cut hand I had sutured, became a staunch patient of the practice.

As each after-hours call was a new patient, and on the face of it, "an emergency", I never knew what the problem was going to be, which added interest and a bit of excitement. Inevitably, there would be the call at about eleven o'clock at night from a drug addict requesting a pethidine injection – they were always very specific about which drug they wanted – ostensibly for an attack of migraine or renal colic.

There was one girl who called me repeatedly. When she complained of renal colic, I would give atropine without the pethidine. As atropine is an anti-spasmodic, it would have some effect if it was truly colic. After the injection, she knew I had given something although not the pethidine she was seeking, and she was very curious to know what I had given. For migraine, a cocktail of largactil and phenergan was given which would have the effect of getting the patient some sleep but, again, without the pethidine. That particular girl always kept her face covered when I visited so that I never saw her face.

There were the poignant times. One Saturday afternoon, I was called to a small house in Beckenham, a low-income area in the southern suburbs in Perth. The husband had chest pain. Not being well-off myself in those days, an ECG machine was not part of the gear I carried round for out-of-office calls. All I could do was to advise hospital. I watched the wife pack a cheap electric razor and a few meagre belongings. The worry and anxiety could be clearly seen. With the uncertainty of what the future might hold for them, the sadness of the situation demonstrated the pathos of human life.

Another afternoon, there was a similar call for severe chest pain. This time, I was too late. The patient was dying. It was one of the many times I encountered the problem that, in doing cardiopulmonary resuscitation, often the patient vomits into your mouth. The ambulance arrived but all attempts to revive the dying man were unsuccessful.

The ambulance gone and the call just being completed, there was a call to Perth Airport. I arrived and was ushered through the back parts of the airport building to a runway on which there was a plane with an Australian insignia on its side. Inside, there was not the usual aircraft seating but couches arranged round the cabin, with tables. One of the air hostesses had earache. The drum was inflamed. There was no way that she would be able to fly, otherwise she might have suffered a burst eardrum. She was extremely disappointed. In the course of the visit I had remembered that the Prime Minister, Malcolm Fraser, was visiting Perth.

Late one evening, there was a call to the house of a prominent Perth businessman. His father, a thin man in his seventy or eighties, had sustained a laceration to the back of his hand. The skin of the entire back of the hand was peeled back and was lying over the forearm, giving a fine anatomical display of the tendons underneath. He refused to go to hospital and insisted that I deal with it. There was nothing that would change his mind. I reluctantly sterilized the necessary instruments, cleaned up the wound, and started to stitch the skin back in place. While working at this, I asked how it happened. Somewhat reluctantly, he said that it had happened in a bar. With difficulty, it came out that it had been lacerated with a metal chair. Even more reluctantly it was revealed that there had been a fight. I worked on and he said that I came from Scotland. I agreed. He said that he had once been to Scotland. He had spent two years in Glasgow, at a place called Barlinnie. Barlinnie was the high security prison for criminals!

About two weeks later, I had occasion to see this old man again. The wound had healed beautifully.

Maternity work also provided night calls. But one morning, we had just woken at six o'clock when there was a call from the husband of a patient just round the corner from us that his wife was delivering. I went round straight away to find that the patient was in full labour. The couple had not been able to afford a bed and the labouring woman was on a mattress on the floor. It was a case of doing it all on my hands and knees. The baby's head appeared, like Oliver Twist, in a caul. By this time, Mary had appeared with my medical bag; I opened the caul, and delivered the baby. Then the ambulance, which the husband had called, arrived and the ambulance men came in. The placenta was delivered and the patient was transferred to hospital for follow-up care.

About a year after the practice had started, we decided that, for once, we would take a Sunday off. The children were loaded into the car and we drove south. We had a picnic lunch in a forest and went as far as Busselton before turning back.

One day a patient, originally from the southwest of Scotland, consulted me. She had an eczematous rash on both hands. I asked what she had been handling. The story emerged that her job was to wash plastic flower pots in a solution. She did not know what was in the solution. Treatment was prescribed and she was asked to find out what chemicals she was handling. This became very difficult as the labels had been removed from the bottles of additives to the water in which her hands were immersed. Despite treatment, the rash became worse and the patient was referred to a dermatologist, Dr Peter Randell, who skin-tested the patient and found that she was highly allergic to chrome.

It was advised that the solution should be avoided at all costs but the relationship between the patient and her employer became very unpleasant. At one point, the manager, who owned the business, had reportedly told the afflicted woman that, in his opinion, both hands should be cut off, at her neck.

In spite of all efforts, the dermatitis became so severe that the patient could not touch anything made of steel, which contains chromium, and even sunlight caused the rash to flare. Legal action for compensation was taken and the local Member of Parliament, who was very supportive, was brought into the picture.

Later that year, the patient was watching an air display on television. At one point she had reportedly said, "Isn't that —'s plane?" naming her employer. Immediately after, the plane went into a dive, crashed, and her unpleasant boss was killed.

A year or two later, the case reached the court. The lights in the court had to be dimmed, as by this time the disease had become so bad that any light exacerbated the condition. The settlement ran into six figures – until then, the largest in Western Australian history, as a special house, in which the unfortunate woman would have to spend the rest of her life, had to be built, with special window glass filtering out ultra-violet light, and an indoor swimming pool.

Another consequence was that, because I had involved the local Member of Parliament, Mary and I were invited to the Governor of Western Australia's garden party that year.

In 1981, I sat the examination for the Royal Australian College of General Practitioners. Prior to the examination I had little or no time to do any studying and decided to try to catch up on necessary swotting on the eve of the examination. I had just started reading when there was a telephone call from the stable where Seonaid was learning riding. She had fallen off her horse and hurt her right arm.

Mary and I drove straightaway to the stable and it was evident that Seonaid had fractured her arm at the elbow. I contacted an orthopaedic surgeon,

Don Webb, gave a pethidine injection to Seonaid and drove her gingerly to Fremantle Hospital. That afternoon was spent in the operating theatre, where the fracture was manipulated under general anaesthetic and plastered. So much for my studying.

For the clinical aspect of the examination, I elected to be examined in my own surgery. The examiners were Dr Howard Watts and Dr Frank Mansfield. I passed the examination and gained my Fellowship of The Royal Australian College of General Practitioners.

In Penang, the children had been given pocket money. With our impoverished circumstances, this practice had discontinued. Early in 1981, they came to us and said that they had seen a black-and-white television set for sale for $100 and, if they saved up that amount of money, could they buy it? Until then we had not had any television. We agreed and they set about doing odd jobs, earning small amounts of money until they had gained the $100. As they had worked so assiduously, we contributed considerably and bought a better, colour television set.

The results of this were somewhat variable. Graeme was then fourteen, Seonaid was twelve and Catriona was ten. Thereafter, Graeme was the best-read, while Catriona read little.

The 1st of August 1981 was my parent's Golden Wedding anniversary. It was quite beyond our means for us to return to Aberdeen to share in the celebrations. The children drew lots to see who would go. Seonaid won. She was then eleven years of age. Arrangements were made for her to travel as an unaccompanied child, which meant that an air hostess would be assigned to look after her. On her return, the air hostess taking her by the hand was the daughter of one of my Sri Lankan patients. This air hostess was later to marry one of the sons of the President of Sri Lanka.

One of the last night calls before I quit the after-hours service was an emergency call to a young woman who was attempting suicide and was having last-minute qualms. We were at the house within ten minutes. Inside the house was silence. I rang the bell and knocked without any answer. On trying the front door handle, it was obvious that the door was open. Being hesitant to intrude, I called the police, who came right away. The policeman opened the door and we went in.

All was silent. We searched the rooms one by one, looking under beds and inside wardrobes, expecting to find a body. It was eerie. When we concluded that the house was empty, the hospitals were tried. Eventually we found that the woman had panicked just after she had phoned the service and gone to Fremantle Hospital. Before leaving, the policeman made sure that all the house lights were on. It had been a frustrating and unrewarding waste of time.

It was about this time that there was a complaint from the Health Insurance Commission that my "profile" was not normal. I was seeing a lot of patients for protracted consultations and had a few "brief" consultations. I was visited by an inspector. It turned out that the inspector was a Scot who had worked in rural areas in East Africa and had this as a semi-retirement job. One of the first things he asked was if I was related to Dr Mary Esslemont. My affirmative answer had the effect of making him most respectful. It was pointed out that, with the structure of health benefits, a series of long consultations was less financially rewarding than seeing a string of short consultations. All that was different was that my style of practice did not fit the norm. The inspector said that he was satisfied and that I did not need to fear another inspection.

Eventually, in April 1982, the practice had grown and was now self-sufficient. After four years, I was able to discontinue my after-hours work. It was a relief. Apart from potential midwifery work, we were now free at the weekends.

In the meantime, I had been sitting the Malaysian College examination by correspondence, and that year I gained my Membership of the College of General Practitioners, Malaysia.

Just over a year after my parents' Golden Wedding, there was a telephone call from my father. My mother had died on 25th September 1982 in Woodend Hospital. Her death was a direct consequence of smoking. My father had been having a meeting of Scouters organizing the Gang Show, when there was a call from the living room. My mother, in trying to light a cigarette, had set the chair in which she was sitting alight. The fire was doused and my mother, badly burned, taken to hospital. However, after a few days, she metaphorically and literally gave up the ghost. She had been unwell and in pain for years, and Seonaid had said that when she had been in Aberdeen in the previous year, one of my mother's hospital appointments had been to the radiotherapy unit, so she had concluded that there was a cancer.

My father had surmised, correctly, that none of us could have afforded to attend the funeral and so he had gone on with the appropriate arrangements in our absence.

With the daily work and without the milestones of holidays, memories of those years are somewhat continual; days ran into weeks, weeks into months, and months into years. It was suggested to my father that he might like to visit us. Due arrangements were made so that he would be with us on the anniversary of my mother's death. He stayed for three months in 1983, celebrating his seventy-eighth birthday in early June, and taking a tour of Margaret River, Pemberton, Albany, then to Greenough and Kalbari. In the meantime, Roger Nicoll from the Southside Medical Service covered the practice for us. At Albany we met up again with Captain Len McLeod, who had retired there.

By this time the practice was busy.

Chapter 32

New Learning

It was during 1984 that a new patient, fresh from Britain, attended the practice. She was English, and had a multitude of symptoms. She showed me a chart that she had brought and said that she had been attending Dr Katharina Dalton in London, having been diagnosed with the premenstrual syndrome (PMS). I had never heard of such a disease and none of my books described the condition. She was being treated with injections of progesterone for the second half of the menstrual cycle.

I wrote to Dr Dalton, who sent me photocopies of her papers researching the illness, and the title of the book she had written, *The Premenstrual Syndrome and Progesterone Therapy.* Progesterone was not obtainable in Australia and a special Government permit was necessary to import it. It was very expensive. I obtained and read Dr Dalton's book, and a long battle began with the Government to see if natural progesterone could be manufactured and sold in Australia. The natural product is very much cheaper than the synthetic progestogens, one of which is actually synthesized from progesterone. Progesterone from the corpus luteum was first discovered in 1929, so that any patent rights were long out-of-date and drug companies were not interested in manufacturing progesterone products. Only one produced the product in injection form and as implants.

Synthetic progestogens, although they have progesterone-like properties on the lining of the womb, have different chemical compositions and their actions on the brain and other organs are quite different. In fact, they tend to increase premenstrual syndrome symptoms because, of course, their action on the pituitary gland suppresses the production of the patient's own natural hormone.

Now cognizant with the condition, the complaints of a number of puzzling patients became clearer. One in particular had presented with headaches, aches and pains, a feeling of being swollen up and a number of other things. I had asked her to come in a week's time for a long appointment so that I could do a thorough examination and give myself a chance to try to diagnose the condition. She did not attend but turned up two months later with similar complaints. When asked why she had not kept the appointment for the examination, she said that she had felt better so had not bothered to come.

The husband of another patient had called me out one evening as his wife had become decidedly queer quite suddenly. They had been visiting friends and she had just started a second drink when she had become almost psychotic, with marked shivering. As the "toxic shock" condition had just begun appearing in the literature, I sent her to hospital, where she was admitted. She had quickly recovered and was discharged next day.

The next month, symptoms recurred and it was realized that when these symptoms appeared, so did the period. She was started on natural progesterone with very satisfactory results.

Then, patients who wondered if they might have this largely unknown disease started coming in. Diagnosis was relatively easy. All the patient had to do was keep a daily diary of how they felt, leaving it blank if they felt well and putting a cross if they were "out-of-sorts". A collection of "Xs" before, and sometimes running into, the period was diagnostic. In those early days, I did a number of hormonal and other studies to exclude other possibilities.

One young lady was somewhat puzzling. She had a long history of ill-health and her previous doctor had eventually given an injection of testosterone which had the result of stopping her periods altogether. Without the monthly menses, how was it possible to establish when her premenstruum was? I ran a number of hormonal studies, which showed that she apparently had no circulating reproductive hormones whatsoever. Progesterone had no effect. Working on the surmise that, in life, oestrogens primed the uterine lining to react to progesterone, I decided to try giving a course of oestrogen followed by progesterone. It seemed to work. Her symptoms subsided and she became much more normal and rational. It seemed that progesterone did, indeed, need oestrogen for it to have its effect.

The complication was that her husband, as carer, tended to treat her in a very parental manner, which resulted in her responding, reactively, in a child-like way. She eventually annulled their Catholic marriage and she married a barrister. Unfortunately, years of illness had conditioned her into a mentality in which her approach to interpersonal relationships was damaged, and that marriage also eventually broke.

Early in 1985, Dr Glenn Otis Bair of Topeka, Kansas, wrote to me inviting me to a conference on PMS in Anaheim, California, and asking if I would present a paper. I was intrigued; it seemed to be an opportunity to learn more about this condition, about which there seemed to be so little information, and what information there was seemed to be so contradictory and confusing.

We were still struggling to make ends meet financially, but it seemed important to learn all I could, and it was decided that I would attend the conference, which was to be held at Disneyland (some people thought "appropriately enough"). Obviously, I was in no position to present a paper but the chairman of the conference, Glenn Bair, persisted, so I decided to describe the patient, with her permission, which she gladly gave, about the need for oestrogen as well as progesterone.

The conference took place in late June and early July. It was my first visit to America, a country which I was, until then, not very keen to visit. It was a very long flight and I eventually arrived in the room in the hotel, tired out. I telephoned Frank Varese, who was running the conference, to let him know I was there. He asked if I was hiring a car, to which I replied that it was very unlikely after a twenty-four hour flight, in a country I did not know, where people drove on the wrong side of the road!

I found America fascinating and the Disneyland Hotel was a little town in itself.

At the meetings I met various people connected with PMS research and met Dr Dalton for the first time.

I had a couple of days or so free after the seminars and used the time to visit Disneyland, Universal Studios and the *Queen Mary*, on which I bought a butter cooler, something I had been looking for ever since our days in Malaysia and which was much less necessary now.

Back to Australia and back to consulting and delivering babies.

In 1985, I was invited to become one of the examiners for the Royal Australian College of General Practitioners, and I have been examining for the College since then.

Next year, on 13th March 1986, Mary was found to have large uterine fibroids.

At about that time, one of the drug companies organized a seminar on cardiac medicine over a Saturday and Sunday in the Captain Freycinet Hotel, which had opened the previous year in Margaret River. We were long over-due for a change and so decided to attend. We had visited the area with my father in 1983 but had then stayed at Stone Cottages, about twelve miles south of the town and had two days of touring in the caves and forests without visiting the town itself. On this occasion, we were captivated by this small resort. As an adjunct to the medical discussions we were introduced to the wineries.

Mary had her operation, during which a five-and-a-half-pound group of fibroids was removed. No malignancy was found. During her convalescence, the College rang up and asked if the practice would accept a GP Registrar for training. Thus Dr Jenny Brockis joined the practice for a period of six months.

With another doctor in the practice came our first opportunity in eleven years to take a family holiday, and Mary, Seonaid, Catriona and I spent a week at the Penang Club. On the first morning there, we went for breakfast and, when the Club "boys" (servants) saw us, they were very pleased and old acquaintances were re-established. Some of the "boys" had served at our wedding.

In 1986, two Australians, Barlow and Chambers, were executed for drug smuggling in Malaysia. It caused an international furore. Our daughters had projects they had to write for school, so we went into the *Straits Times* and the *Straits Echo* offices for material. Of interest was the concern of the news-papers' staff at the consternation the hangings had caused.

We were all invited to a meal at the Penang Club by Ian Meek and Tom Hepworth. There it was mentioned that Dr Wilson had developed a tremor and that it was thought that he was suffering from some neurological disease.

Not long after we had returned to work, one evening at about eight o'clock a man consulted me. He said, "All I want is a pethidine injection. I am trying to 'come off' drugs and I just need an injection to 'tide me over'."

I replied: "If you want to stop drugs, the last thing you need is to have an injection of pethidine." I suggested that if he was genuine in wanting to get off the drug habit, he would be better to attend the Government drug rehabilitation centre. He said that he did not want to go there as then he would be identified as a drug addict and would not be able to obtain a passport.

I asked: "Why do you need a passport?"

He answered: "Because I want to go to Penang."

I said that it might not be a good idea to go to Penang. After all, look what happens to drug addicts there, such as Barlow and Chambers. I added: "The Director for Narcotics in Malaysia is a friend of mine" (which was true).

He then questioned whether or not I agreed with what they did in Malaysia and I pointed out that it cured the addicts of their habit for once and for all. I again added that, in China, if the police saw someone on the streets who looked as if they were under the influence of drugs, they locked him in a cell and, if the prisoner was having withdrawal symptoms next morning, they shot him.

By this time, my "patient" was looking considerably paler, and I reminded him to sign the book as he went out!

During my time in practice thereafter, few drug addicts asked me for narcotics. One of the favourite ploys was to complain of a severe migraine attack. With migraine, my policy was to do a careful examination of the patient. After all, I might be dealing with a patient with meningitis or a brain tumour. One day, a new patient consulted me, ostensibly suffering from a migraine attack. I suspected that this was a drug addict trying to get a shot of pethidine (they were always very specific about which drug "worked"). I did the usual full examination. A query came into the surgery a day or two later as the Medicare number seemed to be in doubt. The Medicare card, it turned out, had been stolen and belonged to someone else. I was able to give to the police a very full description of the person I had examined, including height, weight, and colour of hair. When she was caught, she had on her many stolen Medicare cards.

In 1986, there was an invitation to attend another conference, in Melbourne, on "Hormones and Behaviour". This conference, which lasted four days, only presented widely divergent views on PMS, and I gained the impression that many of those there were only there to be there and to make themselves heard. However, there were some interesting speakers.

One of the symptoms of PMS is a feeling of bloating and being swollen up. When fluid retention takes place in heart or kidney failure, the dependent parts of the body, the legs, usually swell first. In PMS, the swelling seems to be felt all over the body. One of the researchers had found that, in the premenstruum, there is a shift of fluid between the various body compartments, intevascular, extravascular, and intracellular, accounting for the feeling of general bloating.

Another speaker, a Dutch professor of obstetrics, described an occasion where he had made an error of judgment and how important it is to be honest and frank with the patients.

No mention was made of the use of progesterone.

Prior to effective contraception, once married, a woman's life was very often a series of pregnancies. During pregnancy, body progesterone levels are high and, because of the repeated pregnancies, periods are rare. Thus, in the natural state, a woman goes through life with a much higher level of progesterone than in the present day. The use of progesterone in PMS, when seen in this light, becomes rational and very unlikely to be harmful.

Related to the premenstrual syndrome is post-natal depression and progesterone can be used to prevent this life-threatening condition. One of my patients had repeated pregnancies because she felt so much better when she was pregnant than she felt in the non-pregnant state. Unfortunately, after delivery, she would develop post-natal depression and progesterone was effective in keeping this at bay. Interestingly, at one point she developed depression due to other factors (exogenous depression) which was treated by counselling, and she stated that this type of depression felt different from the post-natal type.

Chapter 33

"Life is Not Meant to be Easy ..."

"Life is not meant to be easy, my child,
but take courage: it can be delightful"

(George Bernard Shaw,
***Back to Methuselah*, rev. ed., 1930).**

Since Malcolm Fraser misquoted this in the 5th Alfred Deaken Lecture on 20th July 1971, omitting the second message in the quotation, it has been attributed to him telling us not to expect too much. Problems arise all through life and it is up to us to deal with these problems as they arise.

The trainee Registrar who followed Jenny Brockis did not have the easy personable character of Jenny, who attracted patients. There was eventually a confrontation and she left. We were back to a one-doctor practice but with an increased patient load. The General Practitioner College was helpful, finding a doctor who was looking for a job. Dr Alastair Currie was laid-back and easy-going and got on well with the patients. He agreed to work in the practice for two years as an Assistant. We would have preferred a doctor who would be interested in becoming a partner, but it was better than nothing.

1986 ran into 1987 and life settled down to regular, day-to-day work. A medical practice had started not far away, prominently placed, on a crossroads of the main roads in the locality. The doctor who had begun the group was reputed to have boasted that he would take over all the patients in the district. It was not long before there was a complaint from the Medical Board that the lettering on our signboard was bigger than was allowed, and that I was advertising qualifications that I did not have. An employee was sent out to investigate but she found that the allegations were all false.

A new receptionist, Sue Miles, was employed by the practice. My father paid another visit and we repeated short holidays to Margaret River and Kalbarri. I was also invited to join the Rotary Club of Thornlie, which I did.

This year, there were two conferences on PMS, one run by the International Society of Psychosomatic Obstetrics and Gynaecology at Kia Wah Island in South California and the next, a few days later, in Chicago. The Kia Wah conference was well attended by notable authors on the subjects, but again progesterone was not discussed. At the end of this conference, there were two or three days to spare before the Chicago conference began. The Income Tax Department wanted me to return to Perth between the conferences if I wished to claim them as necessary expenses! Fortunately our accountant managed to scotch this ridiculous idea.

A new Omni Hotel had opened in Charleston, near Kia Wah Island, and I managed to book a room at a very reasonable price, which was their opening gesture. Thus began my love for this historic city.

I explored the town, Fort Sumter, and the nearby Middleton Plantation, and attended a "make-up" at the Charleston Rotary Club lunch. The Club President was Mr Alfred Pinckney, a famous Charleston name, associated with the American Civil War. As I sat at the round table, I read the names of those at the table, most of them Civil War names. At one point, an older man sitting next to me leant over and said "You're Scots, aren't you?" When I affirmed the fact, he said that he had never been to Scotland but his grandfather had been but had got stuck there and had not been able to return to Charleston for six years. On being asked the reason, he replied that it was the time of the "Great Unpleasantness", which is one of the names the people there termed the Civil War. The Civil War had taken place from 1861 to 1865, little more than one hundred years previously.

After the lunch, as I had been looking for some books on the American Constitution, he took me to visit the University, so that I could get some advice.

The few days over, I took the plane en route to Chicago. Not long airborne, I saw from the aircraft window a swathe of land where the vegetation looked younger that on either side – the area where, a hundred years earlier, General Grant had burned "from Atlanta to the sea".

Chicago itself was interesting and I liked the city, which was not at all forbidding as is suggested by the cinema. The stores were fabulous and I had time to ascend, in the elevator, the 100-storey-high skyscraper known as the John Hancock Center, a journey that took 60 seconds with no feeling of movement. This was achieved by the lift slowly accelerating half the distance, and then slowly decelerating. The view from the top was magnificent, looking through two-inch-thick glass windows at the panorama and down 1,250 feet to Michigan Avenue. The skyscraper could be felt gently swaying with the wind.

The conference in Chicago was a segment of a larger meeting of the American College of Obstetricians and Gynecologists held on 18th September 1987. In order to attend, I was made an honorary MD for the event.

During the course of the meetings, the Dalton Society was given its title. Glenn Bair became the first President. Other items at the conference were also of interest. For the first time, I heard of what was to become known as "the triple test" for Down's syndrome and other birth defects *in utero*. After my return to Australia, I was somewhat amused when a pathologist visited me, some six months later, to tell me about the test but found that I knew more than he.

It was also then that I started to learn about the controversies in medical politics, with each faction clinging to their own pet theories about disease and treatment.

Life ran on but eventually Alastair Currie completed his two years and was about to take a trip around the world with his new wife. Again was started the search for a new doctor. The College had a doctor, Craig Hilton, who had just completed his training Registrarship and was waiting to sit his examinations. He joined the practice, but hardly had he done so when he announced that he had also booked a round-the-world with his new wife!

We survived, and when he returned, the practice continued as a two-doctor practice.

Early one morning, just as we put the telephone through to taking calls for the surgery, Mary answered it to the wife of James Frost. The story was that in the middle of the night, Jim had been wakened by severe chest pain. They had straightaway gone to Royal Perth Hospital where they were seen by a young lady house doctor. Jim was thirty-two years old at the time. She had examined him and taken an electrocardiogram which she said was normal. The house officer spoke to the registrar and Jim was told that he had indigestion and given an antacid. They waited a while but the antacid had no effect on the pain. Jim and his wife were told they could go home, which they did.

The pain had persisted and Jim wanted to come and see me. From the sound of the history I thought that it would be best if they returned to the hospital but Jim's wife said, "What if we are sent home again?" As this was possible, although my appointments were fully booked, Mary asked them to come and said we would fit Jim in as soon as possible.

He was seen as the second patient and the story he related sounded very like a myocardial infarction. He had already had an ECG but it is possible that some ECGs, for instance when the infarction is of the septum of the heart, can look almost normal and very difficult to interpret. It would be a waste of time, therefore, and possibly misleading, to repeat the ECG, and I decided to check the cardiac enzymes in the blood. Blood was taken and sent as a priority to the laboratory. James was told to rest at home.

About an hour later, the lab phoned. The enzymes were very high. Jim had suffered a massive heart attack.

I telephoned the day registrar at Royal Perth Hospital and gave the story. I did not want the patient to be sent home again. The registrar said for him to come in at once, I telephoned the patient's wife and explained that he was to go back into Royal Perth Hospital in spite of her doubts that he might not be well received. Jim survived, but with a very badly damaged heart muscle.

Meanwhile in the practice, obstetrics continued to keep me busy. One evening I had just completed a delivery at Armadale Hospital at eleven at night when the phone in the labour room rang. Sister answered it. It was Mary. I had promised to do a domiciliary delivery for a patient, on the understanding that she telephone me right away when the labour began. She lived at Two Rocks, north of Perth. Here I was, in Armadale, in the far south of Perth. Mary asked to come with me in case I felt tired. The journey was over forty kilometres. We set off, driving the full lengths of the Kwinana and Mitchell Freeways. Half way up, talking, I inadvertently left on a side road and had to get back on the freeway again. We arrived at Two Rocks at about 5.00 am.

The delivery went well and the baby was delivered at 6.00 am, just as the sun rose, lighting the sea, in view through the picture window of the bedroom. It turned out to be a beautiful delivery.

The financial situation in Australia was not good. Interest rates were reaching 20 percent, and we had three mortgages. Our situation in the back streets of Huntingdale was still somewhat of a stumbling block. Shortly before this, relatives on both sides of the family had died and, although it was sad that we would not see these people again, we were left money in their wills which eased our very dire financial situation to a certain extent. If this had not happened I do not know how we would have got out of our debts.

In the meantime, a patient who suffered from paranoid schizophrenia had one of his attacks. At one point, he had left his car standing in the middle of the road, all doors open, as he claimed that the car radio was sending him messages. Another time, his wife was discussing him with his psychiatrist when a neighbour came quickly in to say that the patient, who was an electrician, had connected the telephone to loudspeakers and that the conversation was being broadcast to the entire street. He had to be urgently certified. The only Justice of the Peace available was Pat Morris, who was standing to become the new Mayor of Gosnells. Armed with the commitment certificate, the police were contacted to take him to the mental hospital. A police car drew up at the patient's house but the patient, who was an excellent driver, immediately jumped into his car and sped on through Perth, leaving all police vehicles standing.

Mary approached the City Council of Gosnells to enquire why, while we had been denied a surgery on a main road, another practice had been allowed to start a practice in a much more advantaged area. As we had made the acquaintance of Pat Morris who had, by this time, been installed as Mayor, Mary contacted her. Mayor Morris made enquiries but all previous correspondence at the Gosnells Council had vanished. Fortunately we had kept carbon copies of all the letters. The problem now was to find a suitable building.

On the main road, at one of the corners, opposite the shopping centre, there was a row of display homes with a car park, the entrance being from the side street. The manager had heard of our problem and offered us the corner display home, a condition being that they wished to rent it back from us for a year until its use for display was past.

The City Council then stated that we would have to buy the building first, then they would decide whether or not we would be allowed to use it as a medical practice! At least the corruption in Malaysia is open.

Craig and I worked away in the current building while all these arrangements were going on.

There was one episode that nearly had an unfortunate ending. Craig appeared in the doorway of my consulting room, in obvious distress. A patient had come to see him with a severe asthma attack. Despite all his efforts with ventolin inhalation, the young boy was getting worse. I went in and the youth was moribund. I sought a vein, which was rapidly collapsing, and injected hydrocortisone. As I injected it, Craig said that the patient's heart had stopped. Despite this, the boy came to, very fortunately, despite Craig's assertions that the hydrocortisone had not had time to work.

Craig had been with the practice for nearly two years by this time and we had discussed the possibility of him becoming a partner.

In May 1990, the College of GPs had arranged an off-shore conference, lasting two weeks, in Kuala Lumpur and Penang. I had put in a booking and, later that year, a Dalton Society conference was due which I felt I had a duty to attend. The conference was to be in Oklahoma. This time Mary would accompany me and we would also take a holiday in America.

In March or April, Craig stated that he wished to leave the practice at the end of April. After persuasion, he agreed to stay on until the end of May. By this time the new surgery premises were ready. One weekend in April, having finished consulting on Saturday at lunch time, we started work transferring everything – filing cabinets, patients' files, tables, chairs, equipment – to the new premises.

On Monday morning, at 8.30 in the morning, we were seeing our first patients in the new building.

Chapter 34

New Premises

On the morning Mary and I were due to fly to Kuala Lumpur, we thought that there would be time to see four patients. All patients were known to me and four fifteen-minute consultations could be easily accommodated.

The first three patients resulted in no problems, and then the fourth came in, sat down, and said, "My husband has left me."

The couple had been patients of the practice since its inception, had children, and were, to all intents and purposes, happily married. It was a decidedly awkward situation. I could hardly say that I was in a hurry and rush out the door. I am unsure how I managed to deal with the problem within the time frame. Almost certainly I empathized as much as possible.

Consultation with a lawyer would be necessary. I would have explained that I would be away for two weeks. In the meantime it would be good if she could see a lawyer. I would have advised fitting the doors with new locks. I would see her as soon as I got back.

We caught the plane on time. In Kuala Lumpur, we were the first to arrive and were fortunate enough to be given a very nice suite in the hotel. The conference was good. I had only a short time to say hello to Dr Rajakumar as he was there in an official capacity. I also made the acquaintance of Professor Deborah Saltman, who was Professor of General Practice in Queensland and was one of the speakers.

Next week we moved to Penang, where the conference continued at the Mutiara Hotel, Penang's most prestigious hotel, out at Telok Pahang.

Mary contacted Ah Hiang, our former *amah*, whose young daughter, Poh Gaik, came out to visit us. In the hotel Mary received a message that she had a visitor. She went down to the lobby and there was Poh Gaik, resplendent, sitting on one of the large throne-like wicker "peacock" chairs, chairs that no-one else was game to sit on. Seeing Mary, she ran to her, calling out "Mummy". Other wives looked on, startled. Poh Gaik had grown up with our children and had used the same name that our offspring had used. By way of return, the girls had learned a bit of Hokkein and could sing Hokkein songs. Alas, all that learning was forgotten as they grew.

As I attended the conference, Mary visited people in town. One of her first stops was to the Penang Club. As she went in, Tom Hepworth was sitting in the back patio, having a drink. He called out "Mary!" as if she had not been away.

Back in Australia, it was to work as usual. Craig left at the end of the month.

In one of the medical journals, Professor Debbie Saltman, whom I had met in Kuala Lumpur, had written an article discussing the "oversupply" of doctors. I telephoned her and asked, "What oversupply?" I explained that I was unable to get a doctor to help me. She asked if I was in the country and I replied that I was not in the country but in a suburb of the major city of Perth.

In fact, the government was claiming there was an oversupply in order to cut down on medical places in universities and so save money. This dearth of doctors has continued on until the present day.

Very shortly afterward, an assistant was found, Gary Claydon. He was young and was interested in sports medicine.

For the 1990 Dalton Society conference, Mary and I decided that we would make a holiday of it this time. On the eve of our departure, our Financial Manager telephoned. Our savings for retirement had increased painfully slowly. He wanted us to put a sizeable amount into our retirement funds, and mentioned a sum. Mary broke down in tears. To have supplied this amount, we would have to cancel our trip, to which Mary was so much looking forward. We gave a negative answer to the request and took the conference holiday.

We travelled to Britain, then had a tour of Belgium, Luxembourg, Switzerland, Austria, Liechtenstein, Italy and France, including Monte Carlo and Paris.

When the bus had left Rome, one of the passengers from the back came up behind me and to my side. He spoke with an American accent and said that he thought I was a doctor. Another Perth doctor on the tour, sitting across the passage, looked at me. Ever mindful of the stories of litigation in America, I cautiously agreed that I was a doctor.

He asked if I would take a look at his ankle, which he had hurt while descending the spiral stair in the hotel. I replied that, although I was a doctor, I was not registered to practise in Italy and had no x-ray facilities to help with diagnosis. He said that he realized all that but he wanted to know if he could go on with the trip or if he would have to go to hospital. He and his wife had saved up all their working days for this, their first trip overseas.

At the next stop, I examined the ankle. It was tender at the lower end of the fibula. Neither the tibia nor the ligaments were tender. I cautiously said that I thought it looked as if he had a fracture at the lower end of the fibula but that it would need an x-ray to confirm it. I said, that being the case, he could go on with the tour, but that we could strap it up and arrange for him to continue the tour in the back seat, where he could elevate his leg. He agreed to this course of action.

In Britain we saw our relatives, then went on to America, where we visited Washington, New York and Charleston. Washington was impressive, New York unpleasant, and it was the wrong time of year for Charleston, with lots of rain. However, in Charleston, both of us attended the Charleston Breakfast Rotary Club meeting. At breakfast, Mary pointed to one of the dishes and asked what it was. The answer – "Them's grits, ma'am."

The speaker for that meeting was from NASA. He could not get the projector to work!

From there, we went to Topeka in the State of Kansas, where we had been invited to stay by Glenn Bair and his wife. Next day, he took us to Kansas City to watch a match of American football. Mary had been having a problem with blocking of her Eustachian tubes and was using chewing gum to alleviate the trouble. It was delightfully amusing to see her at this football match, in a bright purple coat, chewing gum and jumping up and down with excitement.

Glenn took me along to the Topeka Hospital, where I did a tour, together with a delegation from Russia. The hospital had a computer monitor at each bedside, and had three MRI units. Topeka at that time had a population of about 65,000; Perth, with a population of about one million people, had only one MRI machine! We also visited the United States Air Force base, which was preparing for a possible war with Iraq, and had a tour through the Black Hills, where we saw herds of buffalo. On the way back, Glenn stopped at a winery, the one and only winery in the wide-open prairies of the mid-west, and bought me a bottle of wine.

We next went south to Oklahoma, through the countryside made famous by Bonnie and Clyde. Oklahoma City has a million inhabitants and two Hilton Hotels. We arrived in the evening and sat down for a drink. Mary asked for a brandy and ginger ale. The waiter looked at her rather oddly then went off to bring her back a brandy glass with a measure of brandy and a glass of ginger ale.

Next day the conference was due to start but first we went out to see if we could get some presents for the family. Opposite the hotel was a large store, as large as a supermarket. It sold only riding boots! Thinking about buying a pair of these boots for our younger daughter, we chose a pair and the Glasgow-spoken Mary said to the assistant that she would like to telephone our daughter in Australia before buying them. The assistant then asked us to go on talking in our Australian accents!

Oklahoma City, in the middle of America, is a huge, innocent country town.

From Oklahoma, we flew to Los Angeles. At the airport at Los Angeles, we were met by the American friend who had consulted me in Italy. He said that an x-ray had confirmed the diagnosis and he was delighted that he had been able to go on with the tour. He took us to dinner and we met up with him once more before leaving Los Angeles.

We had booked a hotel in Anaheim, just opposite Disneyland. Mary was very doubtful about Disneyland but agreed to go in. Once in, we had to return another day! Hollywood, Universal Studios, and the *Queen Mary* were also visited, and we had a very entertaining evening at a restaurant called "Crackers".

We ended the holiday at San Francisco, and then completed our circumnavigation of the world, returning to Perth. After her mixed feelings and reluctance at visiting USA, Mary found the place fascinating and the people on their home ground delightful, just as I had on previous occasions.

Chapter 35

Settling in Afresh

Two of the small bedrooms of the display home had been amalgamated to form a larger consulting room. There was another consulting room and a treatment room between the two. The treatment room had an adjustable operating table. A third room had the potentiality of being used by another doctor. There was an adequate waiting area.

Some years previously, the practice, along with 999 others, had been chosen to display a "Doctors Television Network". The television set had been supplied and each month a video came, with a mixture of advertisements, patient advice, and comic sketches. In the course of preparation to see if the practice was suitable to be included, the doctors' waiting times were measured, and I discovered that my patients had to wait an average of thirteen minutes to see me.

There was a reception area with a photocopying machine, and a room behind for storage of patients' files and other paperwork. A separate door led in from the car park to a small room with a patient couch so that a stretcher could be brought in if necessary. This small room could double up as a pathology room where blood samples could be taken by a phlebotomist. There was also a small kitchen where members of the staff were able to have meals.

Our professional accountant, who oversaw our books and handled our tax, was becoming very concerned at the very slow growth of our retirement fund. He advised another financial advisory company and Mary went to see the new person. By this time, she was handling all the money, both practice and personal, and making a very good and precise job of it.

Our new adviser was streets ahead of the previous one, whose management of our accounts was looking after his own income rather than ours. From then on our retirement fund increased rapidly.

Work went on, busy as usual. I would see the patients five and a half days a week. On Saturday afternoon, and occasionally Sunday, I would write reports and letters to consultants.

One of the patients was a diabetic, on insulin. He was very bad at attending regularly, and at one follow-up appointment with Gary, had not appeared. Gary was concerned, and went to his house to make sure he was all right. He did not get a very favourable reception, but did his check-up and made an appointment for the patient to attend the next time.

Again the patient did not appear and we did not see him again. About three months later, another patient, who lived nearby, telephoned to say that the window of the patient's house was covered with flies. Mary spoke to Gary and telephoned the police. Shortly after, the police phoned back. They had found the patient's body inside the door. It had been lying there for three months in the hottest season of the year. They wanted identification. Gary paled and asked if he would have to go round. He was reassured that the police and the coroner would deal with all that.

Graeme by this time had finished school and university and had graduated with a degree in geology. He decided that he would take some time off and had applied for, and been accepted, to assist at Camp America in the Appalachian Mountains. This he completed and had saved enough to do a tour of the eastern states of America. From there he intended to do a tour of South America. Thereafter there were no further telephone calls from him.

Three months went by and we knew that he was due home soon but had heard nothing. Furthermore, he had gained a scholarship to do postgraduate studies at the University of New England at the Lismore campus, which we had to arrange on his behalf.

I had been working hard now for twelve years and, despite feeling tired, was looking forward to Christmas, when I would have a day off. On Christmas Day, everyone had opened their presents. It was about ten o'clock in the morning, I felt very tired and lay down on the couch. The next I knew, I woke and it was getting dark outside. Mary was not too pleased as there was a lot to do in preparation for the Christmas dinner.

Christmas over, I continued to feel exhausted but went on with work as usual. After another week of this, Mary insisted that I see a doctor, so I made an appointment to see Dr John Stokes. I explained to him that I felt tired and told him about the worries we had with Graeme. He examined me, said that the examination seemed normal but that he would do some blood tests. He wondered if I might be a bit hypothyroid.

The results came back, which showed that I was mildly anaemic, that the thyroid stimulating hormone was within normal limits, and that the free thyroxine was a little below the normal limits. It also showed that the triiodothyronine was slightly below normal limits. All other tests showed no abnormality. Free thyroxine may be reduced or increased in the sick euthyroid syndrome with the thyroid stimulating hormone levels not abnormal, so these results were not very clarifying. I was due to see Dr Stokes for follow-up four weeks later.

Graeme had still not contacted us.

We managed to find the name of the tour group in New York with whom he had arranged the South American trip. They did some research. He had completed the tour in Caracas in Venezuela but had doubled back into the country again. We were really worried by this time. There were stories of students who had been lifted from the streets to supply anatomical specimens to universities. Besides the tiredness, I started to have headaches at night and occasionally had to take paracetamol, once even panadeine forte, to get to sleep. I also notice that the headaches tended to come on after even the lightest of alcoholic drinks.

On my return visit to Dr Stokes, Mary accompanied me. I was again examined and again no abnormality was found. While I was dressing after the examination, Dr Stokes asked Mary what it was that worried her. She answered that it was the headaches as I never suffered from headaches. On hearing this, he decided that he would order a special x-ray, a Computerized Axial Tomography scan of the head.

I was, by this time, really worried that I had a malignant brain tumour such as an astrocytoma. Blair Malcolm and some other doctors I knew had died from this.

In the x-ray department, the scan was taken and I waited in the machine. I noticed the radiologists looking at the films but they eventually said that the scan was complete and that a report would go to Dr Stokes. He was to see me a week after the last examination for the result.

I went back to work.

A few days later at the finish of morning surgery, instead of going home for lunch, Mary brought me sandwiches in the surgery kitchen. I was somewhat surprised, and then Mary let me know that I had an appointment to see Dr Stokes that afternoon. He had telephoned in the morning and said that he had the results of the scan and that he wanted to see me.

Mary drove me to the consultant's office. I realized by this time that the scan had shown something. An astrocytoma or a glioma was a distinct possibility which meant that I would not have much longer to live. I wondered how I was going to spend the next, last few months.

We entered the waiting room and then, when Dr Stokes had seen the patient who was with him, we went in to see him.

He put the scans up on the viewing box. I went round the desk to look. I was relieved to see that the brain matter was clear. However, there was a lump the size of a golf ball in the site of the pituitary fossa. It was not one of the highly malignant tumours I had feared, but a tumour that was treatable. By this time Mary, very worried, was asking what was going on and we said that it was a treatable condition.

John Stokes asked which surgeon I wanted to deal with it and I said "Richard Vaughan", to which he replied that that was who he would have chosen himself. He phoned Mr Vaughan, who said that he wanted to see me that afternoon.

In his office, Mr Vaughan fixed up admission to St John of God Hospital and a place at the end of his operating list, on the Friday, ten days later. In the meantime, I had to have an MRI scan and testing of my visual fields. He said that on no account was I to go back to work. To Mary he said: "I'll have him up and running." It was a relief not to have to work.

The MRI scan confirmed the pituitary tumour. The visual field testing showed that I had a visual defect to the left in the upper visual field. John Stokes had missed it on his clinical testing and I had not noticed anything. However, now that I had this knowledge, I discovered that, by quickly and repeatedly blinking, there appeared a green area in the region of the visual defect.

I met Terry McManus, who was to be the other consultant surgeon operating and he described how the operation would be done. Richard Vaughan would approach through the back of the right eye and Mr McManus would operate through the left nostril. The endocrinologist involved was Peter Pullan, whom I knew.

Knowing that there is a risk with every operation, I decided that I did not know enough about Beethoven's piano sonatas and bought a stack of cassettes of them. I did not have time to hear them prior to the operation so I might never have heard them at all!

In the meantime, we had managed to track Graeme at Caracas airport, where he had taken his flight to Miami. We tried to contact him at Miami but he did not telephone. Again we tried to contact him at London airport, and, in fact, got his description. We managed to track him through customs and immigration. Again he did not phone. Eventually he went along to my cousin Peter's house and he telephoned us from there. He was fairly impoverished but had decided that he was going to do a trip in Germany before returning home.

The night before my operation, he arrived back home. He threw his arms round me, sending shock waves of pain through my head.

Chapter 36

Necessary Interlude

I was admitted to hospital on the day that the operation was to take place, and the time was filled with doctor visits and all the other preparations necessary before such an event. There was no time to read, or listen to cassettes. The premedication was given and, an hour later, I was wheeled to theatre. Mary stayed with me all the time. Mr Vaughan came to see me, but the MRI scans had not been sent from the radiology unit. They had to be sent for.

When the scans arrived, Mr Vaughan wheeled me into the anteroom where Geoffrey Gee, the anaesthetist, said a few words, found a vein and sent me to sleep.

When I woke, I was in the intensive care ward. Night had fallen and the lighting was dim. Mary and Seonaid were there. When I opened my eyes, Seonaid burst into tears. Apparently my eyes and face were all yellow from the povidine iodine used as an antiseptic and, of course, there were tubes in my arm, up my nose, everywhere.

Eventually, they left, and I slept fitfully through the night.

Next morning, Peter Pullan came to see me and I was given a breakfast of scrambled eggs. I sat up to eat them, began to feel nauseated and nearly passed out. Intravenous fluids were still running so that food was, in fact, not essential.

After twenty-four hours, I was wheeled back to my room and the day-to-day ward routines began. I felt distinctly sticky and one of the sisters came to help me to shower. She was intrigued by how to wear a sarong! I began to eat again, and swallowed lots of pills. The tubes were removed, one by one. I was able to listen to the Beethoven sonatas at last, and started reading. I had a large jigsaw puzzle to complete, so was kept occupied.

I still felt very weak. Five days after the operation, on the Wednesday, I felt that I was declining. Visitors came and, uncharitably, I wished they were not there. I felt headachy and so low that I would not have cared if I died. It was a long day. In the evening I felt thirsty and took a drink of water from the water jug. It tasted salty. When I mentioned this, the jug was removed and a new jug with fresh water brought back. It was many days later that I discovered that the sodium in my blood stream had dropped, which was a normal complication of that operation. Fortunately, diabetes insipidis did not set in, things came back to normal within days, and I was discharged, having just finished the jigsaw puzzle, which was framed and hangs as a memento of the operation. The necessary hormone replacement tablets continued and I still take them.

Back home, I felt strange not to be working. I started taking walks round the area. Eventually I called in at the consulting rooms.

Of interest, when the patients seen by the respective doctors in the surgery were graphed, the number of patients seen by me had diminished considerably for the few months prior to the obvious realisation that I was unwell. When I was taken ill, we had been very fortunate to be able to obtain a doctor to help Gary Claydon. She was Fijian, and the fact that her grandfather had practised cannibalism was fascinating to the youngsters.

The next stage following surgery was a course of radiotherapy, x-radiation to the pituitary fossa. This course lasted six weeks.

A Rotary friend offered us the use of his holiday home down south in Augusta for a week, an offer gratefully accepted. We explored the countryside and took walks almost daily in the Boranup forest, gradually building up strength again.

At follow-up visits, the drugs were gradually reduced to a maintenance dose, but I was still not taken off sick leave. There were a couple of patients who otherwise would not have seen the locum doctors, on whom I did home visits. There was another RACGP off-shore conference, at the Park Royal Beach Resort in Penang, so the opportunity was taken to attend it. My father was booked for another visit this year and he came as planned.

He was looking older. The last time he came, we had noticed that he was beginning to be a little confused by intricate travel arrangements. He was more bent, and using a stick that was too short for him. However, we had a pleasant holiday with him, and it was arranged that we would return with him to attend the next Dalton Society conference, which was to be held in London, and then drive him back to Aberdeen.

We flew to Singapore for the first part of the journey, landing late in the evening, with a few hours to wait until the connection to London. Eventually boarding took place, the plane started, and slowly taxied to the head of the runway, coming to a halt before getting ready to take off. There seemed to be a delay, then one of the stewards came down the passage, asking if there was a doctor, could he identify himself? Hesitatingly, I raised my hand. This always seemed to be happening to me!

The problem was that, as the plane stopped, an infant had fallen out of the cot and hit his/her head. Could I examine the baby to see if the child could go on with the flight or should come off the plane at Singapore?

I had no instruments and neither did the plane. I did an examination as best I could but said that I would feel happier if the airport doctor would also do an examination. The plane taxied back to the airport building and eventually a Chinese doctor came on. He did an examination and, like me, found no abnormality. He thought that it would be alright for the baby to continue the journey but asked if I would take a look at the child once in a while.

The plane then had to top up with fuel before starting. A delay like this is very expensive for the airline. The steward approached me and said that there were two seats available in the business class but that it was a "smoking area". There were three of us and, anyway, a "smoking area" did not appeal, business class or otherwise.

We settled back, the plane returned to the head of the runway, and, this time, took off. Drinks were in order and we had just got them when the steward came back to us, carrying a bottle of French Champagne. This was very nice; we had our meals with Champagne, and read or watched the television. A little later, the steward asked if I would check the child again, which I did, finding that the baby was fine. Shortly after, along came another bottle of Champagne. This time we asked if the bottle be not opened and we put it in the baggage.

About half-way to London, I was asked to do a further check, and a third bottle of Champagne appeared. We arrived at the airport eventually with our two extra bottles.

My father was delighted to be in London, as he had not been there for many years. With his Scouting connections we were able to stay at BP House at very little expense.

I attended a course on PMS and then the conference, which was held at the Medical Society rooms. In the meantime, Mary and my father explored London – St Paul's Cathedral, a boat trip up the river to Hampton Court – and enjoyed themselves. I was able to accompany them on visits to Portsmouth to see the *Victory* and the *Mary Rose* and to the Tower of London, which we did not enter on account of my father's infirmity.

Eventually it was time to hire a car to drive to Aberdeen. We went out to Heathrow to pick up the vehicle but were told that we had to pick it up in the heart of London, behind Bond Street. "The best laid schemes …"

Much delayed, the car was hired and we set off, negotiating the traffic in the centre of the city. We managed to get on to Edgware Road and were driving north when a truck tried to pass and knocked the driver's side mirror, breaking it. I telephoned the hire company and was given the choice of returning to the depot or going to the agent at Luton. We chose the latter, were supplied with a new car there and started north again. This time there were no mishaps and the drive went smoothly.

After all the delays, we decided to have a night's stop, short of York. At the hotel where we stayed, the owner advised us to use one of the shoppers' car parks near the centre of the city so that my father would not have to walk too far. We set off nice and early, and reached the car park before there were many cars there. We looked for parking meters or attendants but found none. We set off, exploring the walled city, the "Shambles" and York Minster.

After about three hours, we returned to the car, only to find a parking ticket on the windscreen. This time we found an attendant. I was prepared to pay for the three hours but he would not take the fee. He was adamant that he could do nothing. We should have known the rules. The fine was hefty.

Back in Aberdeen, I wrote to the City Council of York explaining that we were visiting from overseas, that notices instructing how payment was to be made were absent, enclosing a cheque for the five pounds owing, and saying that if they were insistent on the fine being paid, I would only pay it provided they paid an equal amount to the Rotary Club in York, or to some deserving charity. I never received any reply, and heard nothing further. I shall never return to York.

We had a pleasant holiday in Scotland then went on a two-week tour of Italy.

Back in Australia, I was back to work. This time, it was Gary Claydon who wanted to have a year's holiday in Britain. We promised to hold his job for him. For the time he was away, we had a number of replacements, and then, when he did return, Dr Claydon decided to work elsewhere. This was a blow. I again had no help and it was difficult to find doctors who would work so far from the city centre. Training registrars was once more a possibility and I contacted the College.

I entered the training programme and began the six-month sessions for the new general practitioners. It meant that I had to spend time on teaching but, on the other hand, they were able to help with the flow of work. An advantage was that these trainees had to be allowed fifteen minutes for each patient, which was in line with the practice policy. I did not want my practice to earn a name for "fast-buck" medicine.

In 1993, the concept of Practice Accreditation was mooted and I took part in the pilot study. This was enjoyable. First, the practices of the doctors taking part in the study were examined for accreditation. Then, in teams of two, we visited practices in Northam, Wongan Hills, Kalbarri, Geraldton, Collie and Perth. I think that the visiting teams picked up some tips for their own practices in the process.

In 1994, the next Dalton Society meeting was due. This time, it was my turn to run it, in Perth. Dr Dalton and her daughters Maureen Dalton and Wendy Holton came out and there was the conference and the Society meeting. A public talk on PMS was held in the Rotunda Hall at the University, resulting in us being face-to-face with about forty PMS women! It went well.

We discovered that none of the Americans attended. The distance and the cost deterred them. Australia was as far from America as we had discovered that America was from Australia!

At this meeting, I was appointed President of the Dalton Society.

In 1995, the premium for indemnity insurance for doing obstetrics did a steep rise. It became too expensive to pay the premium and keep the costs for the patients within reason, so I discontinued maternity work. For years now, more and more GPs had dropped out of obstetrics and I was getting other patients from the district coming to have their babies delivered. I regretted discontinuing this most rewarding side of medicine. There is a lot of pleasure in looking after women in such an intimate moment, completing a successful delivery, and then watching the children growing up.

Work like this was not without its problems. There was the girl who delivered her first baby which did not, at first, breathe. Labour had progressed so fast and delivery was so imminent that it had been too late to give pethidine analgesia, so that was not the problem. (It was discovered what a soothing effect massaging the mother's back had on relieving the pain of the contractions.) After many anxious moments, breathing was established. It was at that moment that the mother decided to quit smoking. She was a long-standing patient of the practice. What she had not learned from advice, she learned from experience.

Another mother had delivered her first child then had stopped attending the practice. Six years later, a report arrived from a consultant paediatrician about the child. In the report was mentioned the "difficult delivery". Litigation was all too common and warning bells flashed. I got hold of the hospital notes and recollections came back. During the antenatal period, the glucose tolerance test had shown the possibility of the onset of gestational diabetes. I had phoned the consultant obstetrician to refer the patient but he had considered that I was well able to manage the care and delivery; the patient should be advised on diet and on glucose monitoring, the foetal heartbeat should be checked once weekly, and the pregnancy should not go beyond its due dates, if necessary inducing labour on or before the expected date of delivery. To this I added one other rule, and that was to use an epidural anaesthetic so that the baby's wellbeing, already compromised by the raised glucose, was not further endangered by pethidine or morphine.

Knowing this, did I have to do a forceps delivery? Looking at the notes, I saw that there was no forceps delivery. The patient had delivered spontaneously. In fact, far from being a "difficult delivery", it had been a very easy, almost pain-free, and simple birth.

However, after the baby was born, the left side of the face was immobile. The paediatric consultant was called in. Investigations then disclosed that the facial nerve on the left side was congenitally missing.

I telephoned the paediatrician whom the child was currently consulting and told him about the history. His comment was, "I thought so." The child had been seeing another consultant until then, and this was the first time he had seen the patient. As my referral, six years old, had never been renewed, I was the GP to whom he wrote.

I heard nothing further. This was an example of how easy it is for malpractice suits to begin.

Another patient with a gestational diabetic curve was also of interest. She was of a strict religious group and was a vegetarian. She was skinny. It was the latest of a number of pregnancies. After the delivery, the warning that diabetes might occur in later life was given. However, the fact that she was thin and already had a strict diet meant that she did not have to change her lifestyle in any way. The only abnormality was that she was genetically predisposed to diabetes.

Just before I ceased obstetrics, one patient was due for delivery at Armadale Hospital. It was the afternoon for Alcoa, so I called in to see how she was going on the way to Jarrahdale. She was proceeding well in labour. I left instructions on how to contact me when delivery was imminent and went on to the mine site.

Nothing was heard, so I called in at the hospital on the way home. The patient was standing beside the bed, holding herself up against it. The baby's head was crowning. The patient was unable to climb up onto the bed. I had to deliver the baby under the patient. It reminded me of a mechanic working under a car.

The normal surgery patients were very tolerant of the fact that, on the occasions when a maternity call came, I had to break off the consultation and dash off to the hospital. The only patient who objected was a nursing sister. She was furious. She apologized later.

1995 was the year when Mary's Uncle Walter visited us for a second time. We took him to Kalbarri and to Margaret River. At Kalbarri, I was intrigued by the large number of flies on Uncle Walter's back. When we returned to Perth I checked him for diabetes, which he indeed had.

Shortly before this, Aunt Molly, my father's younger sister, had died and the share of the estate left to me depended on the sale of her house. By this time, we had seriously considered buying a block of land on which to build in Margaret River. We had looked at some places the previous year but had not found anywhere suitable. This time we were shown an area which was possible and then another area which was even more possible. There were two or three spare blocks but the one which, to me, was most desirable, was one that was not for sale then but was being reserved for sale later. It was bigger than the others. I told the estate agent that this was the one we really liked. She said that it was not on the market yet, but that she would enquire.

From the prices of the others, I mentally worked out what it would cost, more or less. The agent telephoned the owner. He agreed to sell. The price was below what I had calculated. We agreed to buy.

It would be possible to make up the shortfall of the money needed to pay for the land from my share of Aunt Molly's will. Unfortunately, however, the wife of a distant relative disagreed about the money due and the resolution of the will was delayed. We had to take out yet another mortgage. It took one to two years to sort out the will, by which time we had lost a lot of money in interest rates.

On the other hand, we had a block of land in Margaret River. We could, when the time came, build our retirement home on the block.

One Saturday evening, just as we were about to eat, there was a ring at the doorbell. Mary answered the door and I heard the voice of a patient, the one who had persisted in telephoning every evening at eleven o'clock when we first began the practice. I hid behind a screen but the patient wanted a house call. Her brother had just murdered his wife! He had stabbed her in the chest with a knife.

It seemed more of a case for the police than the doctor but the concern was that the patient's mother had come over to the house and she now wanted me to attend the mother. I went round to the house and there was the mother, sitting there. However, the mother did not want to see me – she wanted her own doctor! With some relief, I returned home to dinner.

Towards the end of 1995 there was another visitation from the Health Insurance Commission, despite the fact that there had been the promise that I would not be investigated again. This time it was because of the number of pathology tests I was ordering. Presumably I should have been referring the patients to consultants to investigate. I was not practising unethically; it was that, again, my consulting pattern differed from the norm.

Chapter 37

Penultimate Years

Registrars had been with the practice regularly: Kylie Seow, Simon French, Joanna Teh, and now Jenny Sisson. Jenny was looking for a job and she continued on with the practice.

In 1996, two years had passed since the last Dalton Society conference in Perth, and the next one was due. It was to be held in America again, at the Black Point Inn, in Prouts Neck, Maine, from 20th to 22nd October. We therefore arranged tours prior to the seminar so that we could visit Niagara Falls and see the northeast American fall foliage.

Mary and I travelled first to visit Roswitha Carter at St Leonards in Sussex. From there we attended the Gurkha Regiment AGM and luncheon. Mary had caught cold about three weeks before then and a cough had persisted. After the Gurkha curry, the cough disappeared.

Then on to Aberdeen to visit my father. Arriving there I telephoned "Kitty" Dalton to say we had arrived. The conference had been cancelled.

By then it was much too late to cancel our leave and we decided to enjoy the tours we had arranged. We managed to change our bookings from the Black Point Inn to the Inn By The Sea, which was much less expensive.

Niagara Falls was spectacular and the New England autumn scenery magnificent. We reached the Inn By The Sea and spent the first day walking along the beach and enjoying the views.

The next day was a downpour. We managed to arrange a taxi to take us into the town, but at midday the rain was so bad that all shops closed and we had to get a taxi back to the hotel. Three water mains had burst and the hotel had no water. We were melting ice cubes to obtain drinks. All the other hotel guests left, but of course we had nowhere else to go. The hotel staff were extremely concerned and hospitable. Again we experienced the warmth and generosity of the Americans in their native land.

After the aborted conference, the next stage on our journey was to visit the Grand Canyon. This can only be done by flying to Las Vegas, a place as vulgarly opulent as all accounts describe. The Grand Canyon was, as its name suggests, grand. In the morning, at an unearthly hour, we went in the freezing cold to watch the sunrise. This was followed by breakfast, during which I had to return to our cabin to fetch something for Mary. On returning I remarked about sending me out in the cold, cold snow. When she was non-responsive, I said "Look!" Indeed it was snowing. To return to Las Vegas, we had to do it promptly, and after the wings had been de-iced. The snowy scenery was beautiful and there were good views of the Hoover Dam.

The American tour finished by visiting San Francisco, the Muir woods, the Napa Valley, and Yosemite National Park. It being the end of the year, there was a touch of snow on the way up to Yosemite.

1996 passed, and work went on as usual in the practice. James Frost had been attending regularly for follow-up of his myocardial infarction and damaged heart over the past few years. He had sought legal advice and was suing the hospital and the doctors whom he first saw for damages. Three cardiac specialists were testifying on behalf of the hospital. After many years, the court hearing had, at last, arrived and I was required to testify on behalf of the patient.

I went into the witness box and the first thing I had to do after taking the oath was to tell the court of all my qualifications. The lawyer defending the hospital and the doctors was a fat, belligerent woman who tried to put across a story that I had handled the case badly. The problem with lawyers is that they do not experience the circumstances as they happen. My explanation pointed out that I had done what I reasonably could have done in the time available.

Jim won his case, but of course the hospital appealed and Jim died before the appeal could be heard.

About this time one of my regular patients came to see me. From his history, he seemed to have come from a somewhat dysfunctional family. He tended to go to bars and become involved in fights. When it was disclosed to him how these fights originated, he realized what was happening and avoided such situations. He had been involved with drugs and had married three times. On the occasion of this consultation, he mentioned that he had seen a wonderful film, *Hamlet*, the four-hour version with Kenneth Branagh. He had never before come across the play but described the intertwining of the plot and the intricacies of the story. Previously I had managed to obtain his IQ, which was well above normal. It was an example of how circumstances can affect people.

During 1997, a letter arrived from the Akademi Kedoktoran Keluarga Malaysia (Academy of Family Physicians, Malaysia), which was the new name for the College of General Practitioners, Malaysia, to the effect that Founder Members of the College were to be awarded Fellowships. After some consideration, Mary and I decided we would go to Kuala Lumpur for the investiture. I wrote to Dr Rajakumar. He invited us for lunch at the Lake Club and we caught up with events. He asked how I had first come to Malaya, as it was then.

"The first night I spent in Malaya, I slept on a *charpoi* in a gardener's shed under an *attap* roof."

He said, "You know, you should write your autobiography. That could be the first line."

We have come full circle. However, this is only the story so far. I am still alive and well!

The investiture was quite splendid. The robes were Royal Blue with silver woven thread (*songket*). The Censor-in-Chief of the Australian College examination, whom I had met at the exams, was in the robing room. He was surprised to see me and I explained how I came to be there. I lined up with the other Fellows, the only *orang puteh* among all the Malays, Chinese and Indians. The President of the Malaysian Academy also gave me a questioning look. Later, I met him and described the circumstances. Also being given honourary Fellowships were the Prime Minister, Datuk Seri Dr Mahathir bin Mohamad, his wife and Datuk Dr Lim Kee Jin, whom I had known in my days in Cha'ah, when he was the consultant physician at Johore Bharu General Hospital.

In Kuala Lumpur, I took the opportunity to buy new sarongs, then we returned to Perth.

Shortly afterwards, I was awarded a Paul Harris Fellowship by the Rotary Club of Thornlie, for community services, both professionally and in the Rotary Club, and for having practised in out-of-the-way places in Malaya and in outback Australia.

I was now sixty-five years old, was starting to suffer from "burn-out", and so far we had not found a doctor who would buy, or even take over, the practice.

Graeme was the first of our children to be married, in Lismore, New South Wales, in 1998. We took a short break to attend this country wedding.

Our next Registrar was Derek Scurry.

One day, Jenny Sisson called me to see a patient. The patient was a woman who was of psychopathic temperament and who repeatedly attempted suicide. On one occasion I had prescribed one of the new SSRI drugs. She looked at the prescription and said that these were alright – she had once swallowed one hundred of them in a suicide attempt. She was from Bishopbriggs, from where Mary comes and had once, when a child, set fire to the school.

When Jenny called me, this patient was sitting, completely intoxicated with alcohol, and both forearms were slashed like joints of pork. Jenny said that this young lady refused to go to hospital to get her wounds sutured. I told the patient that what Dr Sisson had advised was the best course of action. She still refused. I asked how she was going to get the lacerations stitched. She pointed to me and said that I could do it.

Mary was at reception. When I explained the situation she telephoned all the patients booked for the next two hours, told them that there was an emergency and rearranged their bookings. I set to work, the suturing not made any easier by the patient who, in her drunken state, tended to roll off the couch. At one point she wanted to vomit and went through to the toilet. There was even blood at the back of the toilet bowl where the patient had clasped the toilet. Eventually I almost needed the full two hours but the job was completed. Despite all the odds, the wounds healed well.

During 1998, I wanted to do a trip back to Aberdeen to see my father, who was ninety-three years old and becoming really infirm. Jenny, however, also wanted leave and I had to jettison plans to see my father that year.

I had decided that I would retire at the end of 1999, whether or not I had found someone to take over the practice. I contacted Martin Harris, who ran a business which dealt with the buying and selling of practices, but no-one was interested. It looked as if we would have to take all the patient files with us when I retired and send them on to the doctors of the patients' choice.

We also contacted Peter Hunt, our friend the architect, to start plans to build our retirement home in Margaret River. One of his young assistants, Brian La Fontaine, had just returned from a two-year stint in London, and it was arranged that Brian would design the house on his weekends at a very much reduced fee. He saw us at our house in Huntingdale and looked at and measured our Malaysian furniture. The building envelope on the block in Margaret River was rather an awkward shape, not very big and shaped like a boomerang. Plans progressed and building started at the beginning of 1999.

At that time, I was on one of the College councils and news came that Professor John Howie was visiting Western Australia. I had known him in the Scouts and the last time we had met was at the conference in Glasgow in 1990. He had become the Professor of General Practice in Edinburgh. He and his wife visited in May and I took them to visit Margaret River, visiting the house site to see how the building was progressing and lunching at Leeuwin Estate.

During that month, also, was the wedding of Seonaid, our eldest daughter.

Chapter 38

End of the Practice

With regard to the future of the practice, there was a breakthrough. A Chinese doctor, whose interests were entrepreneurial, was buying up practices in the Gosnells and Thornlie areas, and amalgamating them into one big medical centre in Gosnells. He had several conditions. He wanted the doctors whose practices he was taking over to work in the new medical centre for a year. The patients would all be bulk-billed. He paid only a nominal sum for the practice he was buying. He boasted that he owned seventeen practices and was worth seventeen million dollars.

The situation was far from ideal. I stated categorically that I was retiring at the end of the year and he accepted that. On the other hand, the care of the patients, the patient files and the equipment, all had a future.

The new medical centre was to open at the beginning of August. In the meantime, I was to work in my own premises as an employee. In the event, the new medical centre did not open on time and I was able to continue working as usual.

A visit to my father in Aberdeen was now a matter of urgency, and, as I was now an employee, and no longer had the responsibility for the running of the practice, I could take a month's leave while one of the other doctors of the group could see the patients.

We flew back to Britain and to Aberdeen. My father was almost blind, was a bit wandered, meals were brought to him, and someone would come in each week to clean the house. The pots were filthy – he was unable to see the dirt in them – the refrigerator badly needed both defrosting and cleaning, and there was a great deal to do. In theory, my brother was living in the upper flat of the house and was there to help in time of need. In fact, the house was a solidly built edifice and any calls for help were unlikely to be heard. It was immediately apparent that any hope of having a holiday to visit other places was not going to be possible.

The month was to be spent as carers. In the middle of the second night, we were wakened by a loud crash in the hallway. We went through. My father had got up and was going through the house when he had fallen, narrowly missing hitting his head on a nest of tables. Next morning, my brother said that he had heard nothing. We were wakened about every third night.

Early on, I noticed that the Lonach highland gathering was to be held on a Saturday. We made enquiries. That day was the day my father spent at one of the treatment centres. We decided to try to get to the Lonach. We drove to Bellabeg where the games were held. It was a beautiful sunny day, which was a change from the usual day of the games. The last time I had attended was in 1952, forty-seven years previously.

There was a new laird. He was the comedian, Billy Connolly. He was accompanied by his house guests, Judi Dench, and the actors Robin Williams and Steve Martin. When the official party arrived, there were girls in a highland dancing competition. The laird ushered his party quickly and discreetly so that the public's attention was not taken away from the dancers.

In the morning, prior to the games, members of the Lonach Society, the villagers and country people from round about, in full highland dress, with their pikes and swords, would march the seven miles up the glen, calling in at all the estate houses, at each of which they would be given a dram of whisky. Following the procession came a horse and cart to pick up anyone who fell by the wayside. In the afternoon they returned to the games and paraded round the arena.

In the course of the morning, Robin Williams had, rashly, agreed to take part in the race to the top of the hill overlooking Bellabeg, a run of about four miles. We watched him completing the course last, and running in, stripping off his singlet and throwing it to the crowd.

With such a professional audience, the Master of Ceremonies needed to be on his toes. At the end of one item, his voice came over the loudspeaker, telling us that the last tune played was "A Man's a Man for a' That." He went on: "This means that we are all 'Jock Tamson's bairns'; that is, we're all cast in the same mould; but it has to be remembered that some are mouldier than others."

The afternoon ended and after a wander around the village and environs, we headed back to Aberdeen.

It was obvious that my father was not managing to look after himself, but he was adamant that he did not want to go into a "home". He was due for a check-up at the outpatient department of the hospital. Prior to the consultation, we managed to have a quiet word with the doctor, explaining the situation. The examination finished, the doctor sat down with my father and said that what he needed was expert care twenty-four hours a day. My father thought, then said, "That's logical." At last, arrangements could be made for him to be looked after.

The twenty-four-hour caring was quite stressful and Mary wanted, if possible, to go over to see the West Coast. With some manoeuvering, we managed to ensure that my father would be looked after for one weekend. We went to the travel bureau and said that we would like to book a bed and breakfast on the Saturday night in Plockton, directly west of Aberdeen. The counter assistant was somewhat taken aback – driving over – staying one night – then coming back the next day?! We said yes, after Australia's distances, it would not be difficult.

It was another beautiful day, over to Inverness, down Loch Ness (no monster in sight), up Glen Morriston and onward to Plockton. We arrived at the B & B and settled in.

During the stay, I asked after the Glasgows. Mr Glasgow had been the excise officer whom I knew on previous visits to Plockton. I remembered, many years previously, introducing my father to him. He had said, "Come in, come in. I'll make some tea. Wait a minute; I've just been over to Talisker. You'll have to put some water into it – it is well over proof."

The landlady, in her lilting voice, said that Mr Glasgow had died ten years previously but that Mrs Glasgow was back in her old house and that she would be pleased to see me. George, the son, had been in the air force but was back in Plockton. Seonaid, his twin sister, had gone to Australia and was living in a place called Wanneroo! Next morning, we called in to see Mrs Glasgow. She had had a stroke but we had a good chat.

Then we set off, back through Speyside, the Lecht Road, and Strathdon, to Aberdeen. We completed our "holiday" and returned to Perth. At least the wheels had been set in motion for my father to be cared for.

Seonaid Glasgow had been married for a number of years and was now Seonaid Mackay. On return to Perth, we telephoned her. She had already had a phone call from her mother and we arranged to meet for lunch – a lunch that went on for four and a half hours.

In the event, due to the delay in the start of the new medical centre, I only had to work for three weeks in the new building. This was just as well, as the bookings were made at ten-minute intervals, which was quite out of line with my own practice and resulted in patients having to wait much longer to see me. Furthermore, there were no facilities to keep children occupied. The result was that the patients were dissatisfied.

Ten-minute consultations occurred as the result of the structure of the Medicare schedule, whereby short consultations, ideally six minutes, were much better financially than longer consultations.

It became an uncomfortable final three weeks. However, it passed.

When the time came for me to finally go, it was very touching to see that my patients, some of very long standing, had held me in some sort of respect. I was presented with an oil painting set and easel and a cartoon of myself, which patients had clubbed together to present.

My last day at that medical centre was Tuesday, 22nd December 1999.

On Wednesday, 23rd December, I finally made house calls on four patients, finishing at eleven o'clock that morning. At five in the evening, I was in Margaret River, in the new house. Mary followed on the following day.

Retiral home, 2 Chardonnay Avenue, Margaret River

Chapter 39

Retirement

Waking the following morning, I shall never forget the glorious red sunrise, seen from the bedroom window.

Furniture was brought from Perth to Margaret River and moved in. The first item to arrive was the gong, sent from Aberdeen. Before we had left from our holiday, my father had said that I might as well have it sent right away and it came out, care of the Aberdeen Shore Porter Society (Established 1498). The empty house in Huntingdale had to be cleaned and painted and made ready for selling.

We set to work.

Christmas Dinner was eaten, more or less on packing boxes. Things were sorted out and furniture put in place. I started to do "make-ups" at the Rotary Club and Mary began attending the church. We explored the countryside. I began evening art classes. There were trips back and forth to Huntingdale, where we had left a mattress on the floor to sleep on. A visit to Sands and McDougall was made to purchase a computer table, and two comfortable armchairs bought. These were to be delivered on the 3rd February.

On 2nd February, Mary had a visit to do in Perth to have her teeth checked and I returned to Margaret River to take delivery of the armchairs and the computer table. Mary remained in Perth to complete the tidying of the house, which was, by this time "under offer". The chairs and table duly arrived and were installed. I waited for Mary to phone to say that she was about to start driving to Margaret River. It was not until 4.20 pm that she telephoned. She said that she would fill the car with petrol then be on her way.

The journey normally takes about three hours and fifteen minutes so I expected her to arrive at, or shortly after, 7.35 pm. It was becoming dark. 7.40 pm arrived, then 7.50. I stood at the window and worked out the most advantageous place to first see the car. At 8.05 pm she was definitely late. I wanted to not believe the possibility that she had been killed in a motor accident and that the retirement to which we had both been looking forward was not to happen.

At 8.15 pm I telephoned the police to ask if there were any car accidents and was told that there was just one at Busselton, but it was not Mary's car and that possibly the accident had held her up. I waited five more minutes then decided to start trying the hospitals. I started with Bunbury Hospital. I spoke with the nurse on reception and was told that she was just being brought in now.

I asked what the injuries were and was told that her left thigh was broken and her left arm. I said that I would be there in an hour, hung up, and left.

I started the journey north. It was dark. I passed Busselton. The mineral sand mine at Capel was eerie, the tall chimney belching yellow smoke. I arrived at the hospital and went in and was shown where Mary was lying, covered with a blanket. She asked me what had happened. "Where is my bag, where are my rings?" She asked me to phone the rector of Margaret River and Dennis Claughton, the former rector at Gosnells, in the morning.

Her left thigh was in a splint. Her left arm was in the shape of a Z. Her rings had been cut off; the bag was still at Harvey police station. The sister showed me the sodden clothes that had been cut off the patient and asked if they could be thrown out. I said yes.

The decision was that she would have to be transferred to Fremantle Hospital by the Flying Doctor Service and I was asked if I wanted to accompany her in the plane. I said that I would drive up as I had to collect her bag from Harvey and would need the car in Perth.

Having seen Mary off in the ambulance at about eleven pm, I drove on towards Harvey, went into the town and found the police station. I knocked and entered. When I said who I was, the sergeant demanded to know where I had been. Having answered, I asked about the handbag and it was produced. I found her address book and telephoned Seonaid, to tell her what had happened and to say that we were going to Fremantle Hospital – Mary by air, and I driving.

I asked the best route to take to the hospital and left. I drove north along the South-West Highway and became worried because I had not filled the car. It was now about two am, and the petrol was running low. Fortunately, the all-night Shell service station south of Pinjarra was open and the car was filled up. I got something to eat as I had not eaten since lunchtime. At Pinjarra, I turned left to join the coast road and then up towards Fremantle.

Reaching the hospital, I went in and was shown where Mary was. Seonaid was already there. She had telephoned Catriona who joined us shortly afterwards. The sister asked if we wanted to be public or private patients. I asked who the surgeon on call was and was told Tony Jeffries. I answered "private", which meant that the consultant would be treating and not just the registrar.

Further tests were done and it was discovered that Mary had a fracture of the second cervical vertebra (the "hangman's" fracture), three breaks in the left femur, a Smith's fracture of the left forearm, a fractured sternum, fractures of some ribs, and later it was found that she also had a fracture of the pelvis. With a fracture of the cervical spine, treatment should have been in the hospital at Shenton Park. However, there were the other injuries to consider, so it was decided that it would not be a good thing to transfer the patient. Furthermore, she should have been in the Intensive Care Unit, but there were no beds available. Thus, Mary was treated in a single room. There should have been a nurse assigned to "special" her, but there was an insufficiency of nursing staff.

I was eventually able to go to Seonaid's home for some rest but I returned at about six or seven that morning, to meet Dennis Claughton leaving the hospital. He had been in to visit her, and, in fact, anointed her in case the outcome was unfortunate.

We both went back up to the ward. Dennis eventually left. Mary went to theatre at eleven that morning to have the leg plated. I stayed with Mary all day, which, incidentally, was of help to the nursing staff as, correctly, there should have been someone sitting with her all the time to "special" nurse her.

Again, I lay on the floor all that night and stayed with the patient. A mattress was supplied.

The following evening I thought I could go back to Seonaid's house and get a night's sleep. At about eleven, the telephone rang and the sister said that Mary wanted to speak to me. She wanted me to return to the hospital, so I went.

At the start of the third morning Mary asked what she was doing here, what had happened? I explained that she had suffered an accident and was in hospital.

During all this time, the arm had only been splinted and the fracture was still unstable. I came back to the ward just as the registrar was leaving the room. He was very quiet. Apparently, he had tried to reduce the fracture, the only anaesthesia being an injection of morphine immediately prior to the procedure, which would not have given time for the morphine to work, besides the fact that it was an entirely unsuitable type of pain relief for such a manipulation. Accordingly, Mr Jeffries took her back to theatre and the arm was plated.

A day or two later, Seonaid's husband, Owen, drove me down to Harvey to try to salvage the contents of the car. When we arrived, the police asked if we could jettison the food which was beginning to go "high". We collected what we could of the other goods and chattels, and then went on to Bunbury, to the yard where the remains of the car lay. It looked like a crumpled up yellow paper bag. We continued to Margaret River, turned off the lights of the house, which had been left on, and returned to Perth.

A week after admission, it was time to try to get the patient sitting up, with a neck support. The first attempt was a dismal failure. On gaining the upright position, Mary was seized with an incontrollable dizziness.

The senior ward registrar had returned from his leave, and a couple of days later, when I came into the ward in the morning, the house doctor met me and asked me to take a seat in the waiting room as the registrar wanted to see me. I waited for an hour, and then when the house doctor was passing, I asked her how long I was to wait. She said that the registrar no longer wanted to see me.

The story came out. When the registrar had visited that morning, he had demanded to know why the patient was not up. It was explained that there had been a dizzy attack and the patient had been unable to tolerate it. He had then wanted to see "the husband" (me) when he came in. It is surmised that, when I arrived, the house doctor had said that "Dr Esslemont" was now here. Presumably, on hearing the word "doctor", the registrar had changed his mind.

Later, Mary described the sensation as like seeing the words scrolling up on the computer screen. The condition described was that of a rare form of nystagmus where the rotatory movement is vertical instead of from side to side. The "hangman's fracture" had damaged the foramina of the vertebral arteries and this was causing the nystagmus.

Time went slowly past. The ward was obviously grossly understaffed. I wrote to the *West Australian* about it and the newspaper printed my letter. The members of the ward staff were so pleased that they posted an enlarged photocopy on their notice board. Shortly afterwards, they were given another member of staff, but I gather that this only lasted six months.

Six weeks passed. An occupational worker visited Seonaid's home to see if any facilities were necessary and Mary was allowed out of hospital to stay there. She was still in a neck brace. Eventually the patient was able to return to Margaret River. The journey was slow as we had to stop every hour for a rest. Back home, the new chairs with the footrests were a godsend.

The neck brace was kept on for over twelve weeks. It was fortunate that a shower had been built in the laundry for coming in from the garden, as this facilitated showering in a plastic chair.

Chapter 40

Recovery

The claim for damages was submitted to the insurance company, who were less than happy. They could not believe that such an abstruse list could be true. A representative visited us. Mary was sitting with her neck brace in place.

The insurance man started on the list and we explained that Mary had been bringing the residue of goods from Perth to Margaret River. He asked about the food she was carrying. It was explained that Mary had done a lot of shopping to stock up the refrigerator. He asked why we had not kept the food to show him. It was explained that, by the time we had called in to pick up the food, it was already "high" and that the police had asked us to throw it out. He questioned the claim for a damaged suitcase. The suitcase was shown to him and it was added that if the case had burst, then the claim would have been far higher, as there was a full highland evening dress suit valued at many thousands of dollars in it. The damage to a presentation fountain pen set was queried. It was shown to him.

By this time, he had seen enough and promised that the claim would go through and as speedily as possible.

Time went on and we started to do some walking. The old railway track just across the road from the house made an ideal strip for walking, eleven kilometres of level footpath to Cowaramup, if we so wished.

There were visits to be made to Perth to see the consultants, Mr Jeffries at St John of Gods, and Mr Woodland, the spinal orthopaedic surgeon, at

Shenton Park. The latter hospital was particularly unpleasant. We had to wait for prolonged periods of time in drab surroundings. On one occasion, we had driven up from Margaret River for only this appointment. We waited till nearly 1.00 pm, and then I asked, "When will my wife be seen? We have to return to Margaret River this afternoon."

The sister said "The *registrar* will see your wife at some point." I stated that we had come to see Mr Woodland. The reply was that that was not the routine and that we would have to come another day. I persisted and asked the sister to discuss this with Mr Woodland as we were his private patients. She disappeared and then came back, somewhat surprised, and said that Mr Woodland would see my wife at his lunch hour. When we saw Mr Woodland, he arranged for future appointments to be at his private rooms.

Mary was still extremely anxious in the car and would only ride in the back seat. After some weeks, she gradually braved herself to sit in the passenger seat in the front. It was months before she tried to drive.

Things slowly came back to normal and six months to a year later, the episode had become a memory. On drives to and from Perth, an alternative route was used to avoid the accident site, but eventually Mary steeled herself to visit the place of the accident, where there were still bits of tile lying about.

At Christmas, she baked a Christmas cake, which we took in to the policemen at Harvey. They were happy that things had turned out better than they might have, and we heard more details. The car had been on fire, which had to be extinguished. The drain had begun to fill with water, which had to be turned off. Mary had to be cut out of the car. On the other hand, the police sergeant said that the car was beautifully and precisely parked! On the way to Bunbury Hospital, the ambulance men had wondered if she would make it alive.

The next two years were years of recuperation. A reminder for Mary to renew her driving licence failed to appear and, during one of our visits to Perth, we went into the Traffic Department to enquire about it. There it was discovered that Mary's new driving license was registered to her at "Margaret River, Western Australia, 2685". The postal code for Margaret River is *6285*. It was little wonder that the police in Harvey, at the time of the accident, had failed to find me, and explained my reception when I visited the police station there. The error in the driving licence took years to be finally corrected.

The local GP, whom I knew, wondered if I would be able to do locums for him when he went on holidays. However, when we went into the matter of indemnity insurance, we found that I would need to work for three months a year to pay for the insurance.

However, I could become an External Clinical Teacher for the College, sitting in on trainee Registrars while they were consulting. I could cover training practices in the southwest, visiting places like Manjimup, Donnybrook, Busselton, Australind, Dunsborough. I enjoyed the work. I could visit places in the area, and it kept me interested in the intellectual side of practice and teaching. I did this work for two years. I also had time to write articles for the *Australian Family Physician*, and seven of these were published.

I continued being a clinical examiner for the College. After two years, I decided that I was becoming too old for this and sent in a letter of resignation. A very nice reply came back, but, at the foot of it was scrawled "P.S. Don't think you have seen the last of us!" There has always been a dearth of practitioners willing to act as examiners and I continued examining, as I seemed to be needed. I enjoyed examining the postgraduate doctors who were sitting for their Fellowships.

In both my own examinations, in London and in Perth, I had felt that the doctors simulating patients were not exactly like patients seen in the consulting rooms. In Britain at the time of my oral examination, the patient was supposed to be a child but was played by an adult. In Australia, the patient was one who had a chronic alcohol habit. In real life, the smell of alcohol reveals the problem, but this was missing in the case presented. When I acted as the patient with a similar condition, I took along a small specimen jar with some wine, dipped cotton wool balls into it and put them into my cheeks. A doctor whom I knew thought I had been on a bender and was relieved when I explained, on later meeting him, how I had done it.

At another examination, I was acting as a rather belligerent newly diagnosed diabetic. I met one of the candidates some time later at a dinner. She said that she had wanted to strangle me! However, she must have passed as she also gained one of the prizes.

In 2000, my father died. He had little in his will to leave, but together with our investments over the latter years, for the first time we were debt-free.

On 2nd November 2002, the third child of our family, Catriona, was married. Mary's friend and Catriona's godmother, Maureen Lindsay, came out from Scotland for the wedding. After the wedding we took Maureen – who had said she wanted to see "real" Australia – north, by way of Cervantes, to see the Pinnacles, and Kalbarri, to Newman, where Seonaid lived with her husband, Owen, who was working there. Then we returned to Margaret River.

Mary started to have dreams which woke her at night and then began to bother her in the daytime also. She dreamed that she was lying under a bridge with white concrete walls. She dreamed that she was dressed in white on a rough surface of stones, that the ground under her was wet. She dreamed that she was going to die and she had decided that, if I wanted another wife, she would not mind. She wished that, if she was going to die, she would like a pillow under her head, which was pressing against a hard surface. The dream started to become quite obsessive.

We went to the bridge over the Margaret River, where we used to walk, going under the road alongside the stream to reach the other side. However, this bridge is built of wood and the scene was nothing like her mind's picture.

She described the dream more fully. The bridge was arched. I began to wonder if she was describing the scene of her accident. However, it was not so much a bridge as a large culvert under the road. We returned to the large drain in which the car had landed, five kilometres north of Brunswick Junction.

She said that this was the scene in her mind, except the bottom of the drain was cemented and not rough stones. I pointed out that the cement work was new – at the time of the accident it was rough granite rocks. The arch of the culvert would have been over her head, the white cement walls were just as she described.

Having seen the place, the dreams vanished.

At Christmas 2002, Seonaid, Owen, Catriona and her new husband, Russell, came to spend Christmas with us.

On our walks, Mary had begun to notice weakness in her left leg. She consulted our GP, Gavan White, who confirmed that there was indeed weakness in the left lower leg, a "dropped foot". A CT scan was arranged at Busselton. On Christmas Eve, the scan was done. While the scan was being taken, the radiographer insisted that the patient lie flat, with the leg fully extended, for a prolonged period of time. The severe pain down the left leg became almost intolerable. After the scan, and while the scan was being processed, we were to do some Christmas shopping. However, the pain had become so severe that shopping was impossible. The scans were collected and we returned home.

Mary was servicing at church that evening and the following morning. She managed to last out these periods but the children did the Christmas cooking.

Next day, we contacted Gavan White, and Mary was admitted to Margaret River Hospital, where she was treated by bed rest and morphine. As soon as possible, she was transferred to St John of God Hospital, Subiaco, where she underwent an MRI scan. In the MRI scanner, she underwent a panic attack – when she opened her eyes in the machine, she was reminded of the air raids in Glasgow during the war, when she was put in a confined space as a protection from the bombing activity.

However, she survived that fearful episode and Mr Vaughan operated on the back at the beginning of January. After the operation, he stated that the jelly-like nucleus pulposus had compressed and distorted the spinal nerve root. It was obvious that the CT scan procedure at Busselton Hospital had forced out the disc fluid, worsening the condition. Eventually, about six months later, we received an apology from the radiologists at Busselton Hospital.

Our first two years of retirement had not been too propitious.

Chapter 41

Real Retirement at Last

We felt we were due for a holiday and a change. When we had retired, the allowance for holidays not taken during our twenty-two years of working life in Australia added up to almost a year. We were now able to take all the vacations we had missed.

In September 2003, we flew to Kuala Lumpur, stayed a night in the airport hotel, then hired a car and drove north to Cameron Highlands, to the Smoke House Inn, where we had spent our honeymoon exactly thirty-seven years earlier.

We did as much walking as Mary's back and leg would allow and visited the Boh Tea Estate. After a few days there, we drove north along the west side of Lake Chenderoh to Grik. When I had first driven this road it was a beautiful winding road running through the jungle on the hillside, above and alongside an equally winding river. Now the road had been replaced by a motorway – easier to drive along but much less pretty.

The Grik Rest House also had been replaced by a modern structure. *Arak* (rice spirit) was forbidden on pain of a fine and/or jail. We had smuggled in some cans of beer which we surreptitiously drank in our room. Breakfast next morning was white bread with a jam made from eggs and honey.

From Grik, we joined the fairly new East-West Highway and turned east to Kota Bharu. The driving, although it was a very modern, well-maintained road, was hazardous. We would be approaching a corner turning to the right with a large truck driving towards us, when a car would appear, passing the truck and on the wrong side of the road!

In Kota Bharu, we stayed at a very modern hotel. Previously our holiday had been at chalets on Pantai Chinta Berahi (the Beach of Passionate Love), which at that time had been newly opened. Now the beach went by another, more "politically correct" name. We revisited the beach but the new name had done nothing to stop the encroachment of pollution, empty bottles, wrappings, papers and tins. It was no longer attractive.

We also visited the museum. My Malay was decidedly rusty, but with everyone around me talking in Malay, I found myself thinking in Malay again, and replying in that language. The local people were intrigued to hear an *orang puteh* speaking in *bahasa kebangsaan* and put me through my paces to see how much I knew.

Leaving Kota Bharu, We crossed the country again and arrived in Penang. On our visit to the College conference in 1992, we had been impressed by the Park Royal Hotel, where we had stayed, but on this occasion we had a very mediocre room. Nonetheless, we visited the various places we knew and met friends there.

I attended a Rotary lunch. Sitting opposite me was Freddy Choong, who, in his day, had been a tennis champion and then had taken up motor car racing. When he saw me he said "long time no see", asked me what I was doing that evening, and then suggested that he would give me a guided tour of the red light district! Fortunately, we were meeting friends that evening.

After our return to Margaret River, plans for the next holiday began. For many years I had wanted to visit Charleston and the plantations there in the azalea season. Also, our previous visit to Yosemite had been in the American fall, when the waterfalls had dried up to trickles.

We travelled to America again in March, breaking the journey in Hawaii, which we had never previously visited, visited San Francisco and Yosemite, and then went on to Jacksonville, where we joined a Tauck tour. The tour guide, Andrea Rovito, was excellent. From Jacksonville, we travelled north, visiting Savannah for a couple of days, and then arrived in Charleston. The flowers in the plantations, the azaleas, the dogwoods, met all expectations. We probably saw them on the best day of the year, as evidently the previous week they were only budding, and the following day a heavy rain storm occurred.

There was a three-day break until the next tour so we stayed on at the

Mills House Hotel in Charleston for those days. Very fortunately, we were able to book ourselves into one of the very popular garden tours on one of these days, visiting a selection of the town gardens.

The next tour began in New Orleans, and visited the areas east, to Biloxi, up the Mississippi to Baton Rouge, west to Louisiana, and ended at New Orleans again. It was the weekend of the jazz festival, so we seemed to get the best of all worlds.

After such a holiday, it was time for R & R.

The family was growing, Graeme with three daughters, Seonaid with one son, and Catriona with one daughter.

In *The West Australian* appeared an article on Baha'i and the Baha'i gardens in Haifa. As my father's uncle, John E. Esslemont, was buried there, I contacted the editor, who gave me the address of Michael Day, the journalist who had written the article. In turn, I contacted him, and he wanted to know if I would like to come and visit Uncle John's grave. Nothing was further from my mind. Visiting Israel did not seem very safe, but the invitation was left open.

It was time to prepare for our next overseas holiday. We wanted to repeat the tour to Savannah and Charleston and also visit the Canyons. Furthermore, the time to visit Yosemite was May, when the waterfalls from the melting snows were at their peak – our previous year's visit had been in March.

Mary wanted to see her cousin, Glen Gibb, in Britain, so we decided that this year we would do a round-the-world holiday, travelling west. This meant that we could visit Israel on the way, if we so wished. We made some enquiries. One of the Margaret River potters is Jewish, from Haifa; she visited Haifa yearly, and assured us that Israel was reasonably safe, provided we kept out of the trouble spots.

Arrangements were made. To visit Israel, we had to travel El Al, from Bangkok. In Bangkok, we were interviewed by a young Jewish man, who quizzed us on why we wished to visit Israel, asked if we spoke Hebrew, and did we have relations there? When it was mentioned that we were visiting my uncle's grave, he became very apologetic and sympathetic. It has been said that Jews are prickly on the outside, soft on the inside.

Our plane landed in Tel Aviv. The railway terminal for the train to Haifa was at the airport. We boarded, and then started north. At the first station, some young soldiers, male and female, boarded the train. In their teens, they looked as if they should have been in school. They were in battledress uniform, they were wearing earrings and each was carrying a rifle.

We knew when we had arrived in Haifa. The Baha'i gardens stretched up Mount Carmel, a landmark.

Michael Day met us at the station, readily recognizable with his aku-bra hat. He took us to the hotel, the Beth-Shalom ("Peaceful house"). He had drawn up an extensive schedule.

He took us to the Sea of Galilee, where we visited the mount/plain where Jesus was said to have preached. That he could preach there to great numbers became clear, for the acoustics were such that a normal conversation was able to be heard and understood over considerable distances. We visited Capernaum and drove round the sea, which is in fact a large lake. Michael later published an article in *The West Australian* describing all that we had seen. Next day, we were shown round the Baha'i gardens, into the shrine of the Bab, met people in the House of Justice, and visited the dwelling and the room where my great-uncle had died nearly eighty years earlier.

On the following day, a trip was made to Akko (Acre), visiting the gardens and shrine of Baha'u'llah. Finally, we visited the cave of Isaiah, in Haifa, and paid our respects at the grave of Dr John.

Leaving Haifa, we went to Jerusalem, visiting and exploring the old walled city, wandering through the covered alleyways of the markets. On the last day, we visited the Dead Sea, Masada, and had a float on the sea itself. We returned to Tel Aviv and then went on to London, by way of Frankfurt.

After stays with Roswitha Carter, Glen Gibb and Maureen Lindsay, we crossed the Atlantic to stay a couple of days in Charleston, a couple of days in Savannah, before repeating the Tauck tour under the expert guidance, again, of Andrea Rovito.

The Canyon tours started in Las Vegas, from where we visited Zion and Bryce National Parks, Salt Lake City, the Teton National Park, Yellowstone and Mount Rushmore. Deadwood is a mining town, now filled with gambling hotels. Wild Bill Hickok was about as wild as his name implies and Calamity Jane did not really look like Doris Day. Denver was disappointing. Arches and Monument National Parks, Mesa Verdi were all spectacular, and lastly the Grand Canyon was well worth seeing again. Finally we visited Yosemite, where the waterfalls were at their most spectacular, the water coming over the mile-long drop in veritable lumps. There were a few days in San Francisco, and then we got back home

Chapter 42

Full Circle

Another year went by, and as neither Mary nor I were becoming any younger, we decided that in 2006 it was time to revisit Scotland. To clinch the matter, we received news that the medical class I attended at University planned to have a reunion to celebrate having been graduated for fifty years.

We planned to return to Israel and then visit Jordan before our tour of Scotland, then go on a cruise to the Greek Islands as Mary had done some forty-two years previously and which she thought I would also enjoy.

Only weeks before our departure, however, war began between Lebanon and Israel, and, on the television, Mary saw a rocket hit the railway station in Haifa where we had met Michael Day only a year previously. The plans to visit Israel were jettisoned.

The holiday to England began as planned, but only a day after we arrived, Heathrow airport was placed under high security because of a terrorist threat. We again stayed with Roswitha Carter, who had come to stay with us in Margaret River only a few months previously, and with Glen Gibb.

On to Jordan. We climbed Mount Hebron, from which Moses was said to have viewed the "land flowing with milk and honey" just before his death. The "rose red city" at Petra was as spectacular as has been described and I climbed the 900 and more steps to Ed Deir, "the monastery" at the top of the hill, leaving Mary to sit under the shade of a tree in the restaurant until I returned.

In Amman we went to the Roman amphitheatre. Six days after that visit, a tourist was shot dead there by a Palestinian.

The pilgrimage to Scotland began by again staying with Maureen Lindsay in Barrhead. The next stop was Ayr. Ayr County Hospital had been replaced by blocks of flats and Ayrshire Central Hospital grounds were now the site of a housing development.

Due respect was paid to Alloway, the birthplace of Robert Burns. We visited the old and new churches there, and celebrated our fortieth wedding anniversary with dinner at the Brig o' Doon Hotel.

Then to Bannockburn and Stirling, to admire the reconstructed Great Hall. Our journey then took us to the Braes of Balquidder, pausing at Rob Roy's grave, then to Oban and the ferry to Mull. Over fifty-three years and on five visits to Mull I had never managed to visit Staffa. On the sixth visit, the weather was excellent, and the long-sought voyage was achieved. It was better than expected. Four days on Mull and two on Iona brought back fond memories and ended with a visit to Duart Castle, where the dowager Lady Maclean showed us items of interest.

After Mull, the next night was spent at King's House Hotel, Glencoe, and "The Glen of Weeping". The somewhat stormy weather added to the atmosphere.

In contrast, sunny weather enabled us to see the Isle of Skye in all its beauty, the Cuillin Hills, clear for once, Flora MacDonald's grave, and at the very end, a visit to Talisker Distillery.

The following night was spent at Plockton. Seonaid Mackay, who had moved from Wanneroo to Albany, and with whom we had met irregularly, was visiting the village and we had dinner with her and another old friend, Jessie Moore. Next day we met again, to go out on a cruise in a boat to find the seals. At the end of the cruise, the skipper, who was Seonaid's cousin, gave Mary a big kiss and I got one from the crew, which I did not mind as she was a quite attractive young lady!

By way of Kingussie and Strathdon, there staying at a bed and breakfast at Candacraig, we travelled to Aberdeen.

About twenty-two of what was left of the class of students attended the reunion. We all looked older and recognized each other after a bit of thought. The time passed all too quickly; too quickly to catch up with how we had spent our lives since graduation. Possibly somewhat rashly I had undertaken to try to get "potted biographies" from those who attended the reunion and then circulate them in the form of a booklet to those who responded. The ensuing correspondence has been interesting and entertaining. I discovered, for instance, that the Professor Forbes who came to Penang in 1974 was the brother-in-law of one of my former classmates; his wife, who accompanied him, being his sister.

Full circle.

Eleven days touring Athens, Delphi, Istanbul, Mykonos, Patmos, Rhodes, Knossos, Santorini and back to Athens completed the holiday, then Mary and I returned to Margaret River.

With a history of eleven years without a holiday, we are now taking yearly vacations. In 2007, it was north to Singapore, then turning left and keeping right on, stopping for two weeks for a tour of Spain, Morocco and Portugal, a week in Washington DC for a conference, encompassing 4th July, a couple of days in San Francisco, three at Yosemite, another three in San Francisco, and finally breaking the long flight home with a week's cruise round the Hawaiian Islands.

At the end of the year, our Christmas present to the three offspring was to host them for a combined holiday with them and their families in Penang for Christmas and New Year. We stayed at the Penang Club, taking over all but one of the rooms of the Club, with Mary and I, the children, their three spouses, and seven grandchildren, fifteen in all.

We were back at the places where we had married and where the children were born. Those of us who had lived there enjoyed visiting memories and meeting friends, and to the in-laws who had not been previously, it was an exciting and interesting experience. There were Penang Club staff members who had been there when we lived on the island and even two who had served at our wedding. We were indeed lucky to have been able to save, in the last years of the practice, to be able to afford such a treat.

After six years in medical school and nearly forty-five years working as a doctor, retirement is a change. I miss the patients, some of whom come to visit me if they are in Margaret River, and I miss the intellectual challenge. However, I do not miss the responsibility.

PART TWO:

Reflections and Perceptions

Chapter 43

A Slow Learning Curve

S trictly speaking, having come to the end I should stop. However, it is not quite the end, and it is a bit like spelling "b-a-n-a-n-a-n-a-...", knowing *when* to stop. Furthermore, if you do not want to read any more, you have the option not to do so!

In one of my biographical submissions, one question I was asked was what are my personal philosophies? An outlook on life seems certainly relevant.

In seventy-five years of existence, three-quarters of a century, have I come to any conclusions about life? What have I learned?

Life is a learning process.

Rather than letting my thoughts, opinions, the results of my experiences die with me when I eventually go, let me share them with you.

Let us start with people – humankind.

> The true science and study of man is man.
> **Pierre Charron 1541-1603**

To explain to patients the relationship between mind and body, I used to compare it with a driver and a car. The driver makes the car go, and steers it. Without the car, the driver goes nowhere.

In the womb, in the baby's mind, is switched on a tape recorder which continues to record every event in life. As a human usually is conscious of only one thing at a time, the other recordings on the tape are "sub-" or "unconscious".

To put it another way, we do not normally feel the feeling of clothes on us. But when we think of it, we do become conscious of the presence of clothes on the skin.

The events recorded on the tape may have been conscious or subconscious at the time of recording or afterwards.

In the following, I have described the baby as "it" to avoid repetitively using "he or she".

The new-born baby has no conscious thinking process other than what it feels: feeling hungry, feeling thirsty, feeling frustrated because it feels hungry and is not fed, feeling anxious or angry because it is frustrated, feeling loving to the presence that feeds it, and so on.

Eric Berne, in his books on Transactional Analysis, such as *Games People Play*, vividly depicts these mental processes as the "Child".

When a child is born, its beliefs are:

1. That it is immortal; it has no thought that, some day, it will die;
2. That it is infallible; it can do no wrong, it can smear the bed with faeces but does not see anything wrong with that;
3. That it is irresistible; everybody loves it.

These are very powerful beliefs and some people never entirely lose them. The "Child" "wants" and becomes angry or depressed when it does not get what it "wants". If it finds that it gets its own way by having a tantrum, it learns to have tantrums. If it still does not get its own way, it turns in on itself and becomes depressed.

Feelings are very important processes to keep us alive. Freud described these processes as "drives". "E-motion" is almost synonymous with "energy".

I can remember describing the importance of feelings to a curate, and how important it is to be conscious how we feel. I asked him to mention a "bad" feeling. He thought a minute, and then mentioned "jealousy". I said that means that God is bad. He asked what I meant? I answered: "*I the Lord thy God am a jealous God ...*" (Exodus, Ch. 20, v. 5). We then looked up the meaning of "jealousy": solicitous of preservation of rights, etc.

As we grow up, we are taught by others, starting usually with our parents and grandparents. This, Eric Berne calls the "Parent". How we respond to teaching may depend on our genetic make-up.

The "Parent" may include beliefs.

Sometimes, the beliefs may be correct, sometimes they are erroneous. Is the earth flat or round? When there is new evidence that contradicts what one is taught, a prudent person looks at the old rule, blows the dust off it, and examines it again, bringing it up to date in time and space. As the years pass, more knowledge accumulates on the tape in our mind, and, hopefully, we sort out all this evidence and start "thinking". This cognitive process Eric Berne calls the "Adult".

Not all of us mature in this way, mentally.

We encounter people who are dependent on others, just like babies are. There are people who sometimes use their emotions to manipulate others, just as they did when they were children.

Others have taken what they have been taught very much to heart. They are very much bound by tradition. Those, whose drive for power is strong, are very much in the "Parent" and believe deeply in authority.

In 1963, S. Milgram published in the *Journal of Abnormal Social Psychology* the results of an experiment he conducted demonstrating the extraordinary lengths normal people will go in following orders given by superiors or those in authority. Sixty-five percent of the subjects obeyed orders which would have had fatal results had it not been a simulated experiment. More details of the experiment can be found in the original journal or in the book *Essential Psychology* by R. B. Burns. People who had a dependent personality would follow orders. Those who were of a "Parent" disposition would consider it justifiable, as an authoritarian order.

An experiment of this nature shows how few people grow up to think entirely for themselves.

A number of years later, Zimbardo and Ruch ran a study with even more frightening results (Zimbzrdo, P. G. and Ruch, F. L., *Psychology and Life*, 1973; New York:Scott Foreman).

Students, chosen for their normality, sanity and emotional stability, were randomly allocated to role-play guards or prisoners in a mock prison situation. Although the experiment was scheduled to last two weeks, it was terminated after six days, because every "guard" at some time engaged in abusive, authoritarian behaviour. The adage "Power corrupts" is not only a trite saying but has been experimentally shown to be factual.

Eric Berne calls the relics of childhood surviving into later life as

Archaeopsychic relics (the "Child"). Being very old and deeply rooted in the brain, they are very powerful. The ideas that have been taught, coming from an outside individual, he calls Exteropsychic functioning (the "Parent"). Coming from an early age, this can also be powerful. Reality-testing, which he called Neopsychic functioning (the "Adult"), being the most newly developed, is the weakest.

From what we can observe, humans differ from animals in one respect.

As Robert Burns put it:

> "Still thou art blest compar'd wi' me!
> The present only toucheth thee:
> But oh! I backward cast my e'e
> On prospects drear!
> An' forward tho' I canna see,
> I guess an' fear!"

To a mouse, on turning her up in her nest with the plough,
November, 1785. Robert Burns.

As far as we know, animals live in the present. They may have memories of pleasurable and painful events, such as shown by Pavlov's dog, but they do not seem to think about the past or future overmuch.

"Primary" emotions, such as feelings of hunger, thirst, frustration, fear, anger, jealousy, are protective in purpose.

Because of our ability to project our minds back or forward, two others emotions may occur, guilt and worry. These could be described as "secondary" emotions. Furthermore, they may be instilled from the outside of us by other people. They are taught.

Let us take a hypothetical example. You are driving, a child darts on to the road and is injured. The chances are that you would feel guilty. Yet, it was an accident and the feeling of guilt may not be appropriate.

On the other hand, if you take things from the supermarket and leave without paying, then a feeling of guilt would be appropriate. It is doubtful if a person doing such a thing feels guilt.

We are all human beings. Being human we are fallible and make mistakes. When purchasing an oriental rug it is prudent to look for the mistake in the pattern. If a mistake is not included by accident, a deliberate mistake is incorporated. "Only Allah is perfect." To consider ourselves to be perfect we are judging ourselves to be equal to Allah which is a contempt of others.

From our mistakes we have an opportunity to learn. If we do not learn from our mistakes, we may become arrogant.

Worry is another unnecessary feeling as whatever you are worrying about has not occurred and might never occur.

Any one person has only two worries: the worry that they can do something about, in which case, do it; the worry about which they can do nothing, in which case what is the point of worrying about it?

If you are sitting an examination in six months' time, then it would be prudent to start working for the exam. If the examination is tomorrow, there would be all too little time for study and you might as well spend the afternoon at a cinema!

What difference is this worry going to make in a hundred years' time?

What has all this to do with learning in life? Apart from the fact that I learned it, it is also the bones of further discussion. Although, for clarity, the further topics are divided into sections, it will be seen that they are all interwoven.

In the first few years of life, teaching would be authoritarian, "do this", and "don't do that".

Depending on the character of the "Child", the answer would be "yes" or "no". There is no intermediate. A response may be "Why?", in which case further interactions will depend on the character of the "Parent", who may say "Because I told you!"

However, if a child does not learn "discipline", it does not learn "self-discipline".

My first teaching would have been from my parents, grandparents and Sunday school, thus it would be teaching in manners and rights and wrongs.

Are manners important?

Debrett, which is considered the classical guide, in the Preface to *Etiquette and Modern Manners*, states: "*Etiquette is founded on good manners, a code of behaviour formulated to ensure the smooth running of every possible social occasion while affording offence to none.*"

Sunday school and church will be discussed later when dealing with religion.

School is the source of the next stage in education.

Undoubtedly, the most important teachings at school are literacy and numeration. The number of people in Australia today who have a literacy problem, that is, cannot read to an acceptable level (including the totally illiterate), is in the region of about 20 percent and yet reading is necessary for, say, gaining a driver's licence.

Other subjects, such as science, history, geography, languages, art, are of secondary importance as not all school leavers need these subjects. Learning to type and learning how to balance income against expenditure also would be useful to prepare the pupil on the passage through life.

However, three subjects are insufficiently taught. They are:

1. How to make money; i.e. how to balance the books.
2. How to get on with other people; i.e. how to live in a civilized society
3. How to bring up children; i.e. how to pass these skills on to a future generation.

Parents possibly do not have the breadth of experience or learning to adequately pass on such knowledge to their children. This means that teachers, at least in the first place, would need training to impart these skills.

Chapter 44

"Save Our Souls"

Church teaching, in my youth, was authoritarian and dogmatic. With my upbringing, and with ministers in my family and as friends, I saw no reason to question my religion (I did even consider, once, medical missionary work). I attended church regularly and, in the course of time, was ordained as an Elder of the church.

My excommunication, for what reason was not discernable at that time, resulted in my questioning my religion. It transpired that a someone, whose name I shall not mention, was making statements to the current minister, and making slanderous statements about my wife. I do not understand why the minister believed that person without question.

My first thinking was that, rather than man being made in the image of God; was it not more logical that God was invented in the image of man?

The fact that the "soul" seemed to be considered so important, and that this minister did not seem to be interested in "saving my soul", was another cause for me to question the church.

As mentioned previously, the next confirmation that I might be right was the fact that God could not perform miracles, as evidenced by the fact that my wish for my grandmother to return to life was dismissed as being silly by the moderator of the Malaysian Presbyterian church.

Another event occurred which reinforced my new beliefs.

Mary was heavily involved with the Girl Guides in Penang, and had the use of the church hall for her Guide Company meetings. The new minister who came took exception to the fact that my wife was not willing to consider converting Guides (some of whom were Malays and therefore Muslim) to Christianity. He used this as a pivotal reason to excommunicate her.

It was now obvious that the church is a club. If someone does not conform to the "rules" of the club, they are ejected.

From where does this belief in "God" come, and why is it considered so important?

It seems to me that human beings have a desire to be looked after, just as a baby is cared for. It seems to me that "God" is an invention to fill a residual, archaic want in the human being's mind. As this "need" lies in the archaeopsychic part of the mind, it has a very strong hold.

Church authorities have a wonderful, power-creating, money-making ploy. There is this imaginary need to be cared for, in the thought processes. Furthermore, in line with the "Child's" belief that it is immortal, the priest ("Parent") dangles a carrot by confirming that there is a life after death, a life everlasting, a "pie in the sky".

Thus, the "wants" of the very powerful "Child" are buttressed by the powerful "Parent" (the priest).

There is more.

The priest can exert his power with the threat that, if you do not do what you are told, "Big Brother" (God) will get you.

When the Bible was first written, about two thousand years ago, it provided a good, if authoritarian, template for social behaviour at that time, advising for instance, against killing, stealing, bearing false witness, as well as giving advice about some rudimentary rules of hygiene.

Humankind has learned more since then, which makes the advice somewhat dated.

Two thousand years ago, Jesus started teaching. He attempted to show how the mindless adherence to antiquated rules was stultifying rational living and gave new advice on social interaction. Modern cognitive therapy is not dissimilar.

There were various interpretations of this tutelage. Stories tend to become distorted over a passage of time with many varied interpretations made.

The four gospels currently in the New Testament, not committed to writing until many years later, give varied accounts of the life and teaching of Jesus, and there were other gospels which were not included.

In the 4th Century AD, Christianity received the backing of the Roman Empire. With this new power, church leaders began to try to consolidate *their* teaching to be the "correct" interpretation. Thus, only a few hundred years after Christ, censorship had started and the teaching was being manipulated to suit the opinions of the powers in the church.

Euhemerus was a Greek mythographer of around 316 BC who asserted that the Greek gods had been originally kings, heroes and conquerors, or benefactors to men, who had thus earned a claim to the veneration of their subjects. Prospectively, then, new heroes become *euhemeri*, becoming divinized. This includes historical figures such as Alexander the Great, Charlemagne, Mohammed (although Muslims would deny this), and it could also apply to Jesus.

The worship of the person of Jesus began, to the detriment of his teaching.

Eric Berne, in *Games People Play*, describes a game, "Gee you're wonderful, Mr Murgatroyd", which has a similar scenario.

To add to the confusion there are a number of types of church, each with their own doctrine. As the centuries passed, more and more interpretations of Jesus life and teaching developed. A hierarchy of priests became the interpreters. This was easy in medieval times when only a minority could read and write, and this ability was mainly confined to the clergy. Thus the clergy, as the interpreters of moral behaviour, became extremely powerful.

There has also developed among certain Christians a judgmental attitude contrary to Jesus's teaching ("Judge not that ye be not judged"). Those who did not conform to the dictum of the church at the time became heretics.

As the power consolidated, those with diverse views rebelled and the church broke up into various sects.

The followers of each interpretation considered that *their* interpretation, and their interpretation alone, was correct. The delusion of infallibility is very powerful. Others were judged evil and practices of extermination began to eradicate those "non-believers". Brutal crusades to the Holy Land, burning of witches, trials of the Inquisition were carried out in the "name" of so-called Christianity.

In 1696, a theology student, Thomas Aikenhead, aged eighteen, because of the bitter cold in Edinburgh, jokingly said "I wish right now I were in a place Ezra called hell, to warm myself there." For this remark, he was hanged for blasphemy on 8th January, 1697.

Such was the effect of church teaching.

What of other religions?

I know little about Hinduism and Buddhism. The former has many gods, as it was in ancient Greece. Buddhism, which developed from Hinduism, is more a way of life. In both, the aim appears to be finding peace after the pain and suffering of existence on earth.

Islam was evolved by one man, Mohammed. Modern technology has shown that the Qu'ran (Koran), unlike the Bible, had only one author.

Mohammed accepted Abraham, Moses, Elijah, and Jesus as prophets and accepted their teachings. However, Islam, like Christianity, broke up into various branches, Shi'ite, Sufi, and Ismaili.

The net result is that all the various religions and sects believe that their interpretation is the right and correct one, for which they are prepared to fight.

Baha'u'llah recognized the similarity between the religions of the Jews, the Muslims and the Christians and sought to develop on them. Baha'i is similar in concept to the previous religions but also accepts the equal standing of the sexes and it does not prosetalise.

Furthermore, Baha'u'llah was concerned with complete harmony with science and in being absolutely truthful as far as is humanly possible. He stated: "In order to find truth we must give up our prejudices, our own small trivial notions; an open receptive mind is essential. If our chalice is full of self, there is no room in it for the water of life. The fact that we imagine ourselves to be right and everybody else wrong is the greatest of all obstacles in the path towards unity, and unity is essential if we would reach Truth, for Truth is one …" (*Baha'u'llah and the New Era*, J. E. Esslemont, Baha'i Publishing Trust, Wilmette, Illinois, 1980).

The one common denominator in Judaism, Christianity, Islam and Baha'i is that there is a single all-powerful God ruling over our lives.

I cannot believe that there is an all-powerful old man, in the Michaelangelic sense, that runs our lives. On one of our trips to the United States, we met a very pleasant Jew who told Mary and me that he did not believe that there is a God, that there cannot be a God who let the atrocities at Auschwitz occur.

Does this mean that there is no God?

Yet, inside us is something, perhaps a spirit, that causes what is an essentially selfish being to care, love and be compassionate for others.

It has been shown that rats who are deprived of progesterone by immunizing them against the hormone, take no interest in, and are, indeed, hostile to, their offspring.

Upbringing and the teaching and example of parents may play a part, so, whatever it is, whether hormonal or neuronal, a combination of both, or something else, there is something in us that guides our feelings and behaviour to other creatures on the planet.

This spiritual feeling is not exclusively human. It has been seen in dogs, monkeys, kangaroos, for instance. Animals are sometimes seen to mourn.

Francis Hutcheson was the professor of moral philosophy at Glasgow University from 1729 until his death in 1746. He believed that people can have knowledge of good and evil without, and prior to, knowledge of God. He was also of the view that, besides his five external senses, man has a variety of internal senses, including a sense of beauty, of morality, of honour, and of the ridiculous. He also decided that everyone's ultimate goal in life is happiness, not, as vulgar people assume, gratification of physical desires (food, drink, sex), but that the highest form of happiness was making others happy. Thomas Jefferson was so influenced by this philosophy that he added "the pursuit of happiness" to his list of the inalienable rights of man in the American Declaration of Independence.

M. Scott Peck, in his book *The Road Less Travelled*, writes: "The religious, who, of course, ascribe the origins of grace to God, believing it to be literately God's love, have through the ages had the same difficulty locating God. There are within theology two lengthy and opposing traditions in this regard, one, the doctrine of emmanance, which holds that grace emanates from an external God to men; the other, the doctrine of immanence, which holds that grace immanates out from the God within the centre of man's being."

Not all people seem to possess the ability to behave positively to others. Positive, constructive, life-giving behaviour could be seen as "good". Negative, destructive, life destroying actions could be termed as "bad", or "evil". In his book *People Of The Lie*, M. Scott Peck states: "Evil, then, for the moment, is that force, residing either inside or outside human beings, that seeks to kill life or liveliness, and goodness is its opposite. Goodness is that which promotes life and liveliness."

"Good" and "evil" are essentially human. Volcanic eruptions and earthquakes are destructive and could be viewed as "evil". The sun, which supplies the force necessary for life, could be viewed as "good". However, these are natural phenomenon. In the human being, *intent* also plays a part.

Thus, if there is a "God", it is in us. Jesus said that God is love. This message has not always been listened to. If you do not like the message, you may shoot the messenger, or, in Jesus's case, crucify him.

I have heard people, professing to be Christians, saying that Allah is different from God, and professing Christians who would not pray with believers in other faiths. In Christianity, God exists as a Trinity. How many Gods are there? Is it important? And, if so, why? And, for that matter, what does it matter?

In my opinion, there is no divine force controlling us, other than the laws of nature, and it is up to us to control our own destinies as best we can. If there is some external, overriding force, it does not seem to be a fair one, nor does it seem to differentiate good from bad.

Chapter 45

Life and Death

With my views on religion, how do I deal with death? How do I deal with my ideas that there is no afterlife?

Death is inevitable. There is no escaping it. No one has ever come back to tell us what it is like "being dead". There is no record of anything that Lazarus recounted of his experiences of what it was like after his death.

Those that believe in an afterlife, if they are certain that they would end up in heaven, are, in a way, lucky. If they go to hell, presumably they deserved it!

There is some comfort from those who have had near-death experiences, as the stories they tell of their experiences seem to have been very comfortable and peaceful.

It has been said that life is a "terminally fatal, sexually transmitted disease". Certainly, it is the belief among Hindus and Buddhists that death is a period of peace after the travails of the material world. There is some comfort in that.

Another way of viewing life is of "filling in the time between birth and death".

The way I have to deal with it is to continue living as happily as I can and accept the inevitable when it comes. Death is inevitable and so falls into the category of a worry over which I have little control. Therefore, why worry about it? However I can help to try to prolong it by living reasonably healthily and happily.

How do I view euthanasia?

Some people are of the belief that euthanasia should be a "right". However, in my opinion, I consider it a "wrong" to ask others to acquiesce or expect them to assist the person to die. In forty-three years of medical practice not many of my patients died. However, none of these requested euthanasia. Furthermore, death is final. There is no coming back if you make a mistake.

People who advocate euthanasia might be more productive in putting their energies into curbing the acts of those who produce the opposite effect from "easeful death", war-mongers or sadistic murderers, for instance.

As an after note, ways to ease death are in existence. Heroin is a kinder drug than morphine but, in our paranoid society, it has been deleted from our armamentarium because it is abused by some, a case of "all or none", or "throwing out the baby with the bath water".

This leaves suicide.

I can remember a potentially suicidal patient discussing her thoughts with me. I pointed out that, as no one has ever come back, how does she know that what she is going to is not worse than what she is experiencing at that time in her life? She did not commit suicide.

On contemplating suicide, it again needs to be kept in mind that it is final.

In the Koran, translated by J. M. Rodwell, (Sura 4, verse 33) it is written: "O believers! Devour not each other's substance in mutual frivolities; unless there be a trafficking among you by your own consent: and commit not suicide: - of a truth God is merciful to you.

"and whoever shall do this maliciously and wrongfully, we will in the end cast him into the fire; for this is easy with God."

I shall live, like the animals, in the present, the here and now, and hope that, when death comes, I am tired of living.

However, I have no intention of dying yet! I have enjoyed the three-quarters of a century of my existence and have plans of enjoying more. I hope that the next quarter century will be as good. There may be less excitement – I do not have the energy for that – there will probably be less about which to write.

Where do we come from before we are born? Is there some "soul" hovering around, waiting for a body in which to enter? There I think we come back to one of our three delusions, immortality.

As I wrote at the beginning, life is a continuum. Logically, in the womb, the first nerve cells, the neurons, develop. When electrical discharges between them begin, our thought processes begin, either consciously or subconsciously. As early as the sixth week of pregnancy, the foetal brain begins to function so well that an electroencephalogram can be recorded. At the other end of life, when these discharges cease, all thought processes come to an end. What we call "life" is, in fact, conscious existence, what we see as our "being".

That being said, how do I explain ghosts?

Only once have I thought I had seen a ghost, a dog who had deceased, whom I saw, or thought I saw, run across in front of me and disappear into our garage, which he had so often done in life. I am not sure that the reappearance was not a figment of my imagination.

Are ghosts really souls, or are they vibrations remaining in the environment, echoing off walls, perceived by attuned personnel? They certainly tend to be connected with places.

Or are they some sort of a so-called "time warp" bringing the past back into the present?

When ghosts are reported to be seen, why are they usually clothed? Are the clothes on the ghost resurrected with the soul, which, I would have thought, would have been in the person, and the person only, the naked being?

Be that as it may, as Big God Nqong said from his bath in the salt-pan, as described in Rudyard Kipling's story, *The Sing-Song of Old Man Kangaroo*, ("Just So Stories"), "Come and ask me about it tomorrow, because I'm going to wash."

Life is not a "right", although once we are alive, to go on living may be a "right". Life is, in fact a privilege, it is conferred. If I had not been born, there would be no "me". And, like all privileges, it is up to us to appreciate the privilege of life.

In life, we are dealt a hand of cards. It is up to us how we play them. "Life is what you make it."

Chapter 46

Governments

Parliament, a word derived from Old French *parlement* (speaking), is a formal conference or council for the discussion of some matter or matters of general importance.

Government is the action of ruling and directing the affairs of a state.

In a democracy, "parliament" would be the word more applicable. However, is it?

In his book, *Common Sense*, a title taken from the catch-phrase and philosophy of Thomas Reid (1710-1796), Thomas Paine relates how the English government was formed by William the Conqueror, whom he describes as a "French bastard landing with an armed banditti, and establishing himself king of England against the consent of the natives". England, in fact, became a French colony.

Thus, the beginning of English rule was a government, run along authoritarian lines.

In this book and in *Rights of Man*, Thomas Paine recounts how the English government strove to retain this power against attempts at reform, and used their powers to pay the expenses of a foreigner as monarch, and to their own financial advantage.

Adam Smith, in *The Wealth of Nations*, also complains of the self-seeking attitude of the government: "It is the highest impertinence and presumption, therefore, in kings and ministers, to pretend to watch over the economy of private people, and to restrain their expense, either by sumptuary laws, or by the importation of foreign luxuries. They are themselves always, and without any exception, the greatest spendthrifts in the society."

Eventually, some reform did occur, with voting rights given to all the population except lunatics, criminals and the Royal family.

"Democracy" is defined as "Government by the people; that form of government in which the sovereign power resides in the people, and is exercised either directly by them or by officers elected by them" (*The Shorter Oxford English Dictionary*, Third Edition, 1967).

In Arthur Herman's book, *The Scottish Enlightenment* (Fourth Estate, 2003), he states that Adam Smith pointed out that a strong national government is necessary for providing a system of national defence, to protect the society and its commerce with its neighbours, to provide a system of justice and protection of individual rights, and to help defray the expenses of essential public works, such as roads, bridges, canals and harbours.

Governments have, since then, gone far beyond this, have subsidized education and health care and, accordingly, taxes have risen.

Now, every voter (apart from the exceptions mentioned) has a representative in parliament to whom he or she can approach when necessary.

Unity is strength and these representatives have banded together into parties in order that they can push through their ideas and ideologies. On one hand, this has merit in that the voter then knows for what his or her candidate stands. On the other hand, it can create problems as some of the candidate's visions may not be entirely rational and may not equate to what the voter wishes. Lobby groups are formed to push forward ideologies. Democracy is a civilized form of mob rule.

To take an example, slavery is popularly held in contempt. The *concept* of slavery has been expanded to include the employment of servants. The decrease in the number of servants has increased the number of unemployed people. The dole has been created to help sustain those who are unemployed but is now used as a form of subsistence by those who do not want to work. Yet, "the labourer is worthy of his hire" (St Luke, ch. 10, v. 7). Would hiring people for a fair wage not be better than developing a class of people who live by depending on others' charity?

Another, more serious problem is that, the fact that there are two or more parties creates a *confrontational* situation rather than a *co-operative* discussion.

Members of parties bicker like children; "if you can do anything, I can do better". It is like a circus or a Laurel and Hardy film.

The "party system" has, in fact, skewed the concept of true democracy.

Members of parliament, as makers of law, are in positions of power and the problems of self-seeking are still there. Many have become career politicians and make a living from their not inconsiderable salary and generous superannuation on retirement, while controlling the lives of others not in such a fortunate position.

We may ask what qualifications these members of parliament have to have this power. From what I observe, it is an ability to speak in public, a so-called "charisma", not necessarily backed by intelligence, voted into positions of power by a populace who can be persuaded to do what they are told.

As Sir Winston Churchill said in a speech to the House of Commons on 11th November 1947, "Democracy is the worst form of Government except all those other forms that have been tried from time to time."

What I have learned in a lifetime is that governments are not to be relied on, and that they do not make good employers, any more than does any large business company.

A possible method of reining the opportunity for unbridled omnipotence in those who are elected to be representatives of the community would be to limit their period in office to a statutory period, say, three, four, or five years; for the position to be restricted to one term only; that they be paid for their living during this period only, without any residual pension at the end.

Chapter 47

Insurance

In *Encyclopaedia Britannica*, insurance is described as: "A system under which the insurer, for a consideration usually agreed upon in advance, promises to reimburse the insured or to render services to the insured in the event that certain accidental occurrences result in losses during a given period. It thus is a method of coping with *risk*. Its primary function is to substitute certainty with uncertainty as regards the economic cost of loss producing events."

I initially came across the business of insurance when I first bought my motor bicycle. The first company approached would not insure medical students. I cannot think why.

Then, shortly after I qualified, an insurance agent described life insurance to me. He stated that I would pay insurance companies regular sums of money which they would invest so that a fund accrued. He and I did not know when I would die, but, when I did so, at whatever age, there would be money available for my funeral expenses and for my dependants if I had any.

There are many types of insurance: for instance, fire insurance, motor vehicle insurance, health insurance, workers' compensation insurance, and others, all with the same stated purpose.

With National Health schemes, the government is a *de facto* insurance company.

The result is that regular sums of money go to the various insurance companies.

Insurance companies have tried to diminish the amounts they have to pay in return, by imposing restrictions. A history of a family illness or a genetic possibility might disqualify an applicant from insurance cover.

In Aberdeen, one of our neighbours made a claim because a sheet of lead had been blown off his roof. The claim was turned down because it was "an act of God". The claimant was the Professor of Divinity at the University.

More recently, these restrictive practices have increased.

In medical indemnity insurance, the premiums for doctors who deliver babies and do operative procedures has steeply increased, so that, by 1995, I stopped doing midwifery because the horrendously increased cost of insurance would have to be passed on to the patients.

In workers' compensation insurance, the insurance companies have retained doctors who are prepared to do such work in order to assess workers' compensation claims, to verify if these claims are genuine (which increases the cost of insurance). The certification by the patient's own doctor was not accepted as reliable or accurate.

Certainly, patients are becoming increasingly litigious, especially after obstetric and surgical procedures, and there are patients who try to obtain monetary advantage after real or imagined accidents if they so can.

If one of my patients was referred by the insurance company to be examined by the doctor retained by them, doctors who often gave reports to please the company who paid them, I might ask the patient if they would like me to be present at the examination, which they had every right to do and which was ethically correct. This was often not popular with the examining doctor and occasionally I was able to point out an examination they had omitted to do.

In *The Wealth of Nations*, Adam Smith (1723–1790) writes about "the very moderate profit of insurers". Nowadays, the result of insurance practices is that money is going into the companies but it is difficult to obtain payment in return. In the major cities, who has the largest and most opulent buildings?

A side effect is that insurance companies wield a tremendous amount of power.

A patient, a qualified electrician whose work was good, had, unfortunately, episodes of schizophrenia. He could not find an electrical company to employ him so he decided to set up a company of his own and become self-employed. The laws of the State required him to have a certificate of insurance. Because of his intermittent condition, he could not be insured and so could not set up his own business.

It has been truly said that insurance companies run the country.

The only fool-proof insurance is to have enough capital to insure yourself!

Chapter 48

Are National Health Services a Serious Health Hazard?

In 1912, my grandfather's brother, Dr John E. Esslemont, together with Dr Charles Parker, an Ear, Nose and Throat consultant in London, set up the State Medical Service Association, with the view to developing a complete National Health Service.

Many years later, another relation, Dr Mary Esslemont, was the only woman and the only Scot who was on the committee that set up the National Health Service in Britain in 1948. Some thirty years later, she was to comment that a monster had been created!

Dr Mary's interest in starting a National Health Service was motivated by the fact that her practice included some of the poorest fishing areas in Aberdeen, Scotland. Her experience was that many of the mothers would put off seeking medical care until it was too late, because of cost. Often, instead of leaving a bill, the doctor would leave a treasury note on the table.

She was later of the opinion that, because of the abuse of free medical advice, it would be better if a fee, perhaps not very large, might be charged at the time of consultation. Some consideration might be given to those who are genuinely in need. For this, some sort of means testing would be required, a concept which is not universally popular.

Thus there were very good reasons for having a State health service.

However, what is this "monster" that has been created?

The American Declaration of Independence states "that all men are created equal". This philosophy is, on the face of it, true and fair. However, is it correct? Some men and women are born more intelligent, or less intelligent, than others. Furthermore, education and training moulds people. Some remain utterly dependent, some are driven by their personality to try to dominate, others mature and exercise powers of thought. Thus people are very different.

At school no one taught us

1. how to make money – that is, how to survive;
2. how to get on with other people – that is, how to get along in a civilised society; or
3. how to bring up children.

In the past, this knowledge was considered to be given by our parents, correct behaviour being directed by the religions. It did not work particularly well in the past and is no better in the present.

National Health Services, of which the British National Health Service and Medicare are examples, strove to make medical treatment equally available to all.

However, two aspects which do not seem to have been taken into consideration by the various governments are that medical treatment is expanding and becoming more expensive and that people are basically selfish and very aware of their "rights".

Thomas Paine's publication *Rights of Man* originated as a response to Edmund Burke's attack on the French Revolution and grew into a proposal for the elimination of poverty, illiteracy, unemployment and war. Although published two hundred years ago, little seems to have changed.

"Rights" has become a very popular catchphrase. When someone *wants* something, it becomes their "right", which adds the advantage and power that it is prescribed by some outside force – God perhaps?

To combat illiteracy, governments have also striven to supply free education.

The net result is that governments are attempting to fund free medical care and free education, all of which is expensive. A possibility might be to increase taxes to the point where all that is left to the householder is enough to feed the family and put a roof over their head, a suggestion which could be very unpopular!

A great many people, other than those involved in actual treatment, are employed in the bureaucracy of running this "monster", with the result that medical services are much more expensive than they need be. In contrast, medical services in Malaysia run at a fraction of the cost of those in Australia and Britain, a fact that was mentioned in a talk by YABhg Datin Seri Dr Siti Hasmah Bt Hj Mohd Ali, the wife of the Malaysian Prime Minister, on the occasion of her being made an Honorary Fellow of the Academy of Family Physicians on Sunday, 19th October 1997.

In Malaysia, the patient consulted the doctor. For this consultation the patient paid the doctor a fee. The transaction was direct. Any disagreement could be discussed face to face. There was no bureaucratic "middle-man".

Thus, currently, governments are paying to train doctors and then subsidising their work and treatment. They try to economise by minimising the number of doctors trained, with the result that there is a shortage of medical personnel, and putting limits on medical care wherever they can, with the consequence that doctors are working, aware that "big brother" is ready to step in if the way a doctor practises strays from the norm. A bureaucratic system includes all the paperwork, the staff employed to manage the system, the advisers, the staff employed to generate the paperwork, the staff employed to police the system, and the rest.

Hospitals are understaffed by doctors and nurses and are reaching the situation that patients are in long waiting lists and medical facilities may not be able to handle crises.

The result is that the general public are becoming unable to pay for good medical treatment. We are returning to the point of origin.

Plus ça change, plus c'est la meme chose (Alphonse Karr, 1808-90).

Medicare, run by an authoritarian government and by bureaucrats, may have a **deleterious** effect on people's health. As the medically qualified wife of the Malaysian Prime Minister said, medical practices run as private concerns, with the natural restraints of face-to-face doctor/patient relationships, in the long run, work more satisfactorily and more cheaply than the "monster".

Medicare and free education are "sacred cows" and governments which try to remove any of these "rights" would certainly be unpopular and result in members of parliament losing their jobs and not inconsiderable salaries.

They have the further disadvantage that they create a dependent society of people who are not prepared to strive for themselves.

As others have noted, "National health schemes in all countries have been abysmal failures and cost taxpayers billions in bureaucratic management while those at the coal face have gone down with the ship" (John Bain, Bunbury, *The West Australian*, Saturday, August 25th 2007). Excusing the mixed metaphor, it is obvious what he means.

The one area which seems to have benefited from the British National Health Service is that of childbirth, in which a system of comprehensive maternal care has produced an improvement in the health of the mothers and the standard of obstetrics.

Unfortunately, this has also had its down-side. The antisocial working hours and the fact that parents now expect a satisfying delivery and a perfect baby, and are prepared to sue if this does not happen, has resulted in doctors opting out of following this line of work. Women and their families rarely sued a doctor for negligence before the Second World War. Nowadays, obstetrics is the speciality most plagued by actions for malpractice.

The net result is, who will deliver the babies of the future? The further question arises: "Will the standard of the present be maintained?"

An aspect that does not seem to have been considered is that some people who are intelligent and have common sense might consider insuring themselves against medical expenses. The scenario which Dr John and Dr Mary encountered really applies only to those who have not thought ahead to consider possible eventualities. Those who can pay for education and medical treatment could do so, leaving government expense to those who are poorer and less foresighted. As mentioned previously, Thomas Payne's contributions have not lessened poverty or illiteracy – the poor are always with us.

If there is no government-run health provision, what are the possible answers?

The first solution is to take a chance and hope that enough money is available to pay medical bills, should they arise. This very often works but sometimes there arises treatment, for instance, for pulmonary tuberculosis, not within the reach of the individual.

The second possibility is to invest in an insurance scheme to prepare for such eventualities. While this system can be helpful, unfortunately insurance companies tend to try to manipulate the odds so that they may put restrictions on to what they insure or put a "cap" on how much they pay out.

This leaves a third option, which is to run a self-managed insurance scheme. This can take two forms: (1) by having a fund in the bank, or, for that matter in a tin or a safe, from which the patient can draw as necessary; (2) by investing money and using the interest to pay medical fees.

Unfortunately there are many who are too poor to afford expensive medical bills or prolonged treatment and who can only rely on the government public hospitals and their limited resources. For these, a "National" (government-provided) health scheme would be useful.

Chapter 49

The Profession of Medicine

The interest of my life began as an interest in, and curiosity about, nature.

As I grew, this crystallized into a focus on medicine. In medicine, I could see my interest in living things continuing, a chance to help other people, and an ability to earn an honest living as a result.

These ideals continued through school, through university, and through my house jobs and in the army.

Once I was in private practice in Cha'ah, I realised that it was not always so easy to earn a living. To survive, money was necessary. I also realised that my knowledge of how to help other people was not always accepted as easily as I would have liked. There was very little "curing" – it was a case of letting nature get on with the job while I tried to guide it in the proper direction, if the patient was willing.

Then, when I was in practice in partnership with other members of the medical profession I learned that not all members of the medical profession necessarily had the same ideals as me. It had become a rivalry between people of the same standing. Doctors are as human as the rest of the population.

Another thing I learned was that the knowledge of medicine was expanding. My graduation degree only showed what I had learned up until 1956, and, in the case of obstetrics, what I had learned until 1960. It was not until 1970 that I learned – when I went into consideration of sitting for the Membership of the Royal College of General Practitioners – that a lot of knowledge about general practice had developed without my noticing.

Over the next two years I enjoyed gaining that knowledge.

On migrating to Australia, the next thing I learned was that my higher qualifications were a hindrance rather than a help in finding a new job. Senior practitioners did not want those in the lower echelons of their practice to have higher qualifications than themselves, so that jobs became harder to obtain. I had already discovered something of this nature on joining the practice in Penang. The senior doctors there had the basic MB, Ch B qualifications. I had, in addition, a D Obst RCOG. The letterhead on the practice stationery, prior to my joining, had the doctors' qualifications. After I joined, the qualifications were no longer stated!

On my first encounter with patients in Australia, in Wickham, I found them to be just the same as in Malaysia. People were people, with their illnesses and their worries.

In Malaya/Malaysia the economic side of practice was simple. You did your best to help the patient, the patient paid you. There were no overtones. In Australia, with the Medibank system, where the basic charge for the medical consultation was paid by the government, there was little or no financial barrier to seek medical advice. This, of course led to patients sometimes seeing the doctor for reasons that they would not have otherwise sought a consultation.

The doctors in Wickham and Kununurra had the same ideals as me and there were no problems. Those in Port Macquarie, however, had different outlooks. Appointments were spaced at a much faster rate than I was used to and what was the norm in Wickham and Kununurra. The Medibank schedule was designed to favour short consultations. If you saw patients at six-minute intervals, the income per hour was better than if you saw them at fifteen-minute intervals. I had now encountered doctors with a different, more monetary outlook towards medicine. Even more recently I have heard of a doctor who described his work, not as a "profession", but as a "business", that is, as a means of making money.

As it was, by starting my own practice, I was able to work in the way I found most comfortable. It did not meet with fast-consultation, fast-buck type of medicine until the very last few weeks of my career, by which time it mattered less.

In prescribing, in Australia there is a great deal of wastage of medicines. A tablet taken three times a day for a week means twenty-one tablets a week are required. In Australia, medications are dispensed in bottles or packages with a certain number of tablets; for instance, to prescribe twenty-one tablets, the packaging may be for twenty-five, thirty, forty, or even fifty. Why not prescribe twenty-one tablets which the pharmacist can dispense from the stock?

There is too much government control, which leads to unnecessary expense. What has happened to common sense?

My next observation was the way that doctors behaved at conferences.

At the first seminar at Anaheim, the doctors were there to exchange views and we all got on very amicably. The next meeting at Melbourne was a much bigger affair. Again the atmosphere was amicable but I had the feeling that presentations were for the purpose of displaying the author's intelligence. Certainly, the presentation of papers helps to enhance a doctor's climb up the academic ladder. On the other hand, I learned a lot to clarify the mechanism of hormonal changes from this conference, but it did not change my treatment of patients.

When I went to university, university fees were charged. I was fortunate to have a family who clubbed together so that I could go to university and qualify. It meant, however, that there had to be a drive on the student's part to compensate for the expense.

So it was with the doctors in Malaya/Malaysia, but, by the time that I had migrated to Australia, the Australian government had scrapped university fees and students had relatively cheap tertiary training.

The pecking order to achieve medical training now depended on the potential student's scholastic achievements. Only school students who had attained the highest marks could enter a medical course. This may have resulted in a shift in the attitude of the new breed of doctors.

The prize winners and most brilliant at school tend to be conscious of their own ability and to be somewhat arrogant of those whom they consider intellectually inferior. Interpersonal transactions become, in Eric Berne's terms, Parent/Child. They tend to look at patients in a more objective, detached way, like chess pieces to be manipulated.

Another factor comes into play. Like many money-holders, the government did not want to spend more money than necessary. They had the theoretical advantage of knowing population figures and therefore could project how many doctors were needed.

There was also a drive to have more female doctors and more women wanted to become doctors. Eventually there were more female than male medical students.

In addition, doctors were frustrated by the fact that their professional lives interfered with their family lives. I can remember the faces of our children when the promised outing to the beach was abandoned because of the fact that a baby was on the way. Doctors have a high incidence of broken marriages and suicides. More and more doctors wanted nine-to-five jobs and the increased number of professional women wanted time off to have children and to raise them.

The government's projected figures became skewed.

In 1990, I was finding it hard to doctor the practice.

At first, the government said that there was an "over-supply of doctors", and then they said that there was a "poor distribution of practices" (it is always someone else's fault). After some years, the shortage of doctors was so obvious that doctors were invited to come to Australia. Country jobs were the hardest to fill. Doctors were not willing to revert to the discipline of arduous hours of work when there were easier positions available.

The day of the family doctor who is there to meet the physical and psychological needs of the individual patient seems to be slipping away, to be taken over by doctors on shift duty as in hospital casualty departments.

Unfortunately, with the decline in the spiritual services available, people are being left to fend for themselves. There is a growth in counselling facilities available, filled by excellent practitioners who are, however, unknown to the patient. There is a dearth of known faces to whom those in distress can appeal.

The profession of medicine has always been a follower of fashion, whether it be the belief in the four humours, in blood-letting, or in a "septic focus" being the cause of arthritis.

Today, it is no different.

Sixty years ago, eggs, being a protein food with lots of iron, were considered to be good for you. Forty years ago, eggs were believed to be injurious to the health because of the cholesterol content, today they are deemed to be beneficial.

A recent fashion is "evidence-based medicine". Essentially, all medicine is "evidence-based". The removal of the appendix would not now be performed for appendicitis if it had not been found, at the turn of the nineteenth/twentieth centuries, to work. But what is now expected is that the ideal of a "double blind controlled trial" be undertaken before a proposed treatment can be accepted. There are at least six problems with this concept.

1. Patients may be looked upon as guinea pigs.
2. Medical ideas become, of necessity, retrospective.
3. What happens to the patients who are used as the "controls"?
4. If the number of subjects is too small, no conclusion is possible, so that nothing is "proved".
5. If any of the groups in any way differs, no statistical conclusion can be reached. The statistics become "flawed".
6. The researcher may skew the data to prove the theory.

Furthermore, research requires funding. Much of the funding comes from pharmaceutical firms, who are, naturally, interested in promoting their own commodities. How much bias comes into the results and how many studies are never published because the results are not to the advantage of the researchers or their promoters? Where does thinking and imagination come in to the picture?

A recent development is the increase in the diagnosis of ADHD (Attention Deficit Hyperactivity Disorder). Children with this condition are more and more often prescribed drugs for the condition. It was noticed in the waiting room that some mothers with children to be seen sat with their offspring, reading to them and being actively involved. Others sat reading a magazine while their children ran wild through the waiting room. The latter, more often than not, were considered to be suffering from ADHD. The conclusion seemed to be that, rather than the children being "hyperactive", perhaps they were, in fact, being given less attention than was good for them.

An aspect of attention that seems to be lacking seems to be firm discipline.

The drugs that are being prescribed consist of adrenergic medications. Surely firm discipline will have the effect of releasing adrenaline into the child's system?

It has been claimed that brain imaging has shown changes, implying that the condition is "physical" as opposed to "psychological". Is it not also possible that psychological factors in growth can affect the physical development of the brain?

In an era where discipline and corporal punishment is frowned upon, are we producing an ADHD generation?

Has the profession of medicine become coldly scientific, and what has happened to the art of medicine, the compassionate caring of patients?

"Patient-Centered Medicine" is a new development. The patient's opinion is taken into the determination of what is, in fact, the patient's illness, in an "Adult" to "Adult" situation. After all, it is the patient who owns the disease, in a manner of speaking, and it is the patient who has the ultimate responsibility for the condition.

Chapter 50

General Medical Practice

In Britain, the birth of the "speciality" of general medical practice occurred about a hundred and fifty years ago, in the middle of the nineteenth century. A detailed account can be found in Irvine Loudon's book, *Medical Care and the General Practitioner 1750–1850* (Clarendon Press, Oxford, 1986).

The history is very complicated and the concept was strongly opposed by the Royal College of Physicians and the Royal College of Surgeons, who saw the concept of a "general practitioner" as a competitor for their services and therefore a threat to their income. The College of Obstetricians at that time was having problems in establishing itself and was not heavily involved.

An attempt was made to found a College of General Practitioners about 1850 but it was over a hundred years later, in 1952, that the Royal College of General Practitioners was begun.

Despite the opposition, general practice survived, but with political consequences affecting status and the economical well-being which has differentiated general practitioners and other specialists. The phrase "just a GP" survives to this day.

Thus, to succeed financially, a medical graduate will be drawn to specialities other than general practice so that he can charge higher fees.

A number of things have contributed to the survival of the generalist.

Accessibility is the most obvious factor. A specialist charging fees beyond the reach of the financial means of those less well-off will become less accessible.

In his own way the general practitioner can be as well qualified as any other specialist. Until about seventy years ago, with the advent of, first, the sulphonamide drugs and then penicillin, treatments which actually *cured* disease were practically non-existent. The only four available were quinine, digitalis, fresh fruit and vegetables. The most important function of a medical practitioner was to provide the comfort of his or her presence and skill in diagnosis and prognosis. This was well within the capabilities of a good general practitioner.

Other factors which have contributed are the facts that surgeons are, primarily, *doers*. Their success lies in the skills of their handwork. Physicians have, historically, been rather unpopular figures, possibly because their approach to disease is scientific, dealing with the disease rather than with a human being who is ill.

A good general practitioner deals with the psyche as well as the soma. He or she knows the patient, knows the patient's family, is familiar, friendly, and able to deal with all except a few medical conditions. A good family doctor combines a broad clinical approach with continuity of care, together with a pastoral role.

Chapter 51

The Future

After over two thousand years, little has changed, despite the teachings of Jesus, Mohammed, and all the knowledge available. Ninety years ago we had "the war to end all wars", to be followed twenty years later by another, possibly more horrendous. Since then there has been practically continual conflict.

Not many of us are alone in the world. There are few Robinson Crusoes. On the other hand, we are all individuals. This has the result that the way we live has its effect on other people and other people affect us.

Basically, we are all selfish but have learned to live with other people to very varying degrees.

About sixty years ago, my grandfather, somewhat optimistically, wrote the first booklet in a series of four, *It's Coming Yet – Pioneers of a Better World*.

Roughly, about a third have learned to think for themselves, about one third are dependent and want others to make all the decisions, and another third want to be in charge, to have power.

There are no signs that it will ever be different. To change, parents would need to learn how to bring up their children, to teach them how to make money and subsist, and how to get on with other people. As the parents have themselves learned from their own parents, who were also not taught, and whose concept is "what is good enough for my parents is good enough for me", the situation is unlikely to be any different.

There are many people who are ready to advise others how to run their lives and there are many others who think and act in a way they think that others expect them to think and act. We are all ourselves and it is important to be true, to yourself and to other people. Constant truthfulness earns respect from others. One lie, recognized as a lie, can destroy that trust, for years if not for ever.

It is helpful to treat other people as you would like to be yourself treated. In Charles Kingsley's book *The Water Babies* are two characters, Mrs Bedonebyasyoudid and Mrs Doasyouwouldbedoneby, which says it all.

A Muslim friend has pointed out that great teachers of the past, living in different periods in history, in different countries, preached the same message.

Islam

No one of you is a believer until he desires for his brother that which he desires for himself. Prophet Muhammad (*Sunnah*).

Confucianism

Do not do to others what you would not like yourself. Then there will be no resentment against you, either in the family or in the state. *Analects 12:2.*

Buddhism

Hurt not others in ways that you yourself would find hurtful. *Udana-Varga 5,1.*

Christianity

All things whatsoever ye would that men should do to you, do ye so to them; for this is the law and the prophets. *Matthew 7:1.*

Hinduism

This is the sum of duty; do naught onto others what you would not have them do unto you. *Mahabharata 5,1517.*

Judaism

What is hateful to you, do not do to your fellow man. This is the entire Law; all the rest is commentary. *Talmud, Shabbat 3id.*

Taoism

Regard your neighbour's gain as your gain, and your neighbour's loss as your own loss. *Tai Shang Kan Yin P'ien.*

Zoroastrianism

That nature alone is good which refrains from doing another whatsoever is not good for itself. *Dadisten-I-dinik, 94,5.*

The message is: *Mutual respect.*

History is peppered with instances of gross intolerance of people towards each other, mainly instigated by the respective clergies and in complete disregard to the edicts pronounced by their great teachers.

My experience of the depressing effect of continual denigrating remarks and body language to the point of contemplating suicide taught me of how we can affect others. I have learned not to rely too heavily on others, not even God. "Life is what you make it."

And what will happen to the world and all humankind? It has been theorized that the sun will expand and swallow up the earth in billions of years to come. What then?

The latest "doomsday book" prophecy is global warming. Some say that it is caused by our release of products of combustion; some say that it will happen in any case. It seems logical that products of combustion will add to the effect. An increasing human population will produce more combustion. Surely one of the logical solutions would be to put a stop to the expanding population, as was mooted thirty to forty years ago. Why has this concept not been put into action? A possible reason is that business thrives on an increase in production and sales which in turn means a necessary increase in population.

The demise of species causes concern. As the weaker die out, others evolve.

Since its beginning this planet has been undergoing change. Earthquakes and volcanic eruptions will occur. Research into plate tectonics and continental drift suggest that, some day, massive catastrophes will take place.

The next "doomsday" scenario is that an increasing number of the population are becoming obese, which, in turn, may lead to an epidemic of type 2 diabetes. Strictly speaking, each of us is responsible for ourselves. Those that overeat and under exercise may well become obese, develop diabetes and die sooner, which, to be cynical, will lead to a reduction in the population and result in fewer pensioners to look after. It is a form of "Natural Selection".

It is not really our place to tell others how they "should" lead their lives.

There seems little point in worrying about the future and what "might" happen. We really have little control over these events. Do something about what we can control and avoid worrying about things over which we have no control.

My wife and I are planning more trips overseas. We might as well enjoy life while we can.

Life has had the "highs" and the "lows". If there were no lows, we would not appreciate the highs.

Just as in athletic training, muscles need to work against resistance to gain strength, so, in life, people require to overcome problems in order to develop character.

The highlights?

My life in medicine, my years in Malaysia and Hong Kong, My time with the Gurkhas, and above all else, my marriage and family. My father's words, "a happy marriage is beyond all price", say it all.

I hope that you have enjoyed reading my story as much as I enjoyed writing it.

Addendum

M y grandfather, Peter, was born in 1870 and married Mary Jane Gordon in 1895.

His recollections, written in 1957, in his eighty-eighth year, read as follows.

> *I had witnessed for some time back, how old things soon pass out of recollection .... It is interesting to have some distinct record of them.*
>
> *FAMILY JOURNAL by Geo. Esslemont. 1858*
>
> *Lately, I have been interested in the family history on my father's side. It throws a flood of light on the conditions of Aberdeenshire at the time. My great grandfather was a shoemaker, in humble circumstances. He died at an early age – a month or two before my grandfather was born. Early death was all too common in those days, and looked upon as the Will of God. His son, Peter Esslemont, took a small farm and married. He became the proud possessor of a horse and an ox. The family of ten followed, of whom only five grew up. The conditions of life were hard, but in those days, youngsters started work on the farm at a very early age. Economically, healthy children, able to work, were valuable. The united work of the family enabled the father to take a rather larger farm, which became comparatively*

prosperous, but, alas, one of those terrible epidemics visited the farm, and all of them were stricken down with fever. The father died, and two of the daughters, shortly after. George, the ninth child – my father was the eighth – died of consumption, now called tuberculosis, in his apprenticeship, and a sister, Elizabeth, the only child born in the larger farm, Mains of Shiels, and another sister, Jean.

My grandmother must have been a woman of extraordinary energy, and ability. The mother of a family of ten, being left with the responsibility of the whole family, before she had reached the age of forty seven. She lived till her eighty first year. All her four remaining sons became prosperous, and influential, her eldest as a farmer, the other three as merchants, against incredible difficulties of comparative want of education in the ordinary sense of the word as far as schooling was concerned, but their Spartan upbringing fitted them greatly for success in their calling.

The eldest son, James, carried on the farm, after his father's death, and heroically managed to double the farm by bringing rough, uncultivated land into cultivation. His reward was £100 extra added to his rent. Mary, the eldest daughter was the farm help.

Of the three other sons, Alexander became an apprentice in his aunt's wholesale and retail grocery business in Aberdeen. Peter became an apprentice draper, and the founder of the firm of Esslemont and MacIntosh, and took a leading part in public life in the Town Council, becoming Provost and Member of Parliament for East Aberdeenshire, till he was made chairman of the Fishery Board. John Ebenezer, my father, was the youngest son who grew up. Their story is perhaps a typical one for the north east of Scotland. The houses they lived in mark the growth of the town, westwards and to the suburbs.

My cousins, George and James Esslemont, entered their father's business. Along with MacIntosh, George and James became the active heads of Esslemont and MacIntosh's after their father died. George, in addition to taking charge of the wholesale side of the business, entered the Town Council, and latterly became Member of Parliament for South Aberdeen. George died at a comparatively early age, but his wife took up public work, and became one of the pioneers in Aberdeen, for child welfare. She is now in her ninety first year. The work is continued by her daughter, Dr. Mary Esslemont. Both mother and daughter have been honoured with the degree of Ll.D. by Aberdeen University.

The younger son, James, took charge of the retail department. He had a successful business career, but also died early. In both cases, their sons carry on in the business. James had a passion for horses, and a passion for gardens. He owned 'Langley' in Forest Road. He had a carriage and pair of lovely bay horses, that were much admired in Aberdeen.

I had two younger brothers. William, two years younger, was an advocate. He wrote a book on 'Scots Common Law', and was a lecturer at the University for many years.

John, my youngest brother, during his college career, took diphtheria, but recovered sufficiently to become assistant to Professor Cash. He took a scholarship for research, and was in Germany for a year, but becoming engaged to be married, passed on the second year to Dr. Tom Fraser his year of scholarship resulted in his marrying a German lady.

My brother, John, in some respects, had an extraordinary career. He had found difficulty in accepting the general doctrine preached at the time. He became interested in Baha'u'llah, a Persian prophet. Baha'u'llah considered himself a successor to Christ, and his teaching was, to my mind, far in advance of the average orthodox method of expounding Christianity. My brother wrote a book which expounded this teaching. This book was translated into fifty two languages, and was looked on as the standard summary of Baha'u'llah's teaching. The book was gone over by Baha'u'lah's son Abdul-Baha, who became the exponent of the Bahai faith, and also by a grandson, Shoghi Effendi, who was the guardian of the faith. It led to the publication of a short synopsis of the Baha's teaching by myself, entitled 'A Life Plan'. My brother died, while on a visit to the Bahais, and was buried at Mount Carmel. A beautiful shrine from Aberdeen marks the grave, which has been visited by a few Aberdeen friends.

My maternal grandfather was a tailor, of whom I have very distinct recollections. He began in a humble way, and after his marriage, he went to London, to learn cutting. He worked with great industry, building a successful business. He used to say he never went to the country without a tapeline, and he never came back without an order. He had a great knack of friendship. His customers were his friends. He used to speak of 'a fine man, and a good customer'. He had a clear tenor voice, and was deeply interested in music. I can recall distinctly his singing of 'Ilka Blade o' Grass deps its ain drap of dew'. He was a keen temperance reformer, and did much to try and save poor Broomfield, who wrote that beautiful psalm tune 'St.Kilda'. Broomfield was an alcoholic addict, and my grandfather sometimes paced the street with him, while he was in the tortures of the alcoholic craving. It was a curious incident that made my grandfather so energetic a temperance reformer. His father, my great-grandfather, was a very godly man, and conducted family worship night and morning, but, as was the general practice at the time, he took more than was good for him on market days. He insisted on conducting family worship when he was drunk. It so disgusted my grandfather, that he vowed he would never take the stuff.

My mother was the eldest child that grew up. She had inherited her father's fine voice and devotion to music. At the terrible time when our family was all laid down with Scarlet fever, one after the other, and when my elder sister at ten and a half, suddenly died of the trouble, I was so ill that the doctor gave no hope of my recovery. I remember the horror that I had when the fever went to my head, on thinking that Union Bridge was falling on me. At that time, I had been in the infant class of the Trades Hall School, which was entered at the foot of the Union Bridge. But I remember that, during convalescence, the one thing that soothed me was when my mother sang, and played some of her songs on the piano. In those days, there was practically no provision in hospitals, and most illness was nursed at home. What it must have been for my mother to nurse the whole family through an attack of scarlet fever, and at the same time nurse a young baby not a year old, and, when we were getting better, a girl in my uncle's employ, who had taken the fever. But, just the same, the terrible strain of those years broke my mother's health permanently. Up to that time, she was a marvel of good health.

My mother's brother, Henry Davidson, became successor to his father in the business of William Davidson and Son, Tailor. He inherited his father's musical gifts, and became an energetic Sunday School teacher. He founded, along with myself, the Belmont Musical Society, in connection with Belmont U.P. Church Mission, which met at that time in the buildings vacated by the Trades Hall School. In my early married days, at Affleck Street, we met there weekly. We had great times. Until the present day, I hear stories of those who came through the class, and those associated with it. Harry's eldest boy, Arthur, was one of the early victims of the first World War. My uncle never really recovered from the terrible shock, and was himself, killed in a motor accident. My father, and my uncle George Esslemont, both wrote family journals. As my uncle George died at nineteen years of age, my father's is necessarily the longer of these, and is full of pictures of life a hundred years ago. They shed a lot of light on education, hard work, treatment of disease, and belief in the 'Hereafter' in those days.

My father wrote this of his mother, who was born at Balnakettle, Udny, 13th June, 1799 – 'At that time boys got very little schooling, and girls less. I do not think that my mother was at school at all, but was somehow taught to read, and in after life, became a very good, and intelligent reader; she also learned to write, and could do so very fairly, considering the very little training she received .... She was tall and dark haired, and as her hair remained, and scarcely changed colour, as also her teeth, she looked rather younger than her years. She had a good memory, was observant, and had read and heard a good deal, and could give intelligent account of Church life in the north, from the beginning of the century, and was always specially interested in the U.P.C. Sheils, Craigdam and Aberdeen. Could sing very well, and was fond of singing, but had never been taught the theory of music. She was devout and prayerful, and had a high sense of duty, and enjoyed Church Ordinances regularly.' She lived to be eighty one years of age. It is interesting that my wife's parents lived to celebrate their diamond wedding, and my father and mother celebrated their golden wedding.

At my father's golden wedding was the minister that married them, the bridesmaid, and the best man. The minister had baptized all their bairns, assisted at our wedding, and baptized all our children, and my eldest son, Gordon, when he was engaged to be married, went to tell him, and he asked them to kneel, and gave them a blessing in old patriarchal style. They felt it was almost like a wedding. He died a fortnight later.

On the 31st July, 1895, Peter Esslemont and Mary Gordon [my grandparents] were married in the Free Church, Kemnay. It was a lovely day. The Aberdeen friends came in a four in hand coach. My father and mother, my brother (the best man), and

myself, came in a carriage and pair. It was something of an occasion. Mary Gordon's father was a Kemnay merchant, and elder in the church. Dinner was provided in a large marquee in the garden. It was a glorious gathering in ideal surroundings.
On Friday, 29th July, sixty years after, the directors of John E. Esslemont Ltd. entertained the staff to dinner, and the staff presented the bridge and bridegroom with an oak trolley table, and silver tea service to celebrate their Diamond Wedding.
The fourth generation to join the business was represented by our grandson, Alan, home on leave from National Service with the air force.

On Sunday, the 31st July, the actual anniversary day, the ringer of the St. Nicholas Bells asked the bride and bridegroom to choose a hymn for the occasion. We asked a favourite hymn of our eldest little girl, who passed on aged four and a half years – 'Oh what can little hands do'. On the Sunday morning, a beautiful day, every verse of that little hymn pealed out on the bells. It seemed a message from the sky from the great company who had gone on before. We had a quiet dinner for the family and grandbairns on that day.

On Monday afternoon, we had an At Home in the Northern Hotel. There was neither a four in hand, nor any carriages with fine horses. Instead, a car park had to be reserved for a hundred cars. There were eleven of the original wedding party, including two bridesmaids, and the Rev. Principal Urquhart, who was an Arts Student at the original wedding. Now a retired Principal of Madras College, he gave the toast of the bride and bridegroom. My elder son, Gordon, presided at the gathering. The Lord Provost gave greetings from Aberdeen citizens. The Marquis of Aberdeen spoke for the county. George Gordon, brother of the bride, spoke for the Gordon clan, and James Esslemont, Edinburgh, a cousin, spoke for the Esslemont family. Mr. Gordon declared, that, judging from the family and the grandchildren, the Gordon-Esslemont Blend was 'Good as Gold'.

My brother Alan adds this rider:

> *Peter Esslemont lived to be ninety one, and Mary Jane, his wife, to be ninety five. Her mother, lived to just a few months short of her century, and her sister, Netta, who latterly lived in Canada, lived to be one hundred and seven years old. Her last visit to Aberdeen was to celebrate her ninety ninth birthday, and she travelled across to Scotland by herself. When I asked her if she didn't feel a bit lonely travelling herself, she said 'No.' All sorts of people, who she had never met, were coming and speaking to her all the way across and she thoroughly enjoyed it!*